BLOKE

The photo journal

Peter Slater

FOR THE LOVE OF

blokes

mate1

/meɪt/

noun

suffix: -mates; plural noun: mates

1.

the sexual partner of a bird or other animal.

"a male bird sings to court a mate"

2.

a fellow member or joint occupant of a specified thing.

"his table-mates"

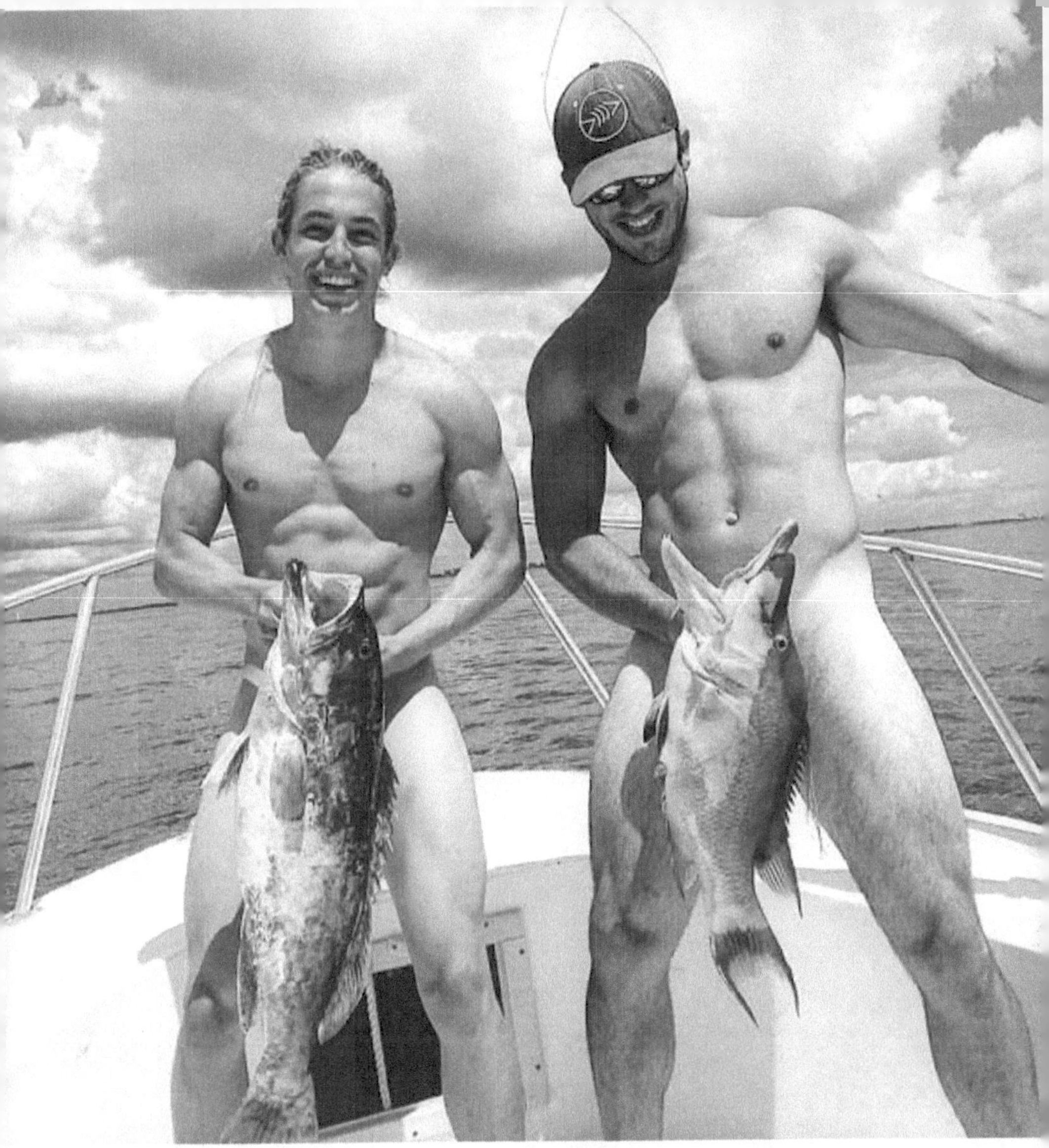

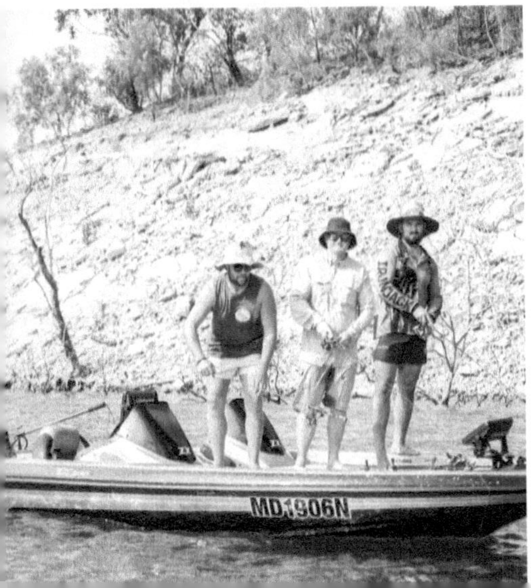
MD1906N

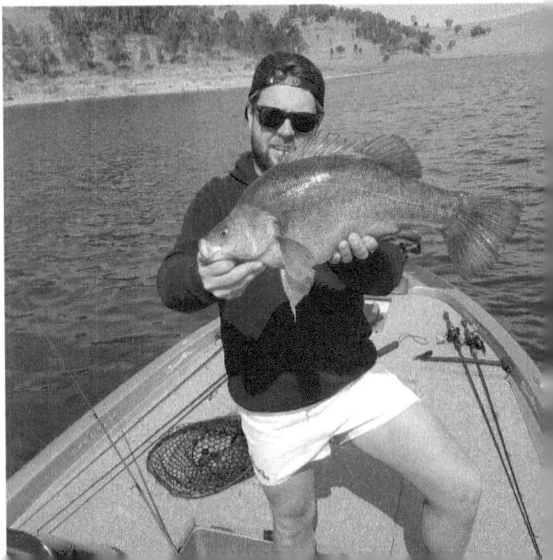

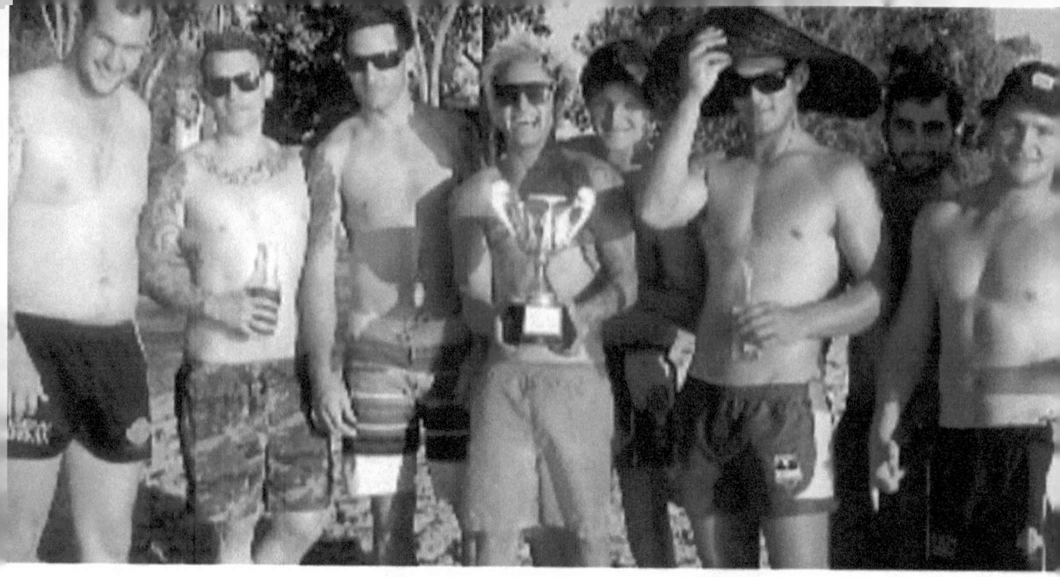

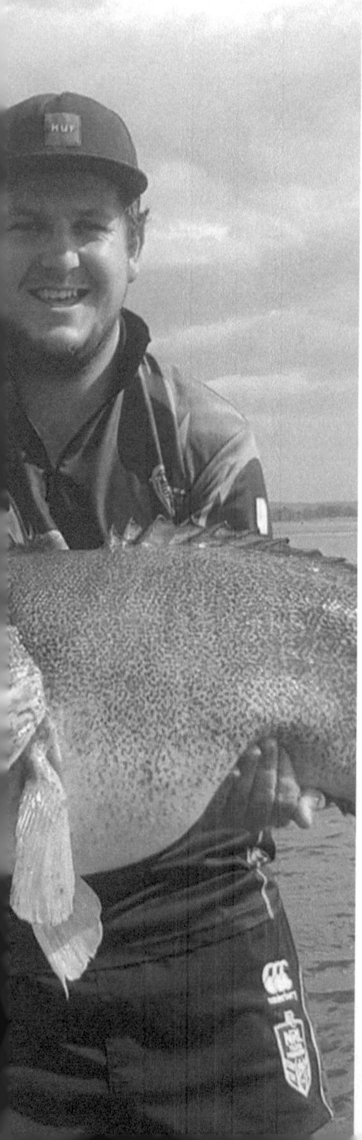
HUF

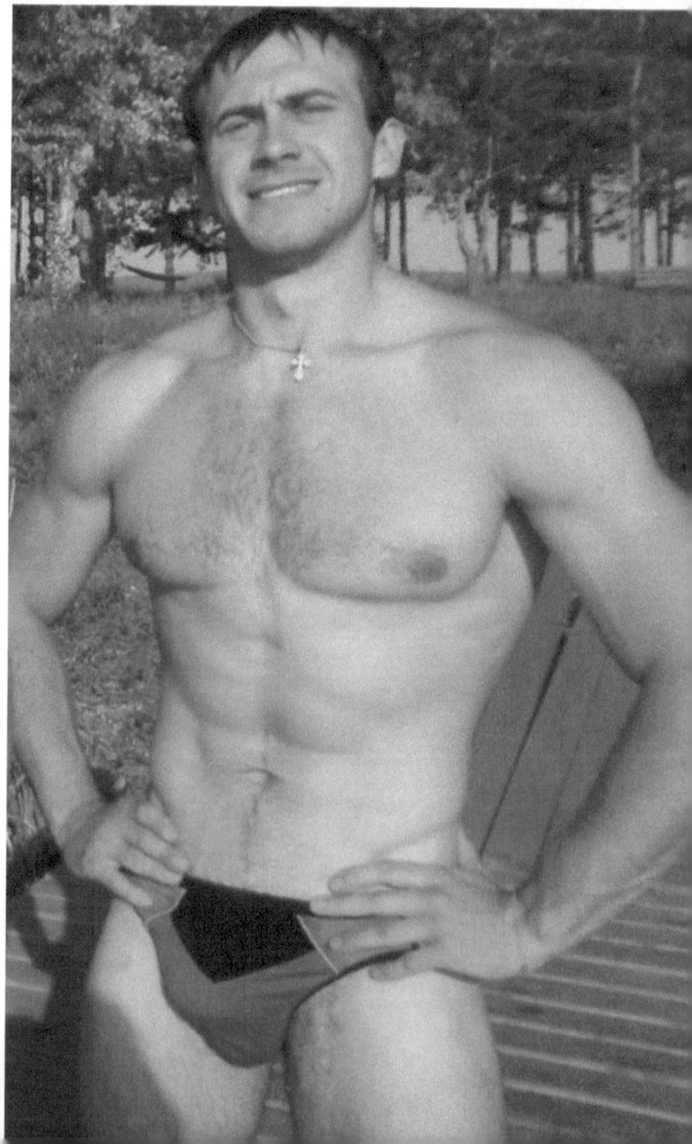

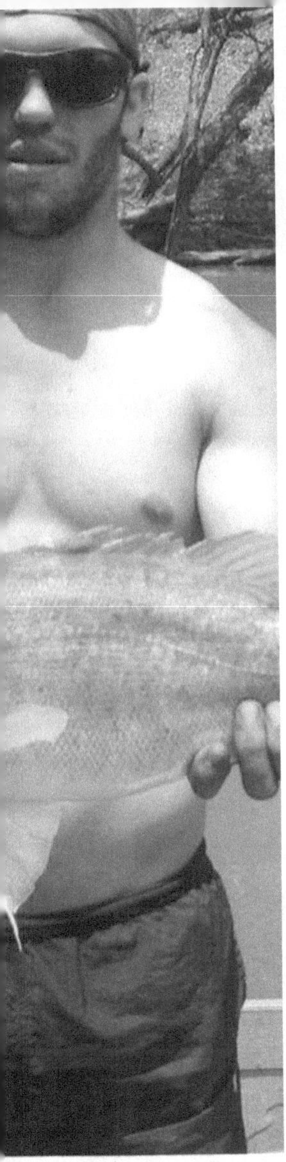
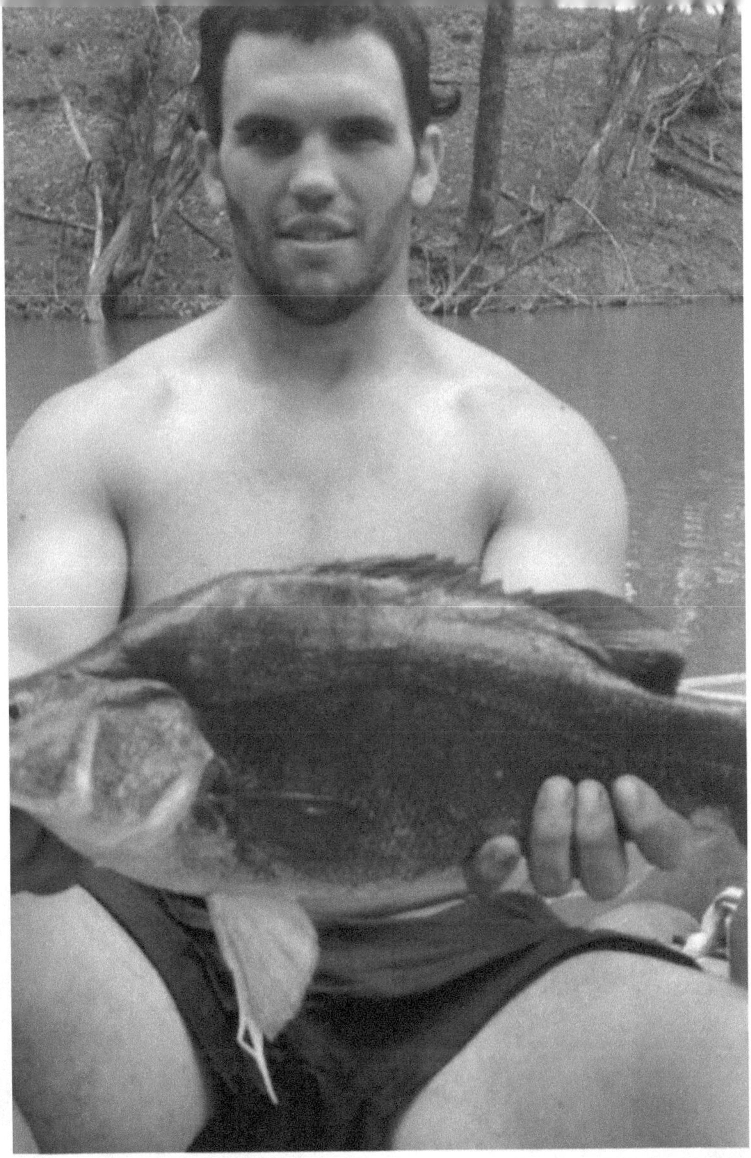
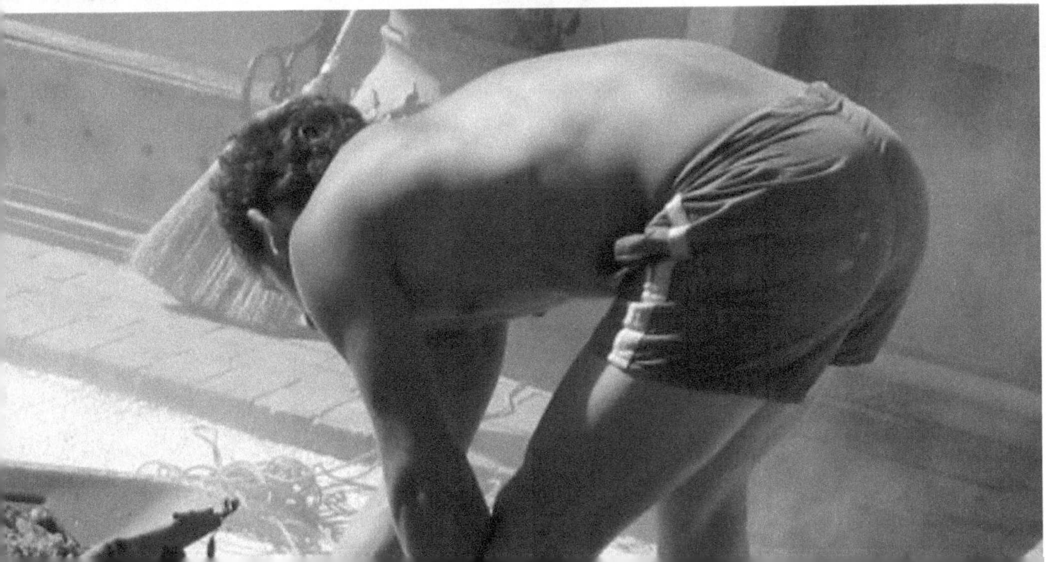

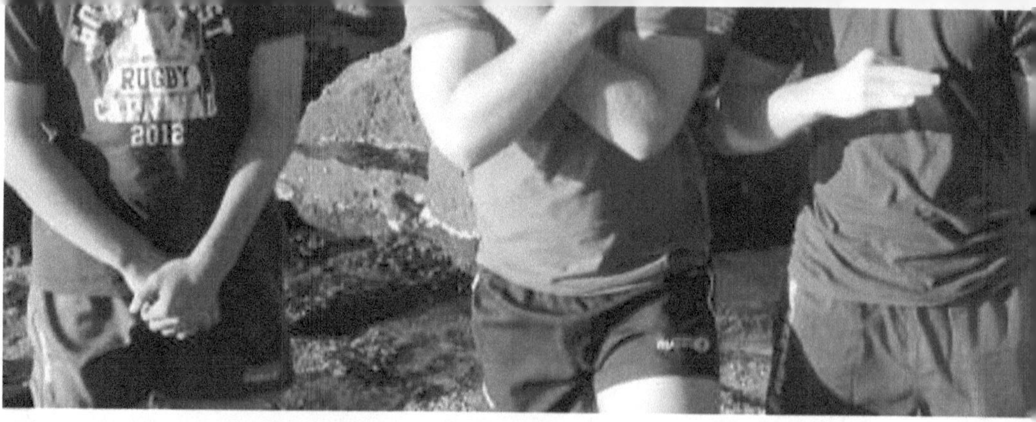
RUGBY
2018

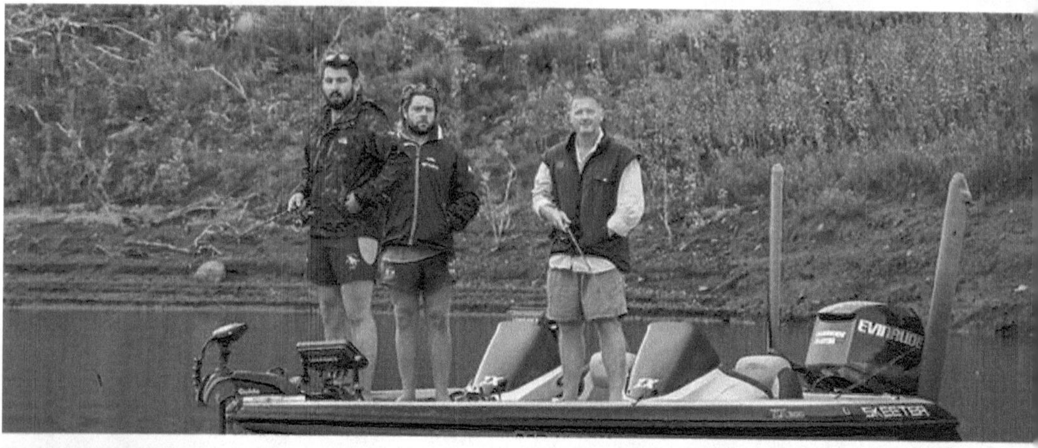
EVINRUDE
SKEETER

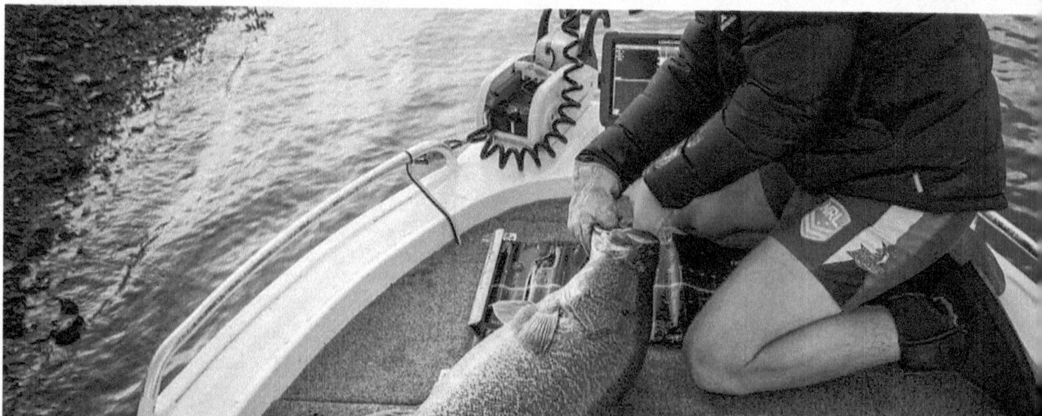

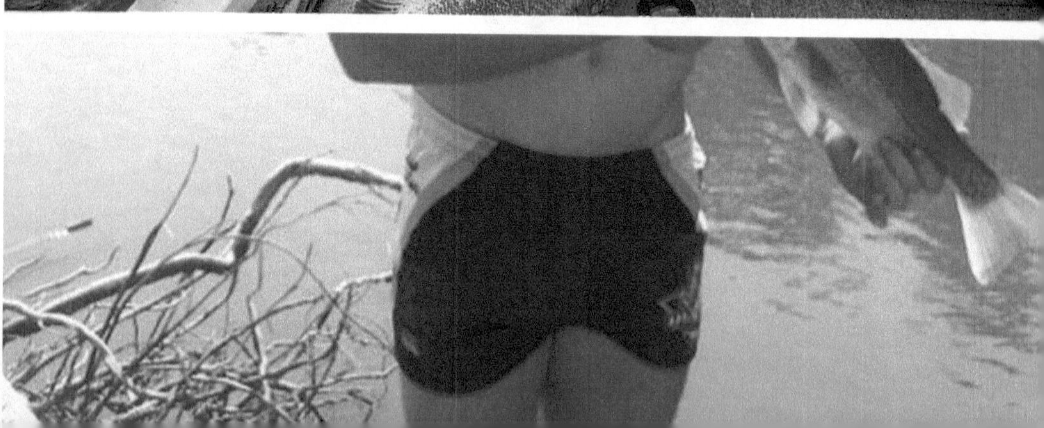

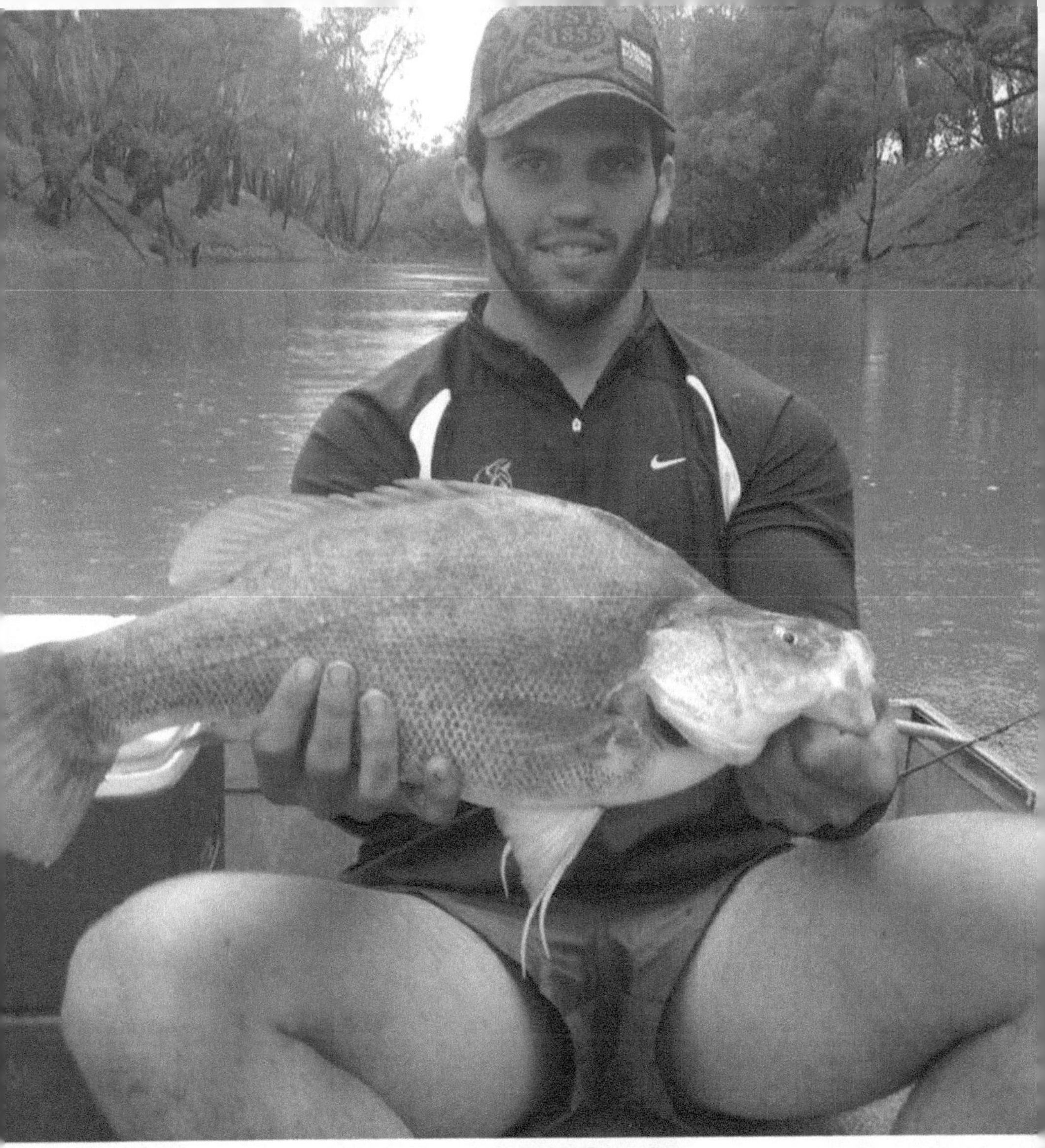

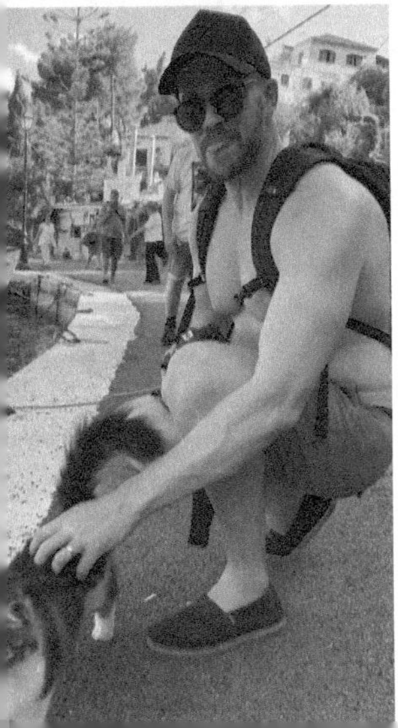

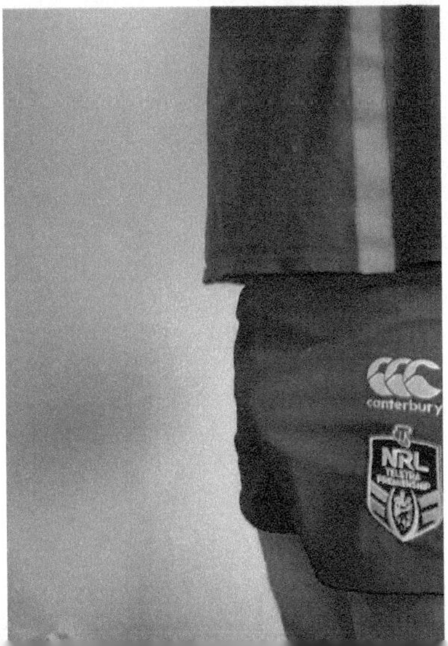
canterbury
NRL

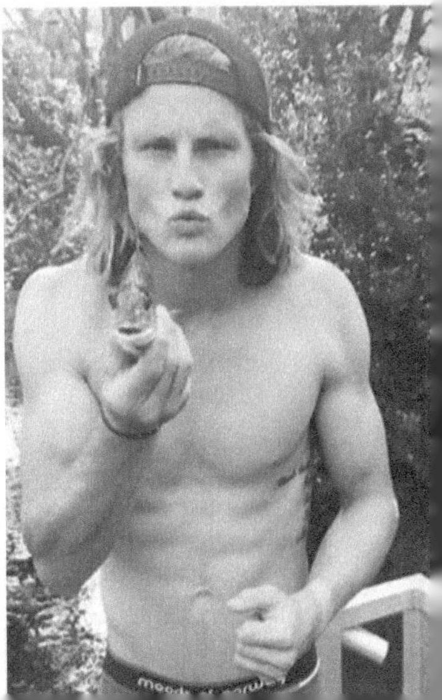

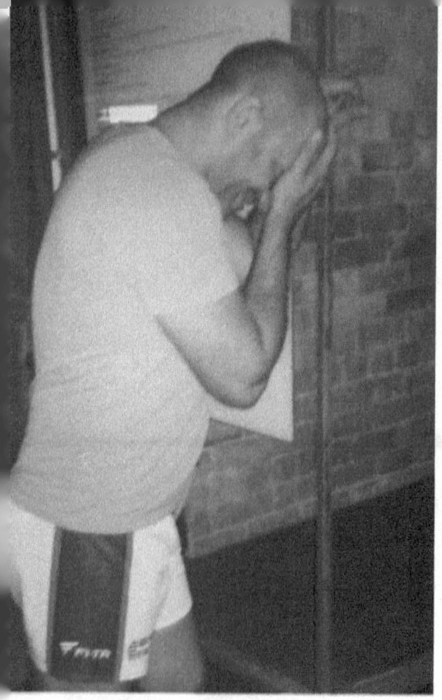
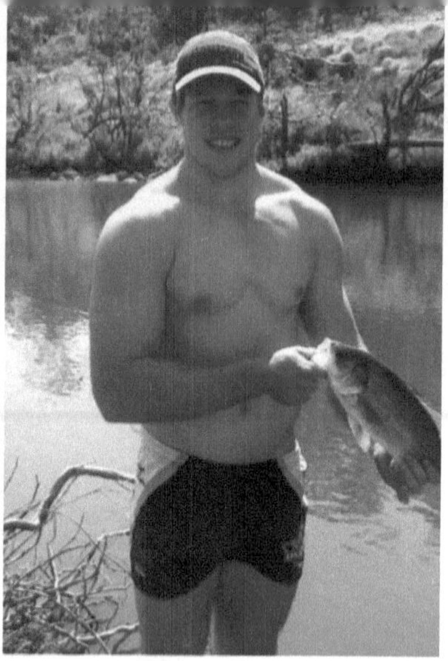
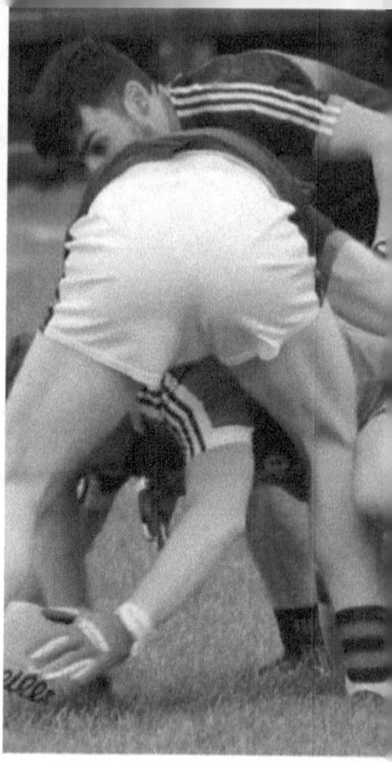
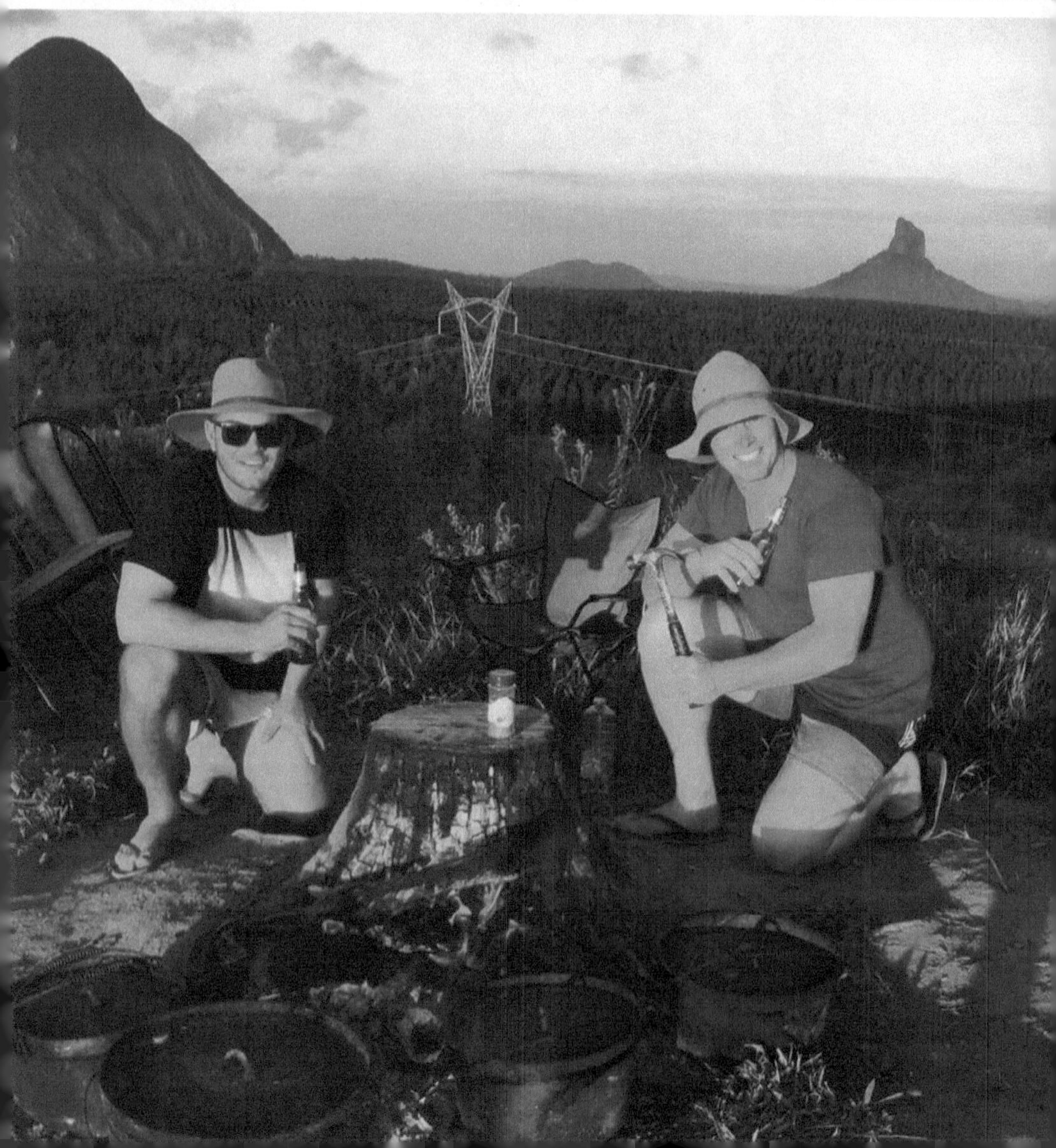

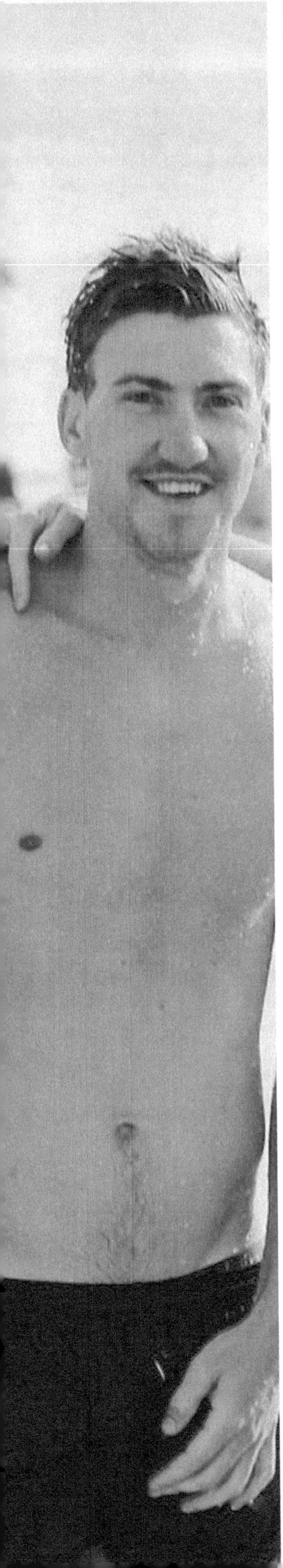

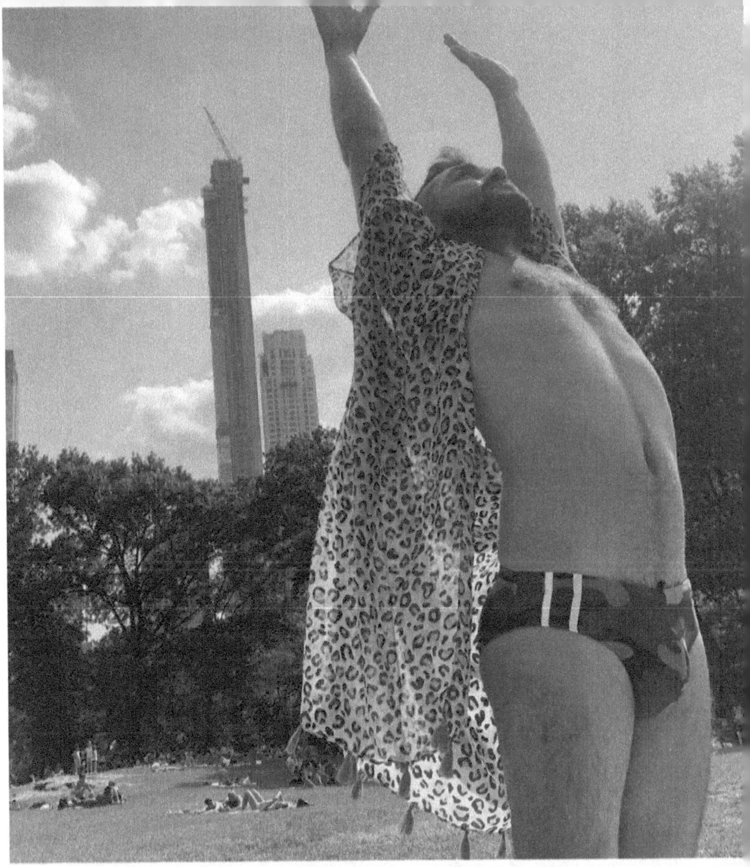

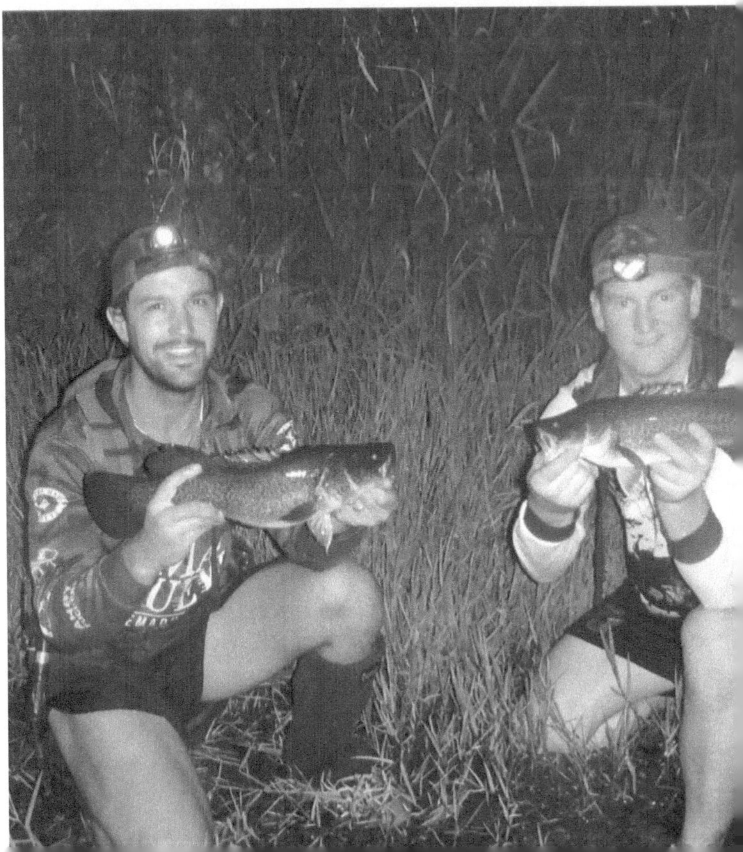

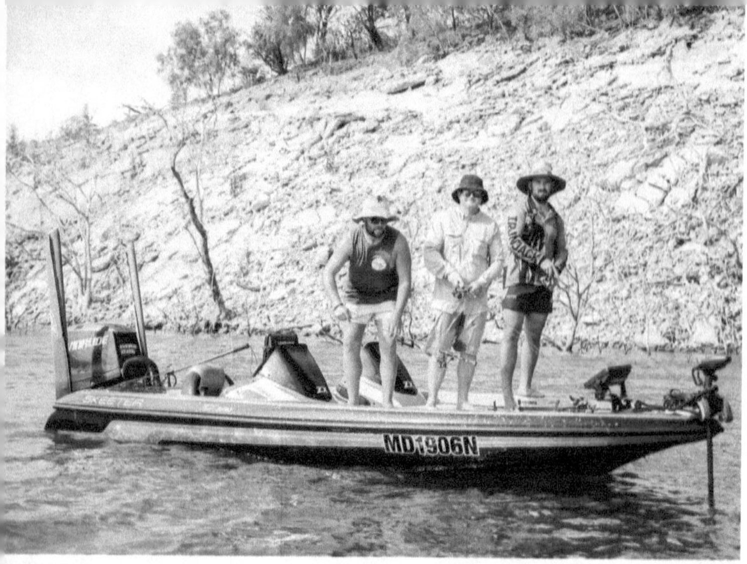
MD1906N
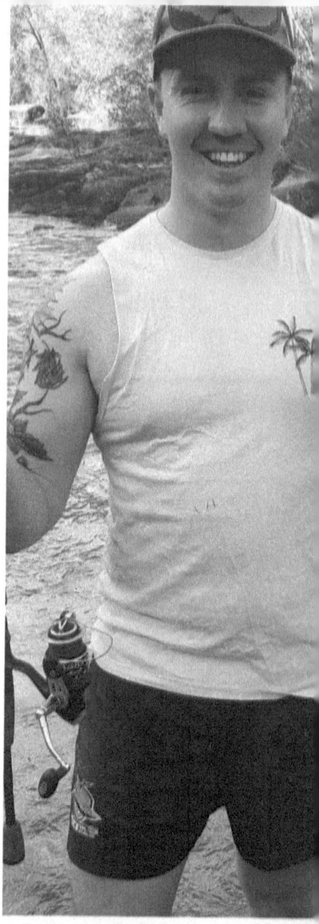
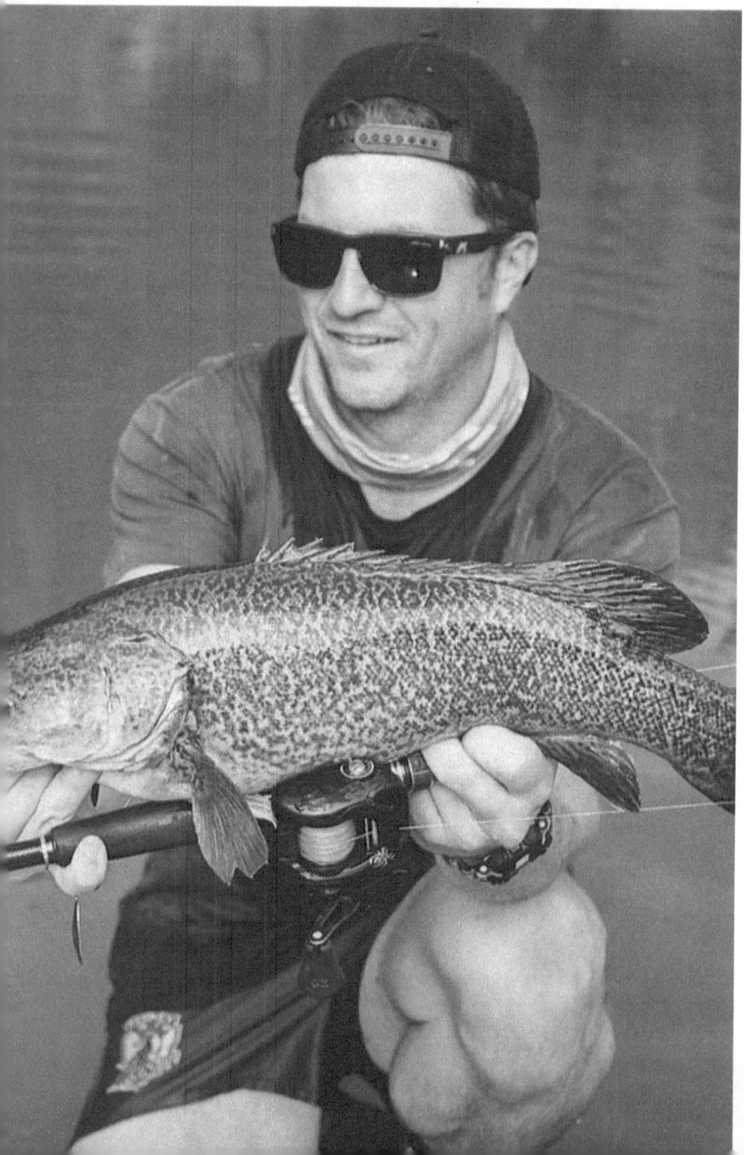
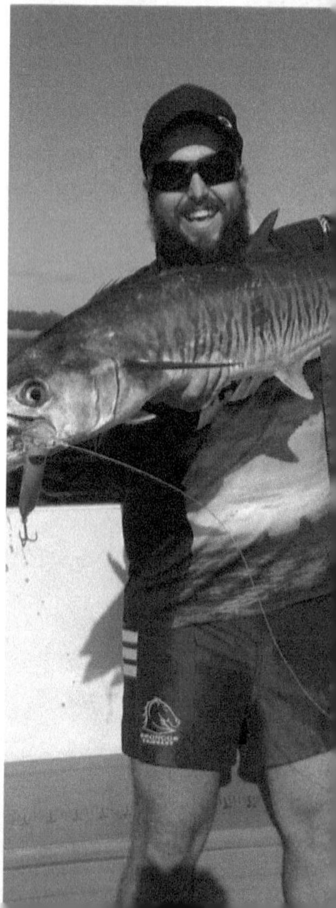

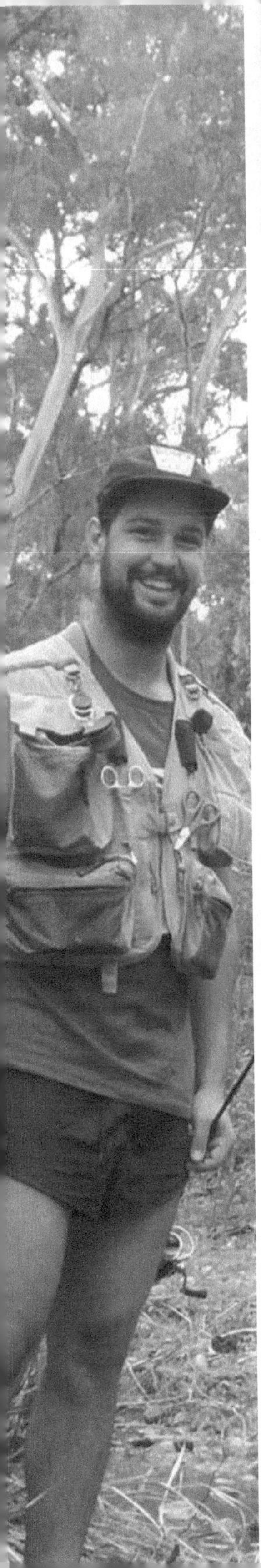

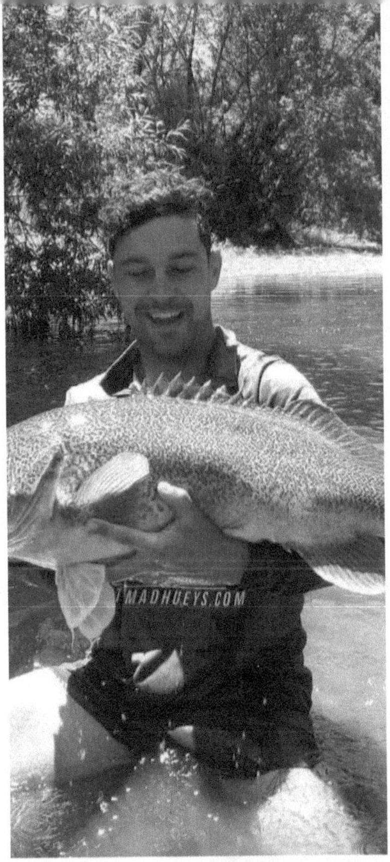
MADHUEYS.COM

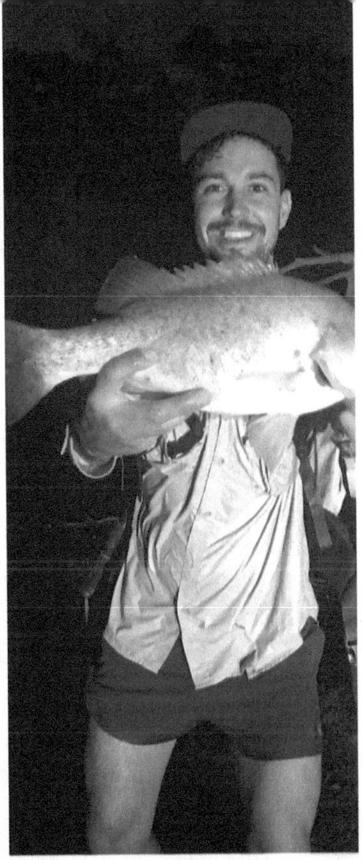

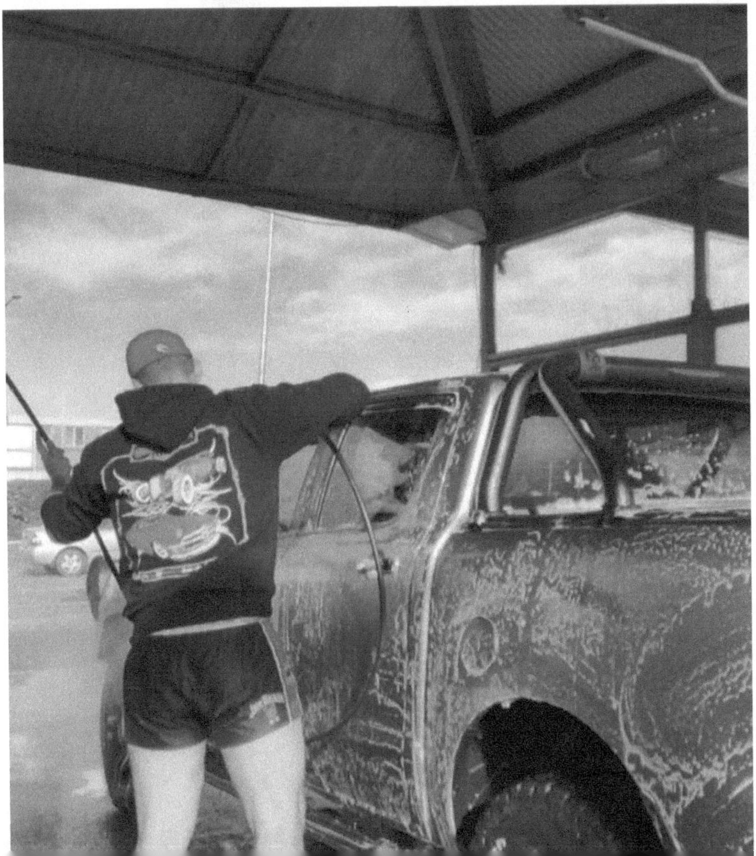

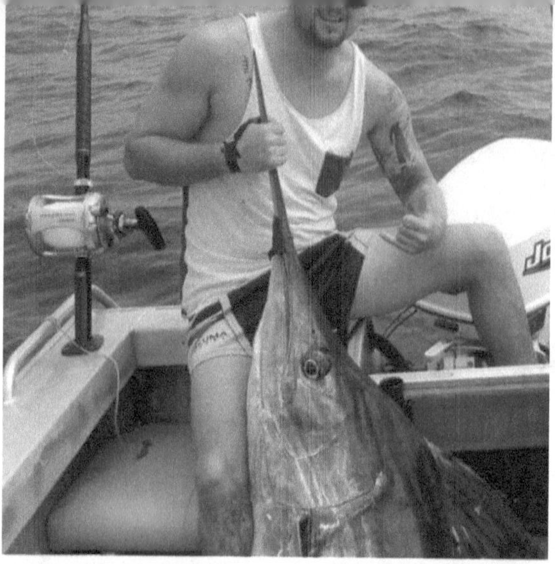
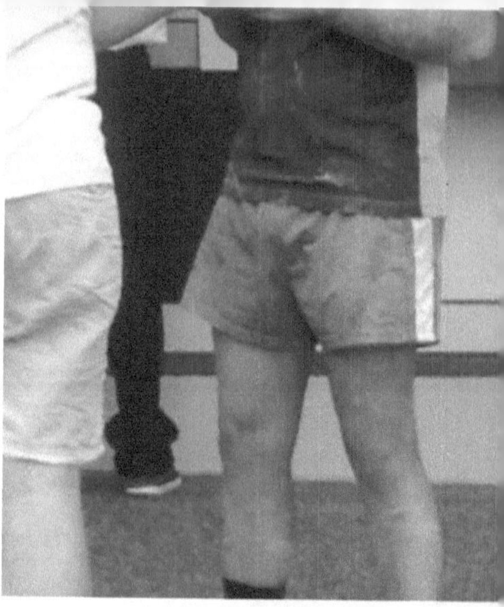
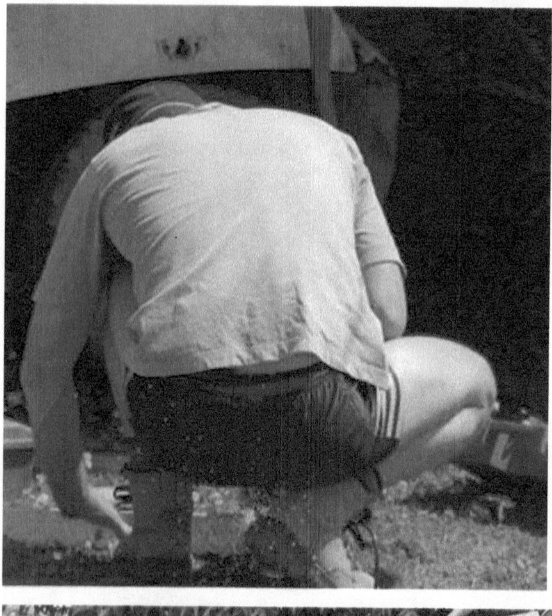
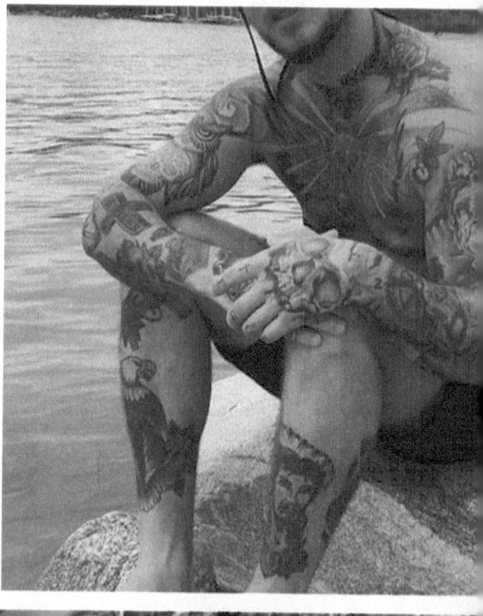
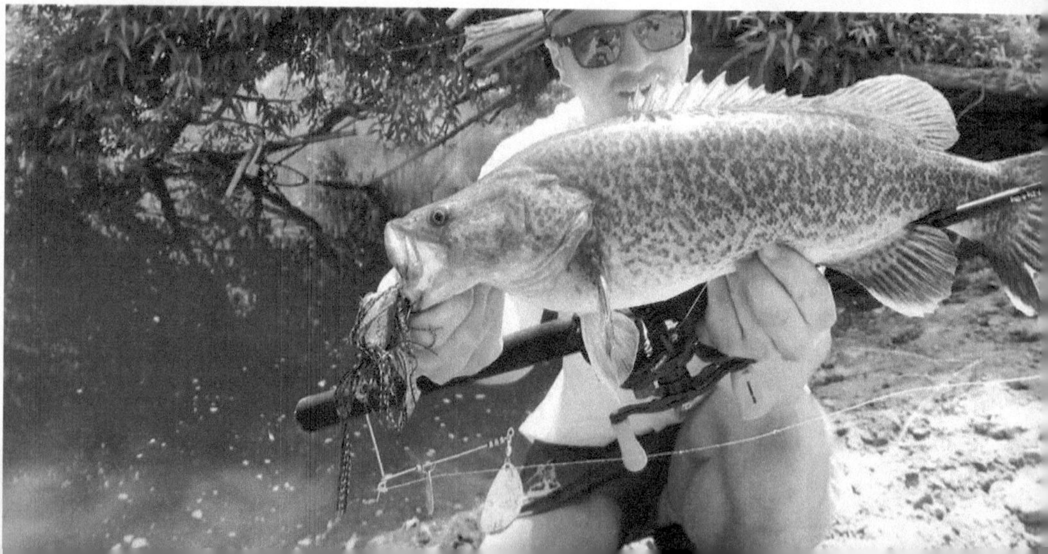

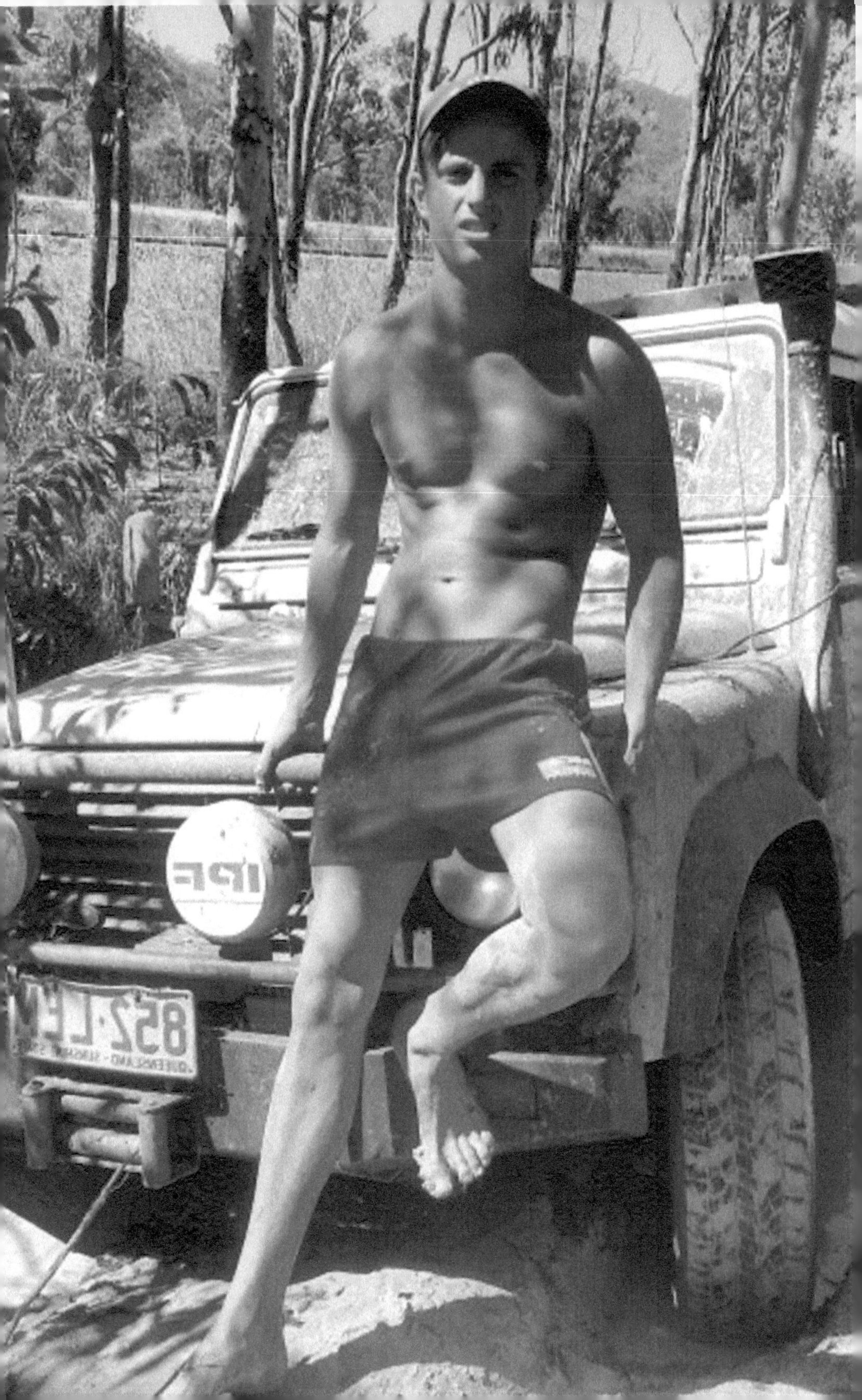

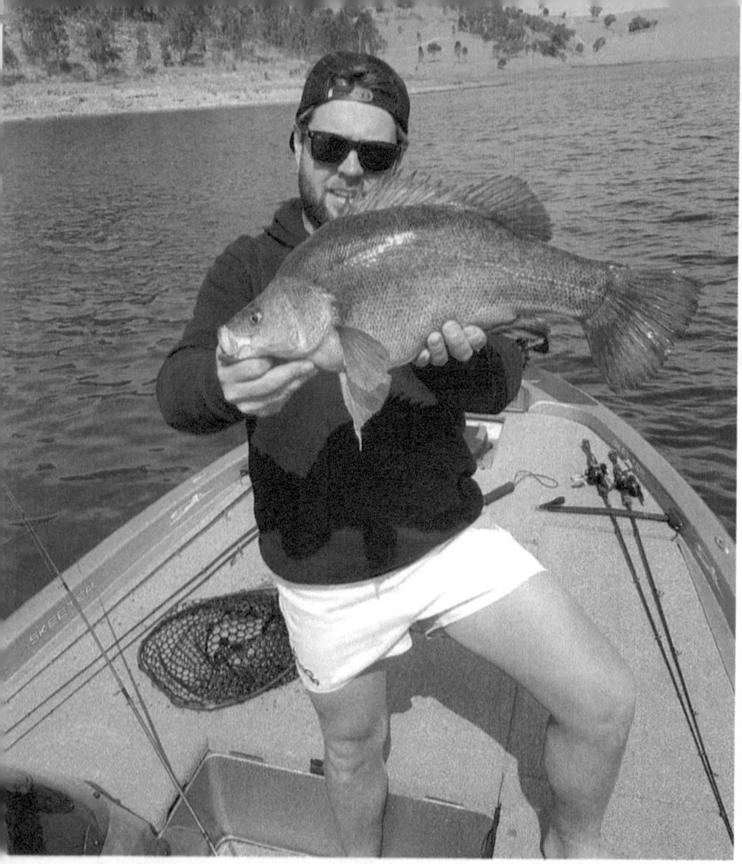
SKEETER

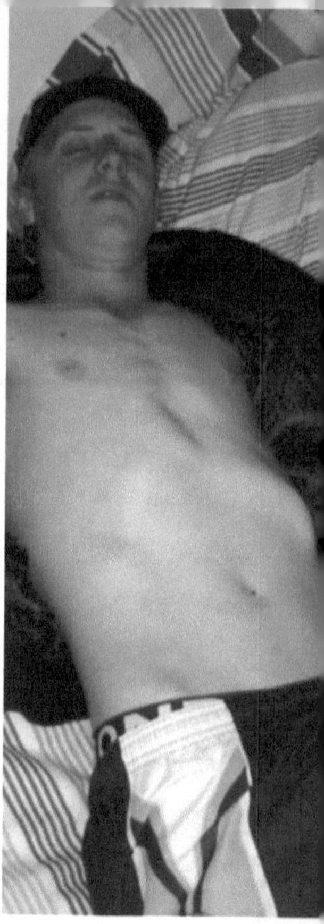

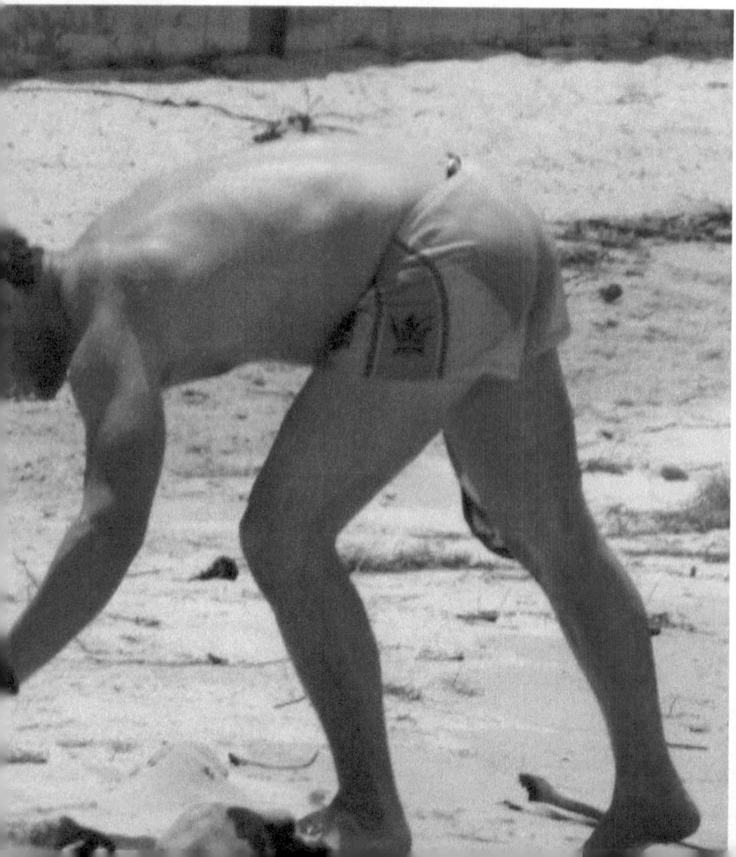

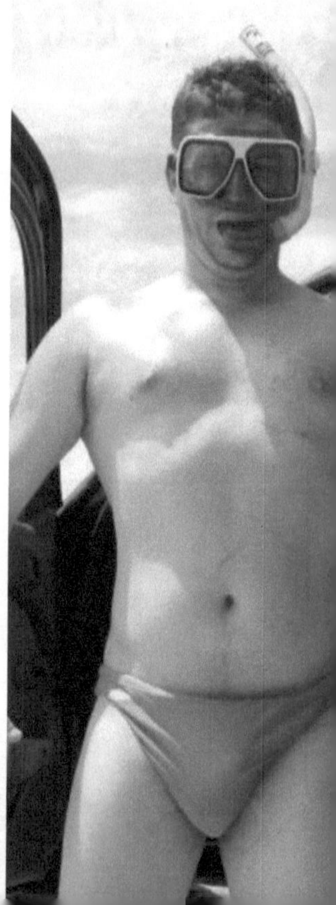

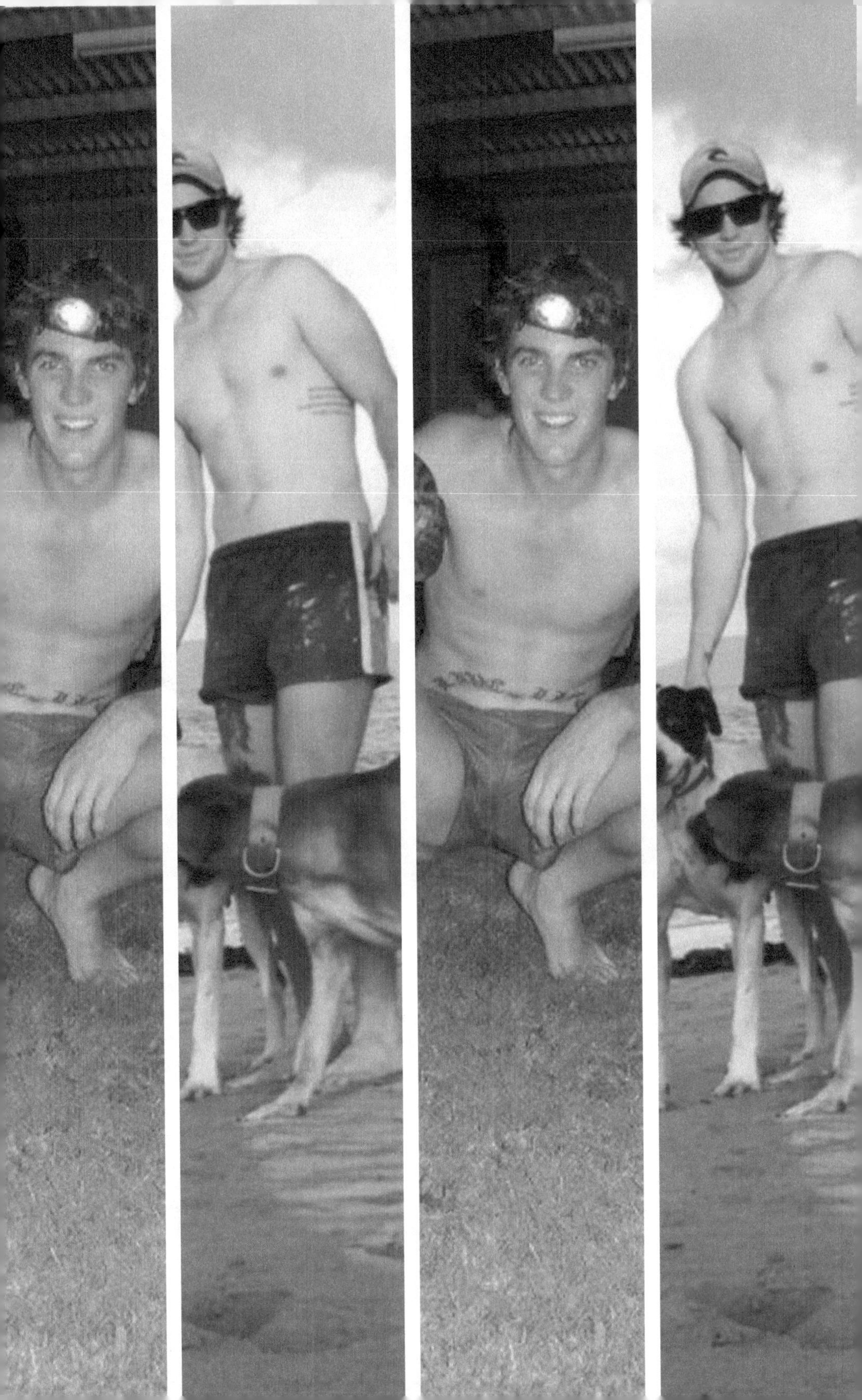

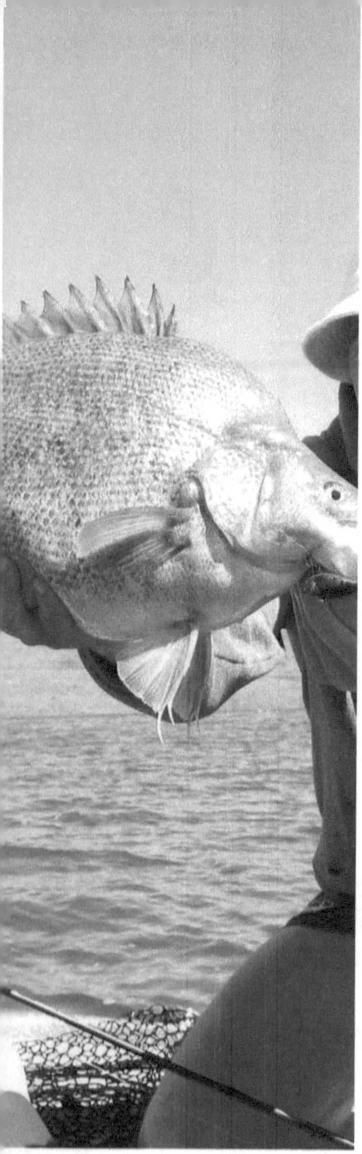
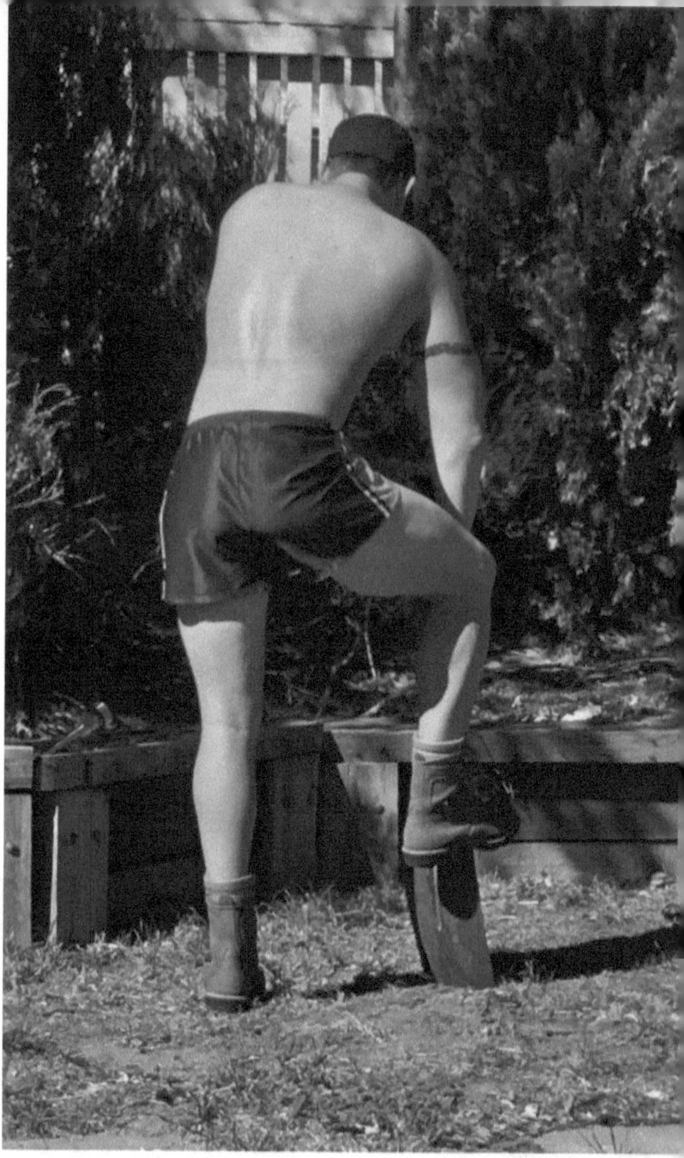
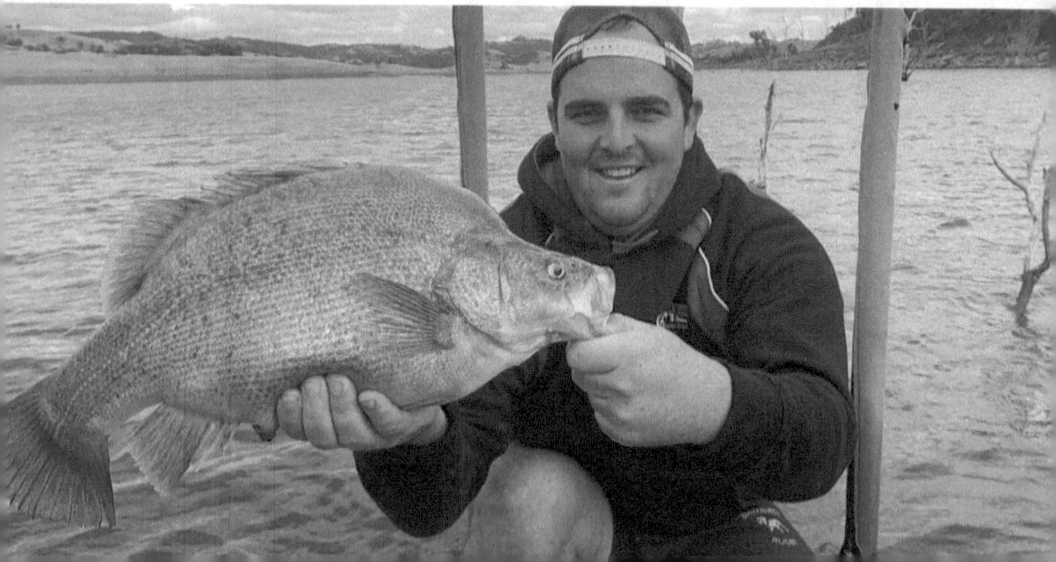

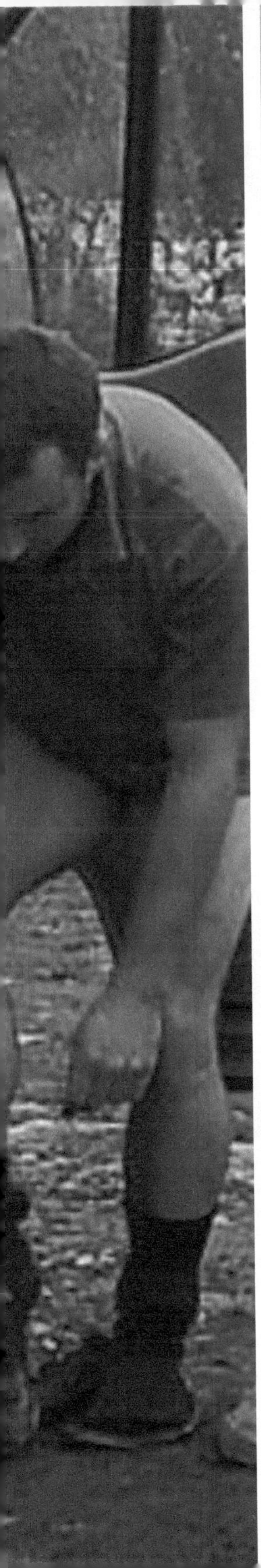

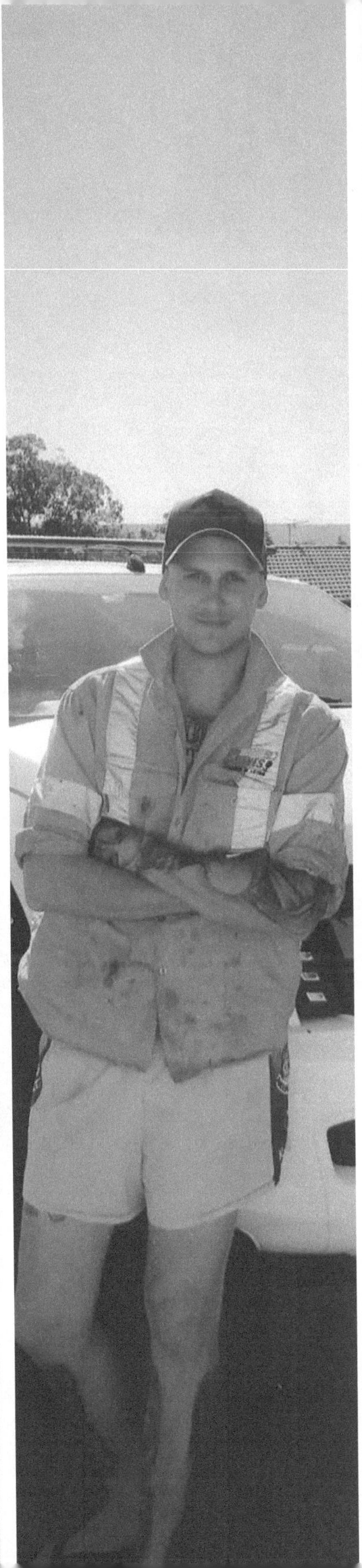

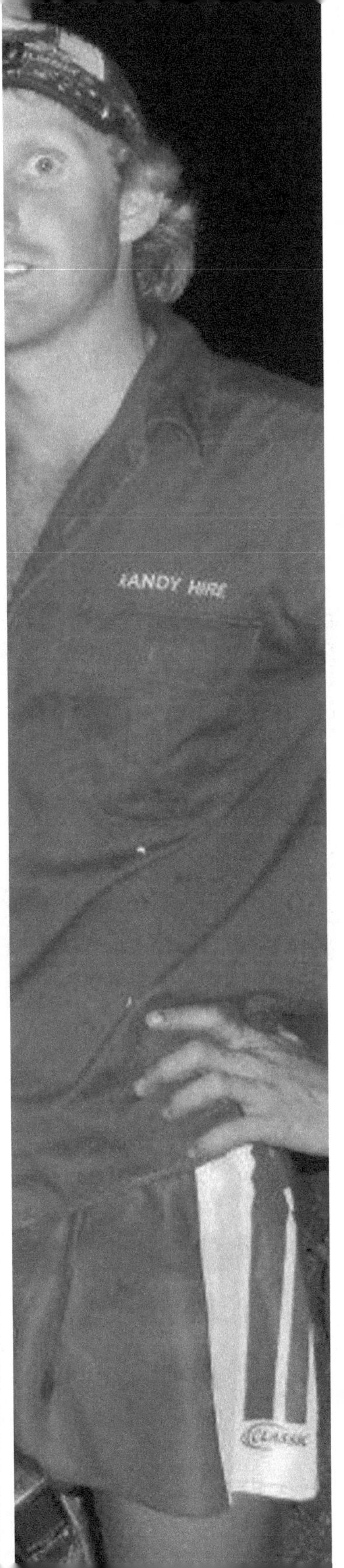
ANDY HIRE

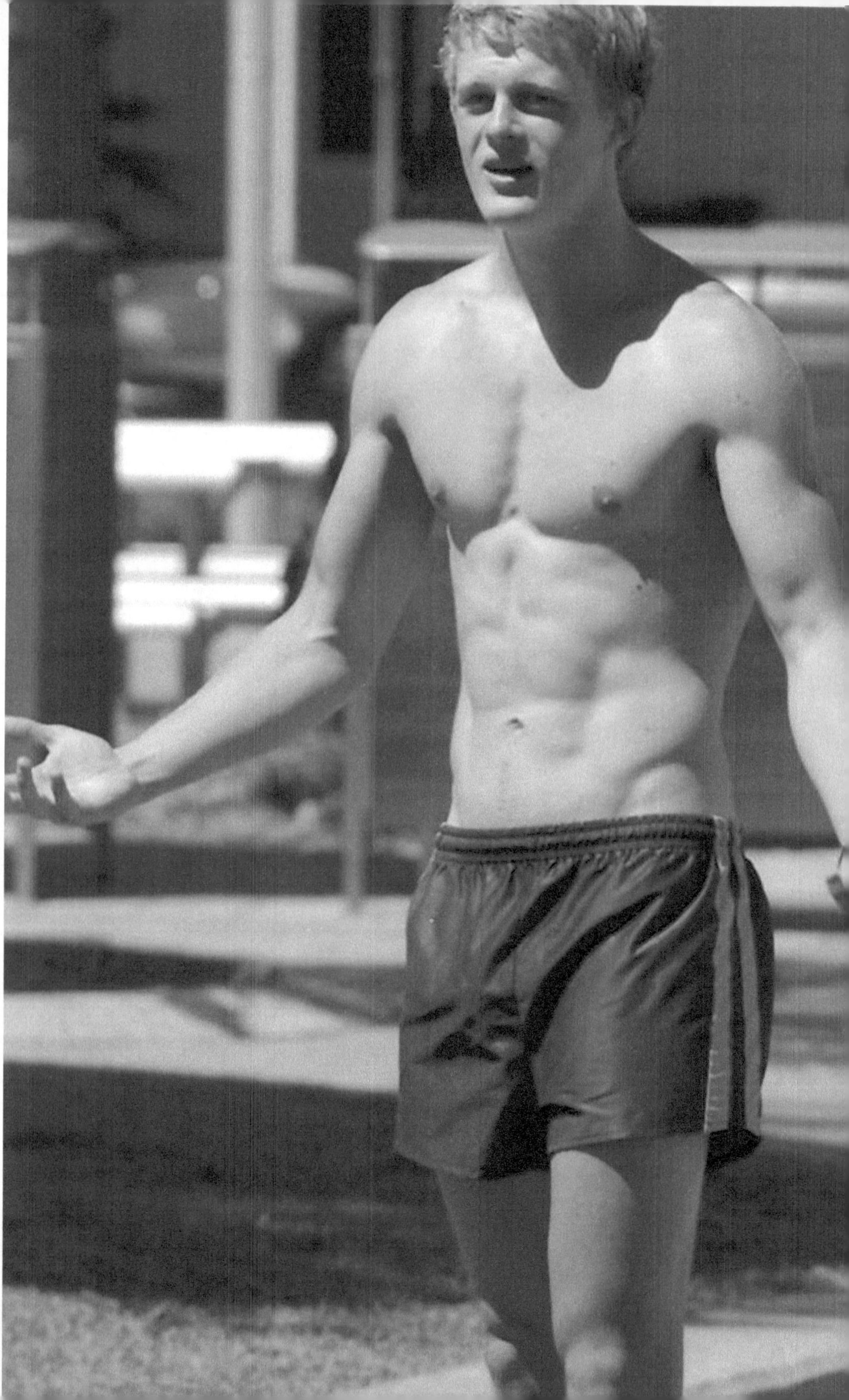

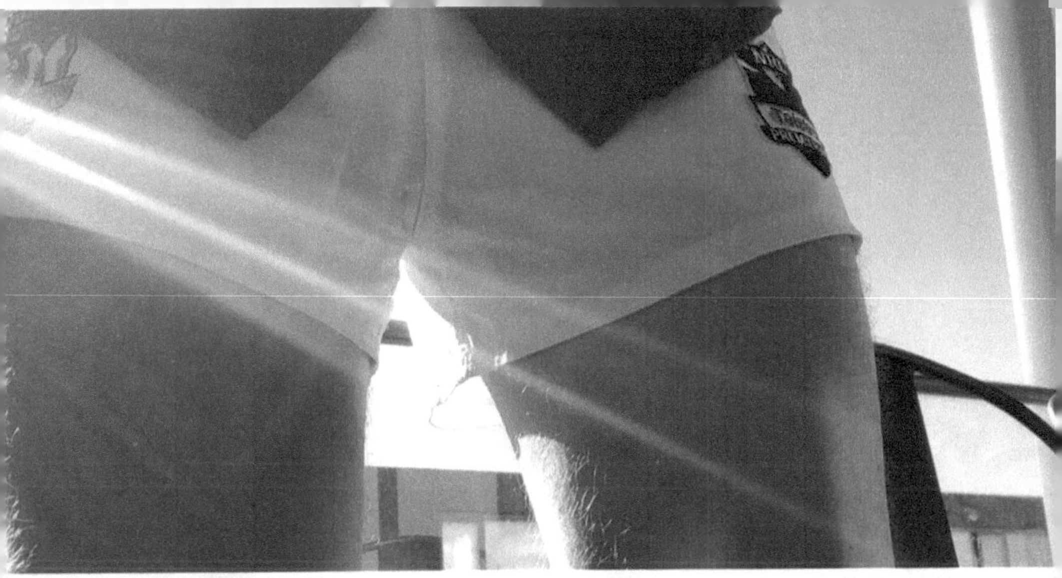

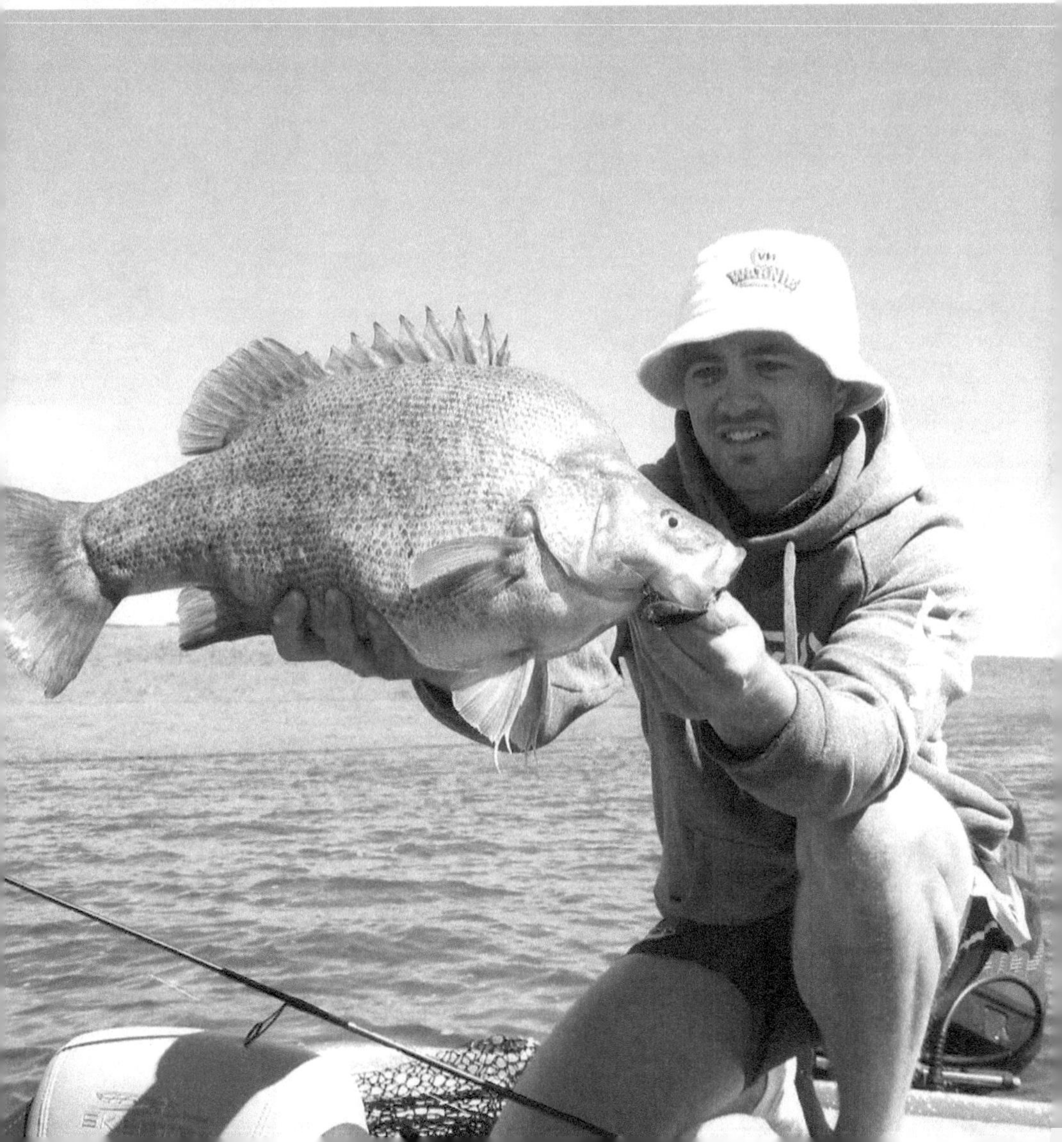

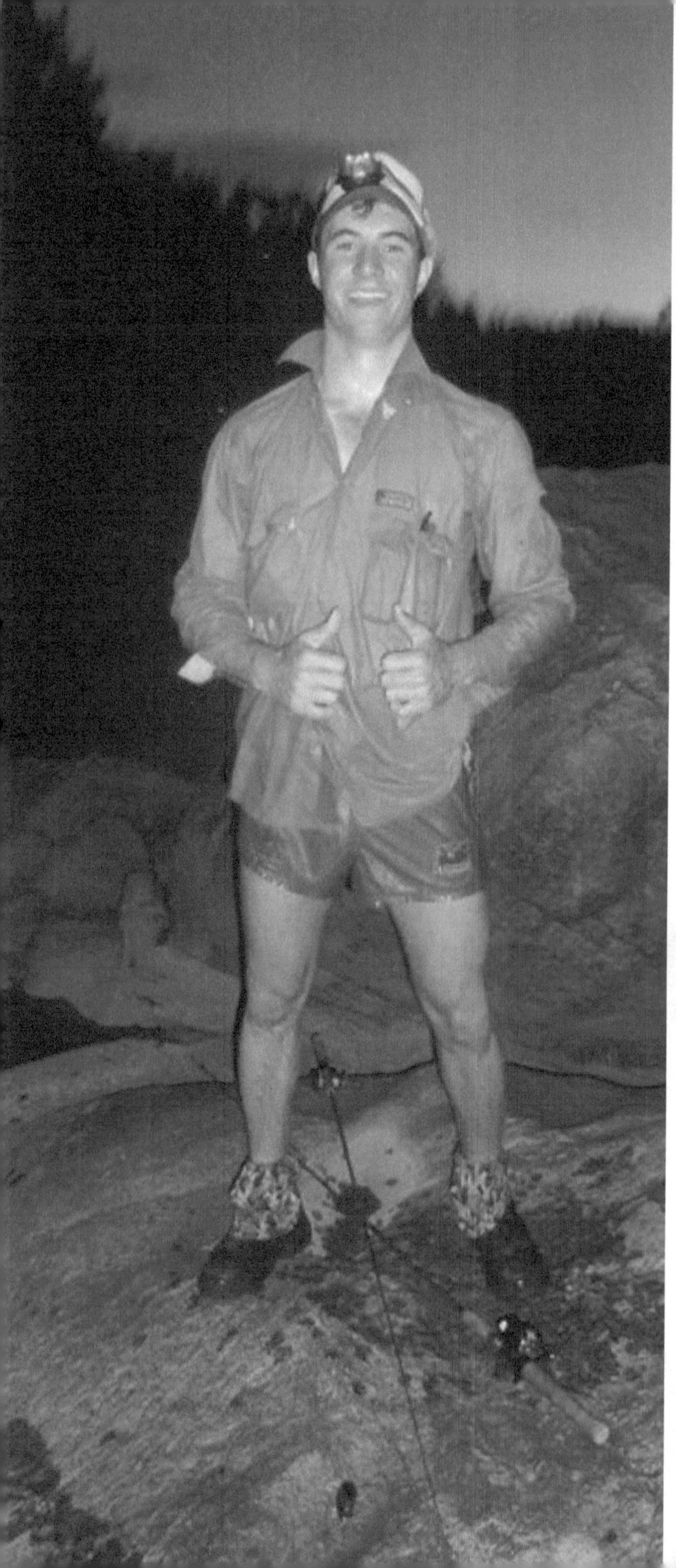

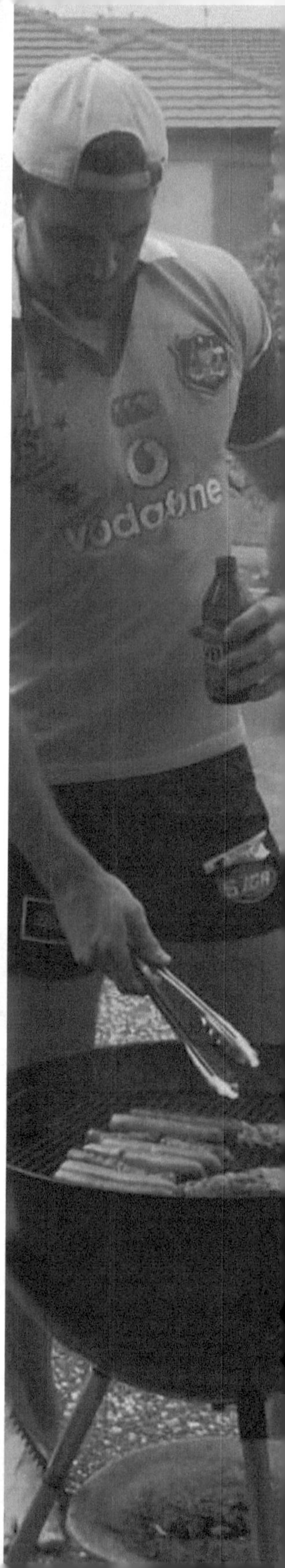
vodafone

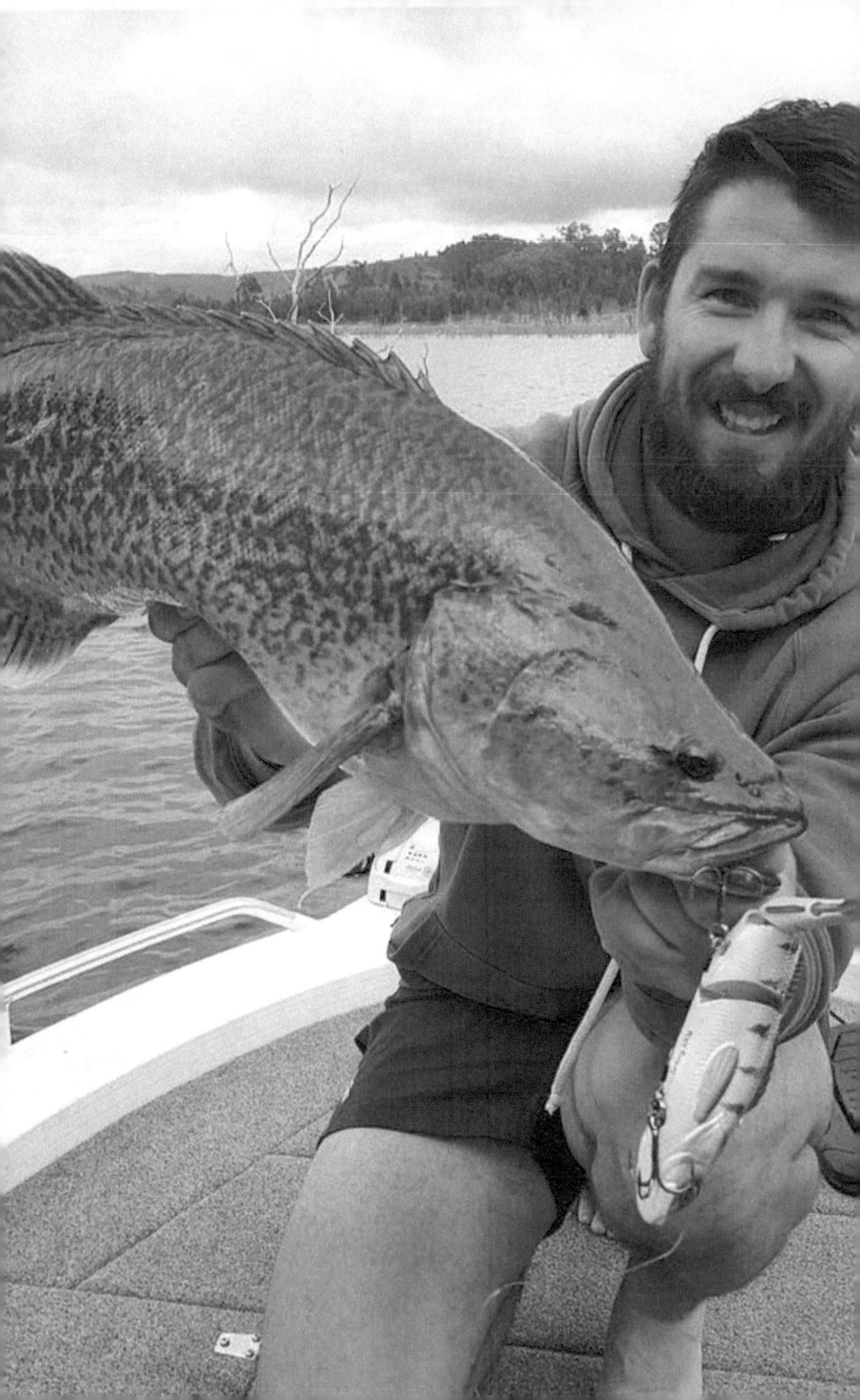

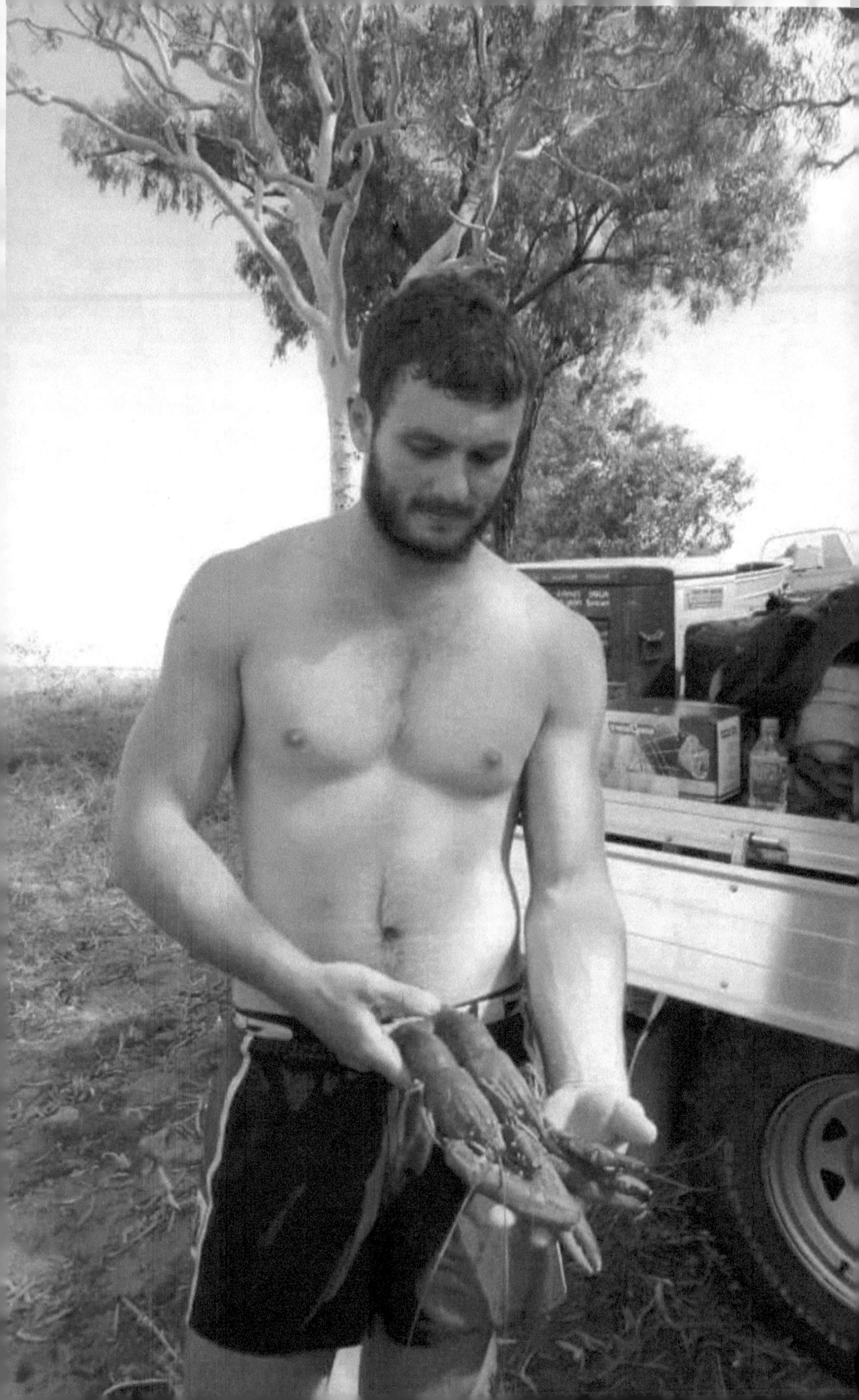

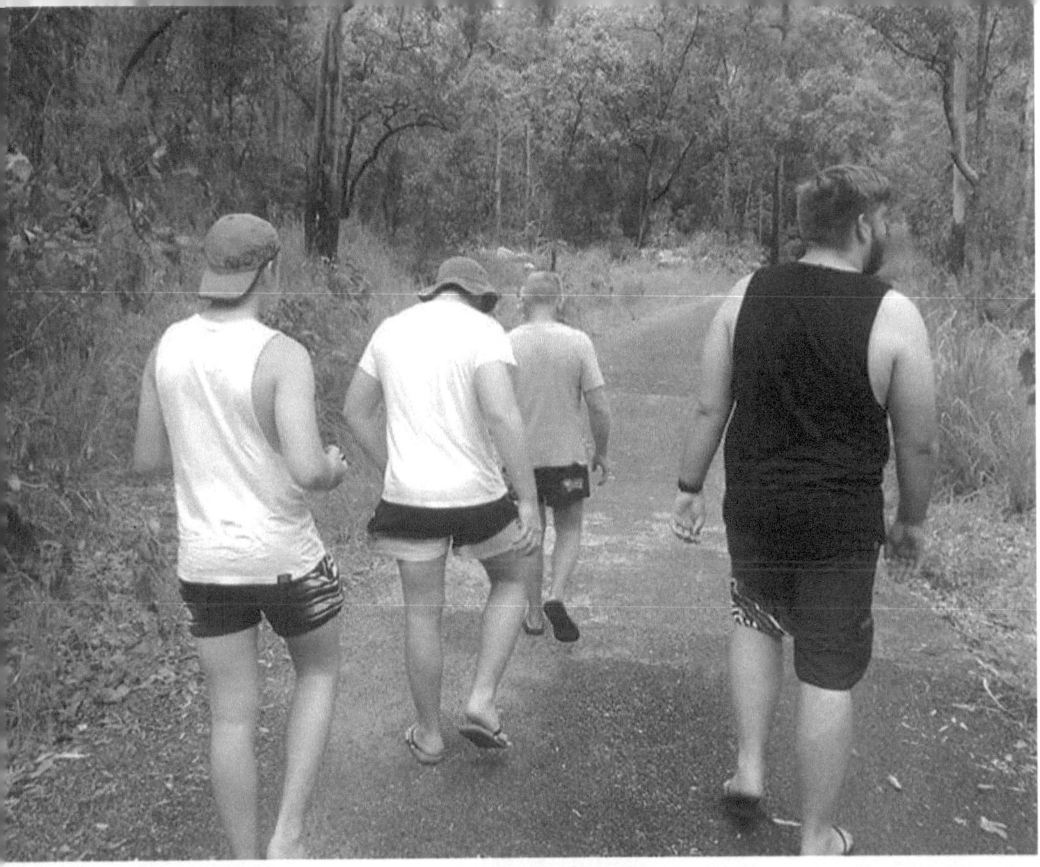

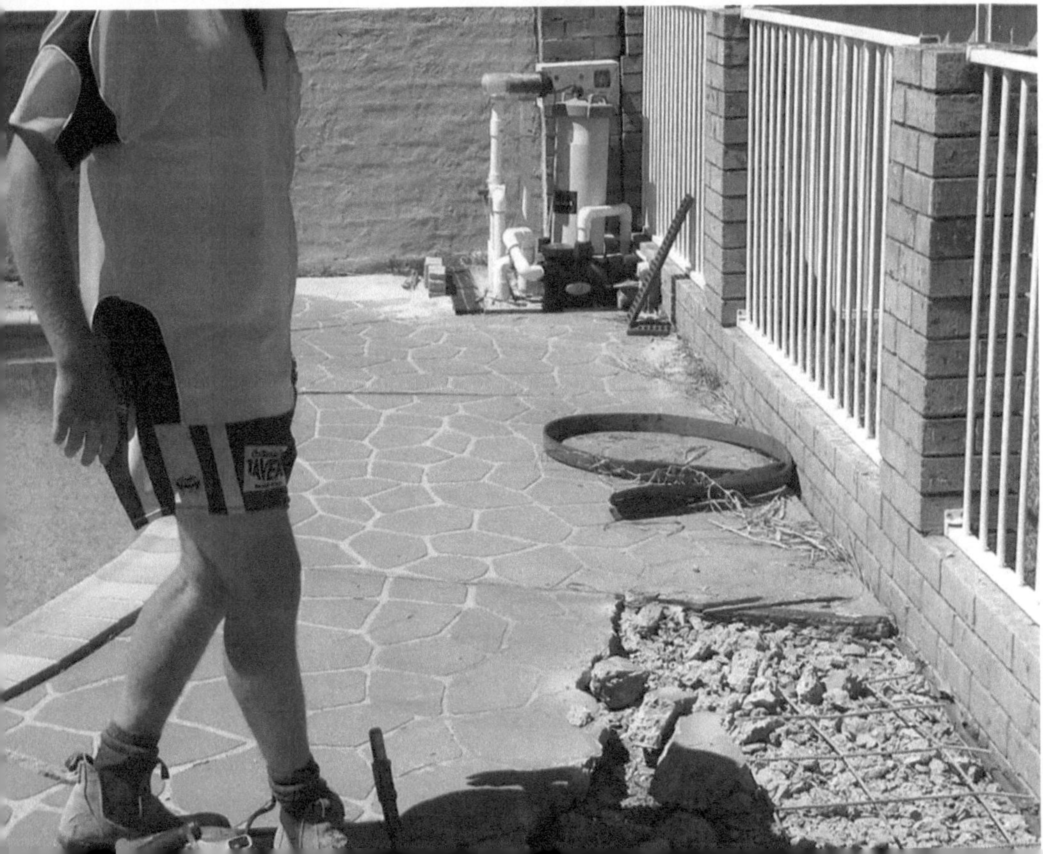

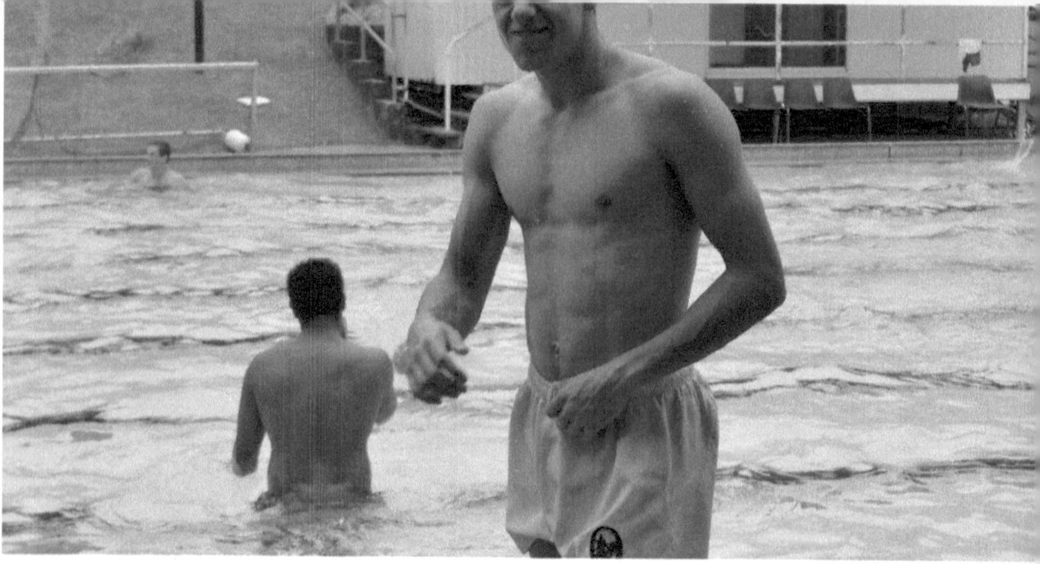

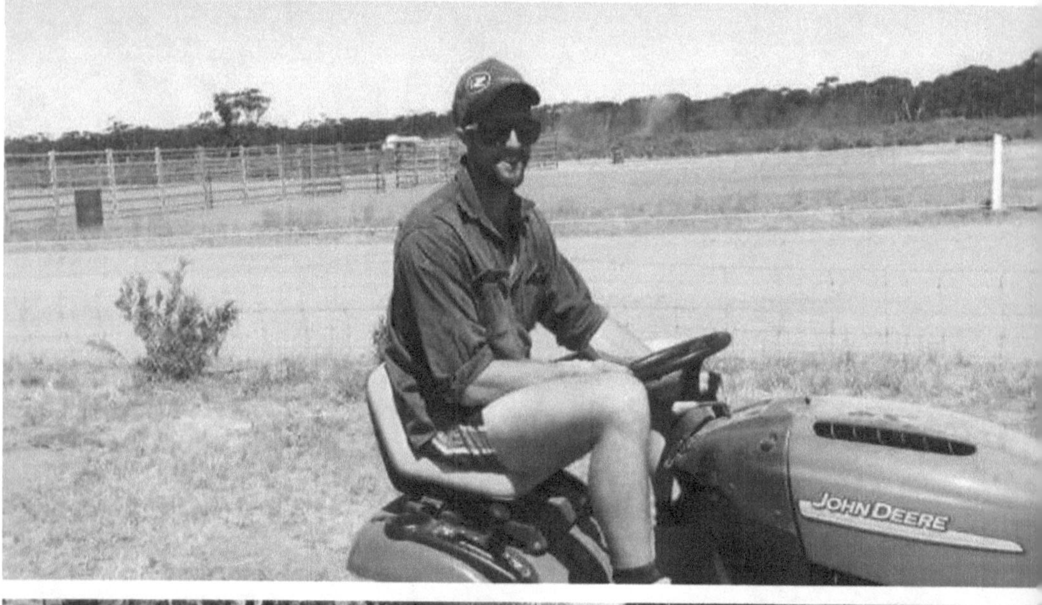
JOHN DEERE

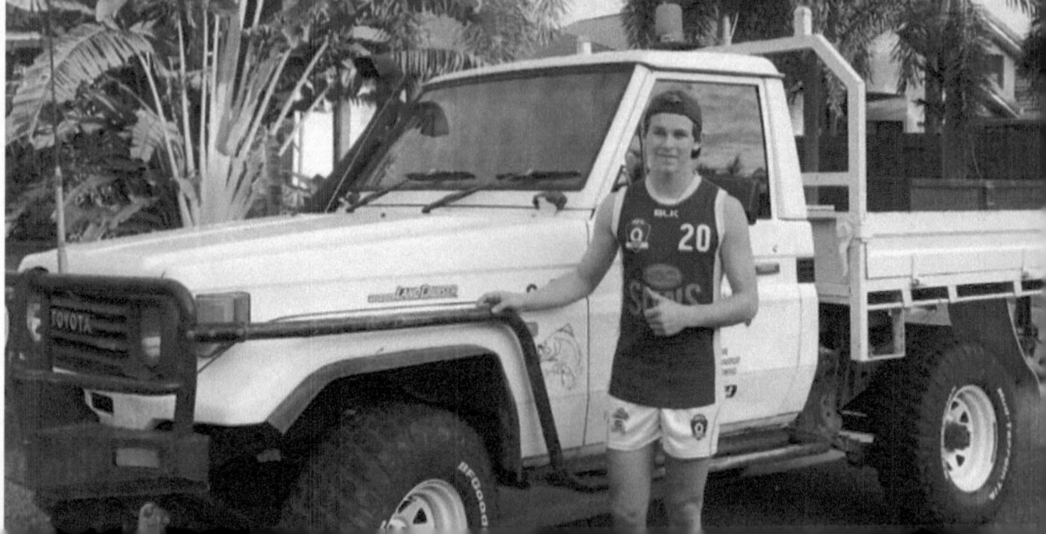
TOYOTA
20

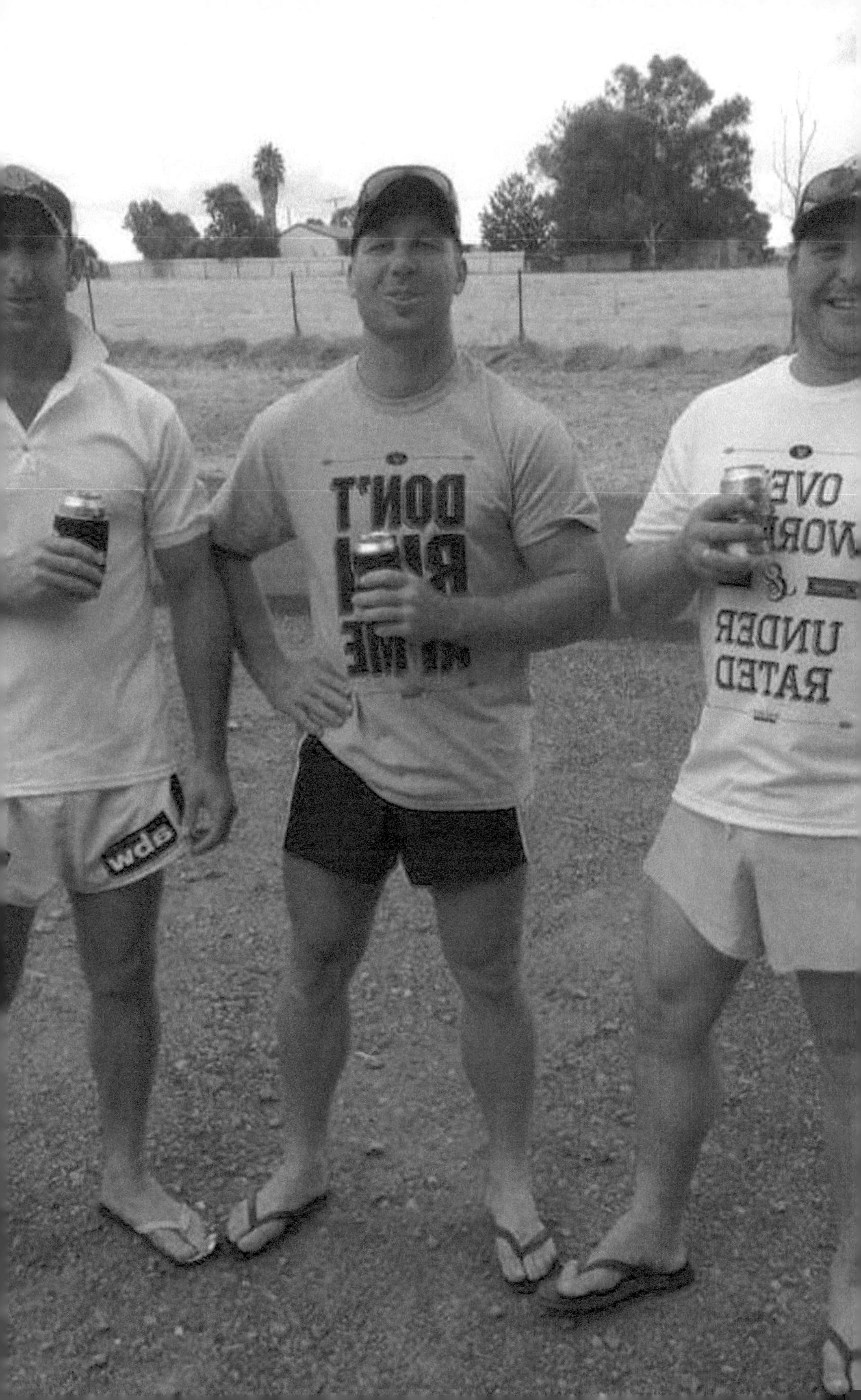
DON'T
UNDER
RATED

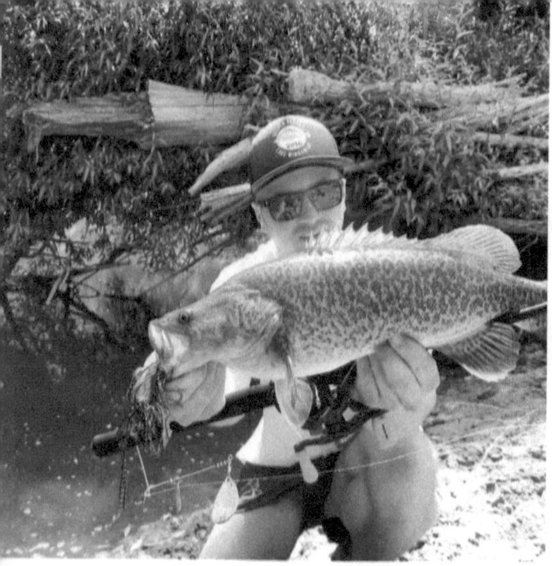

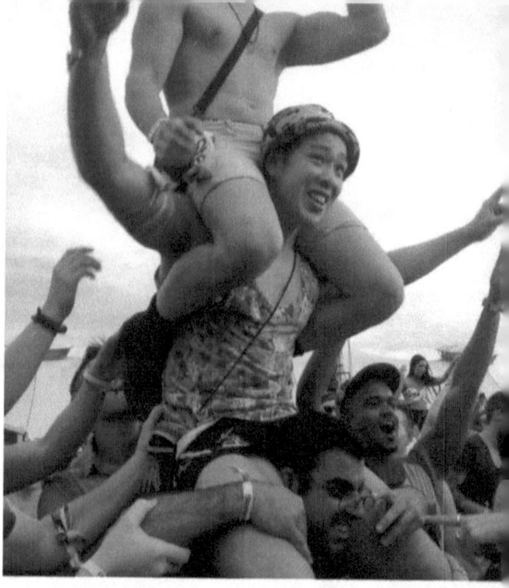

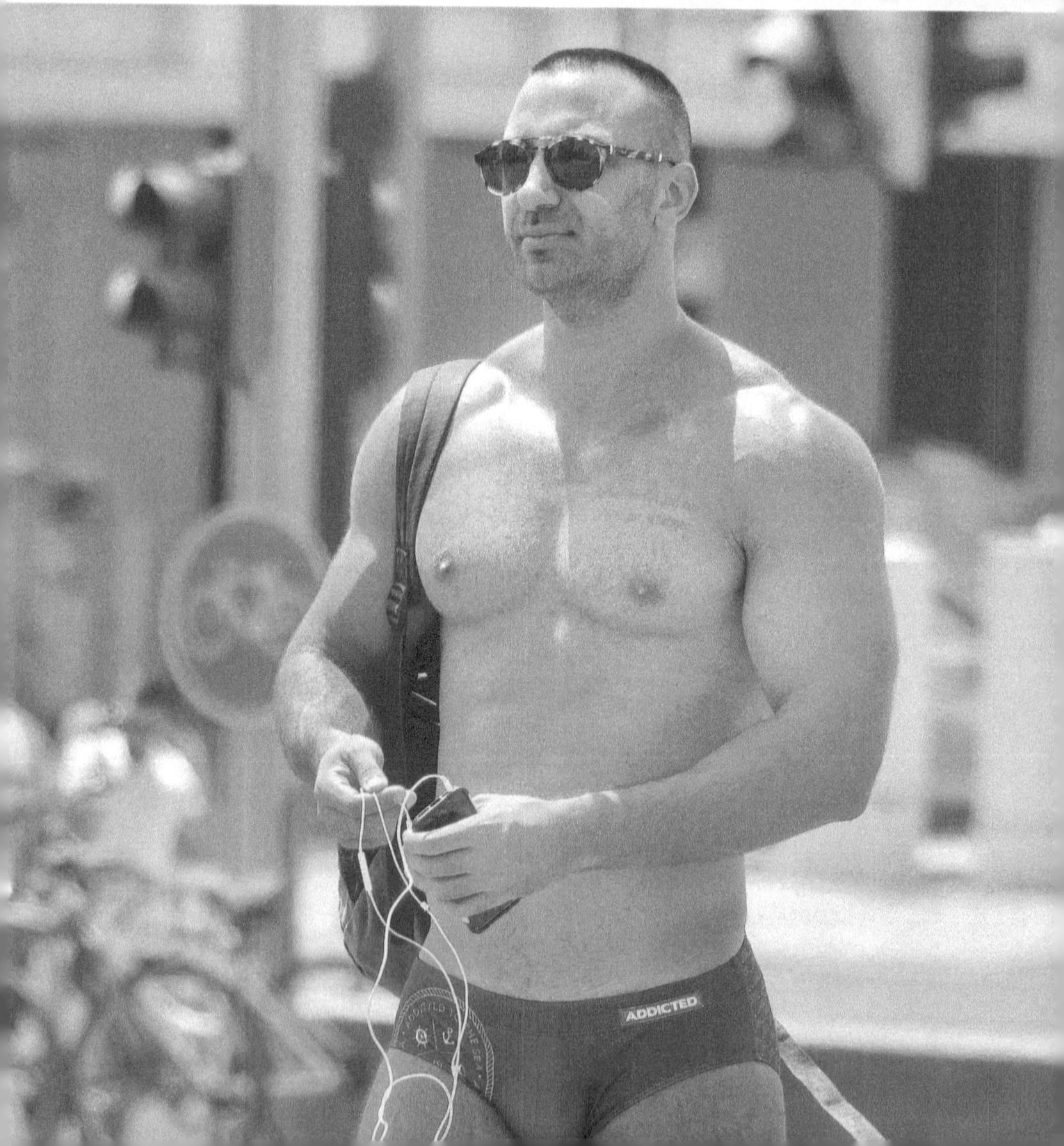

ADDICTED

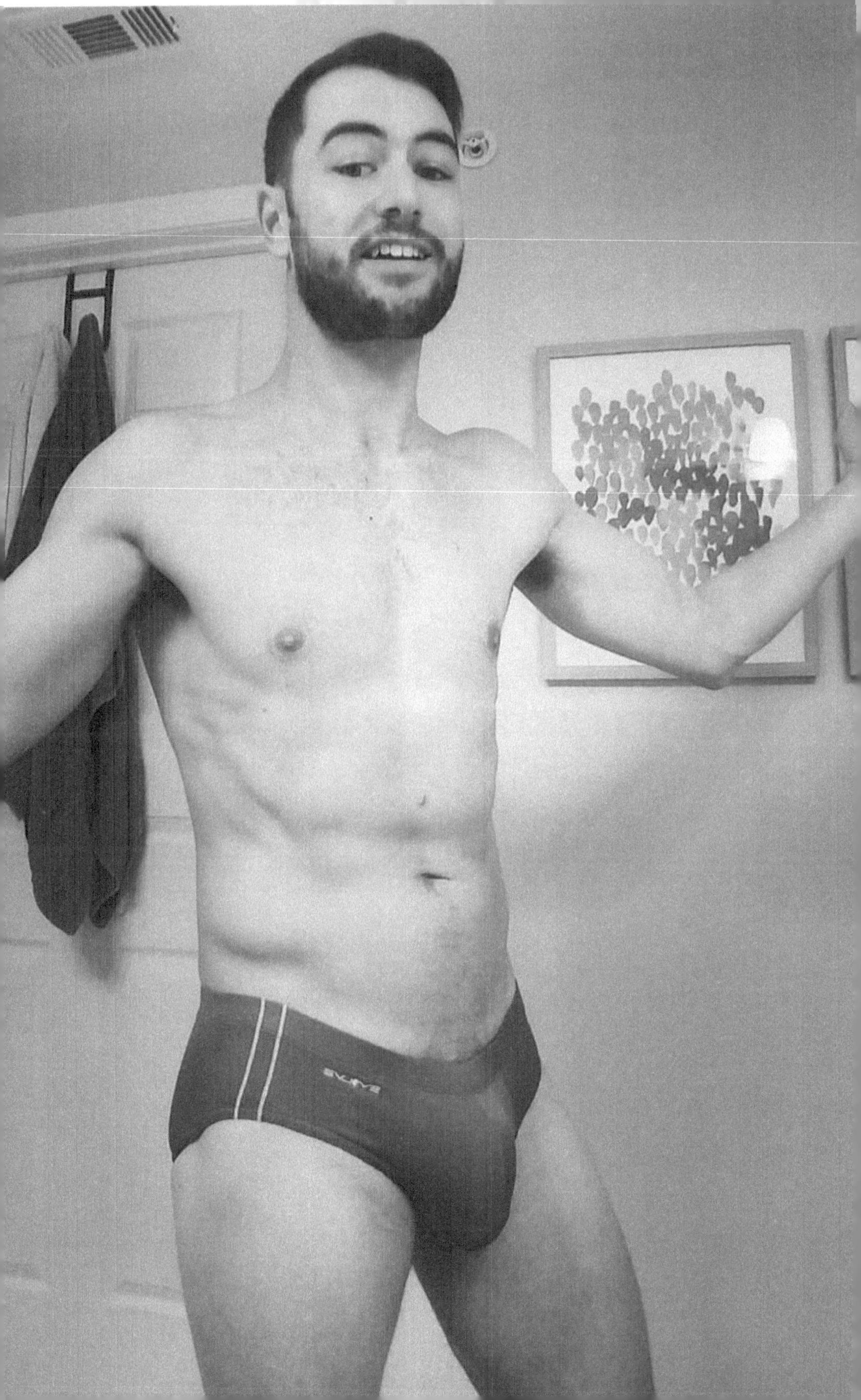

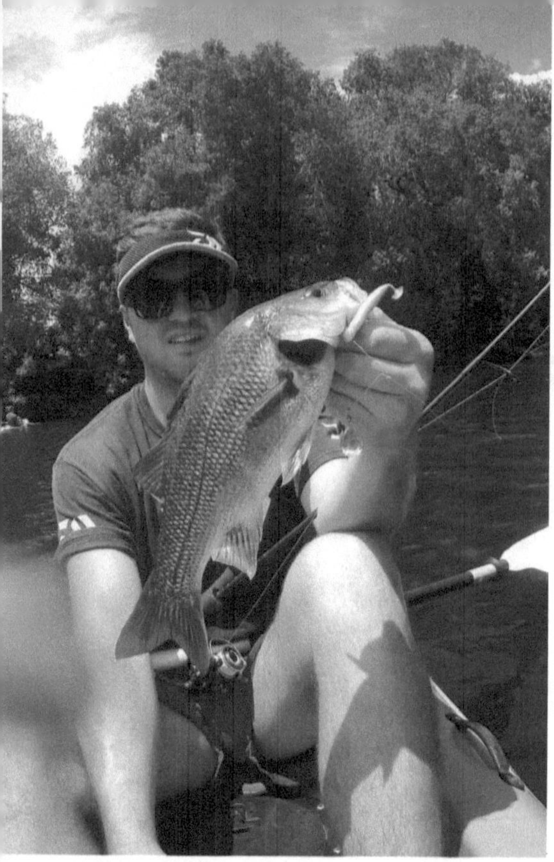

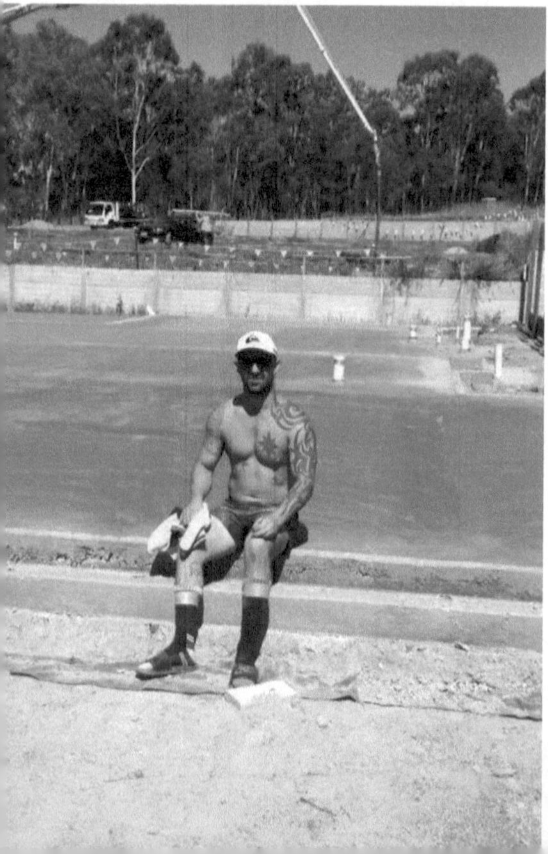

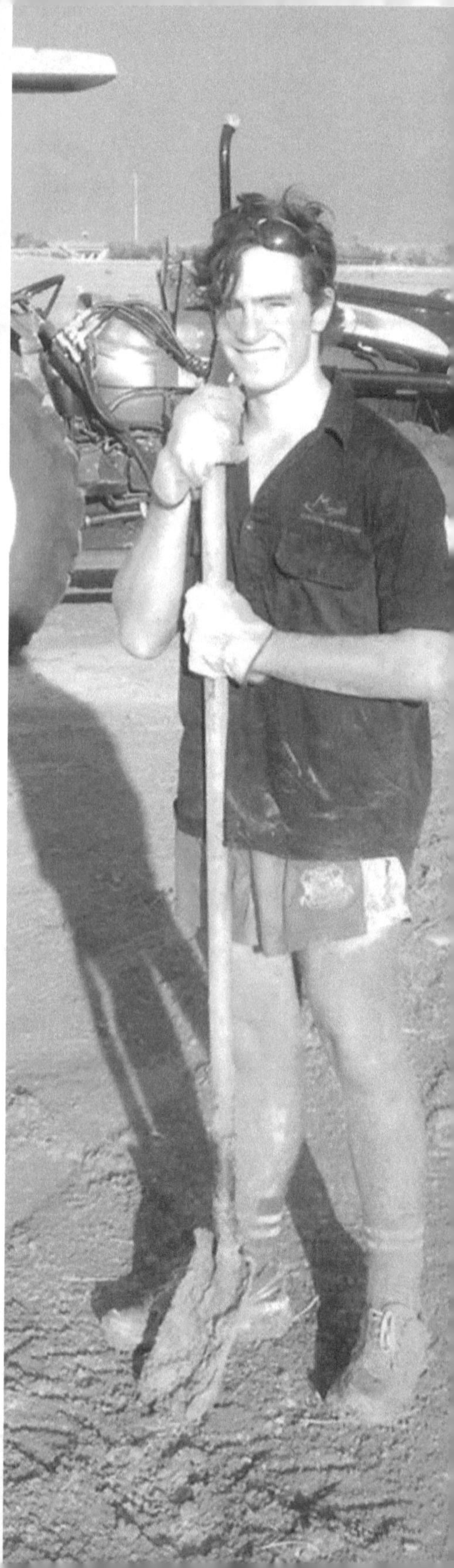

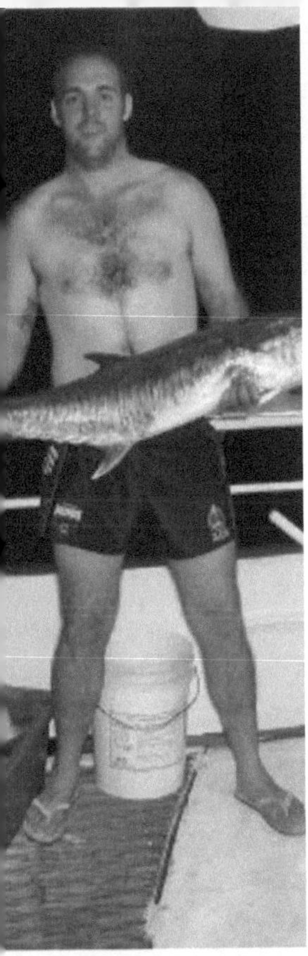

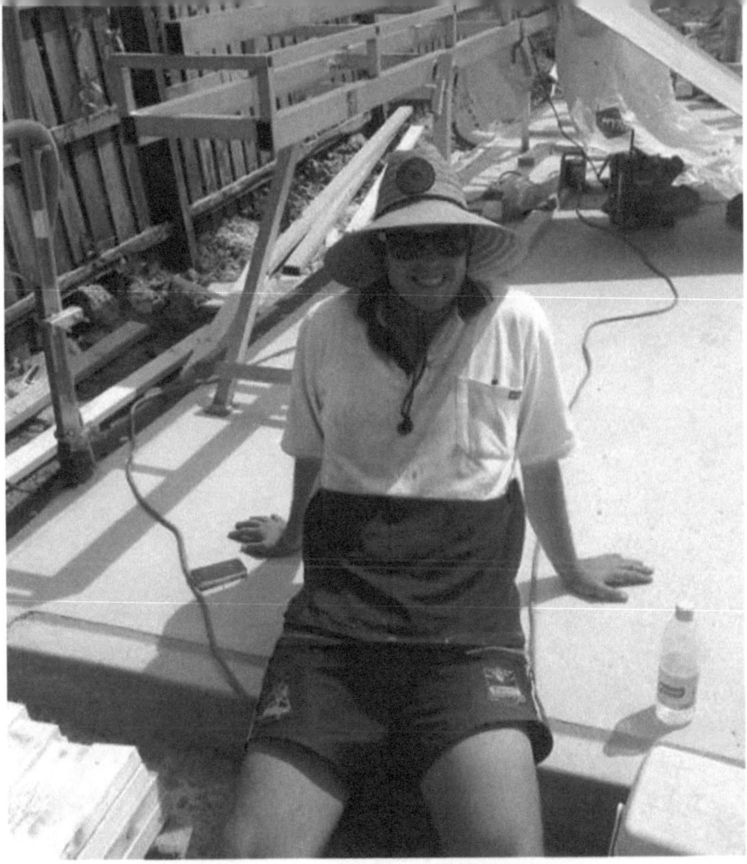

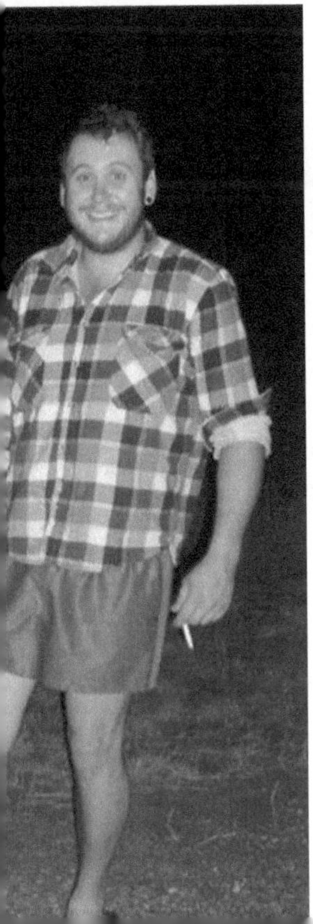

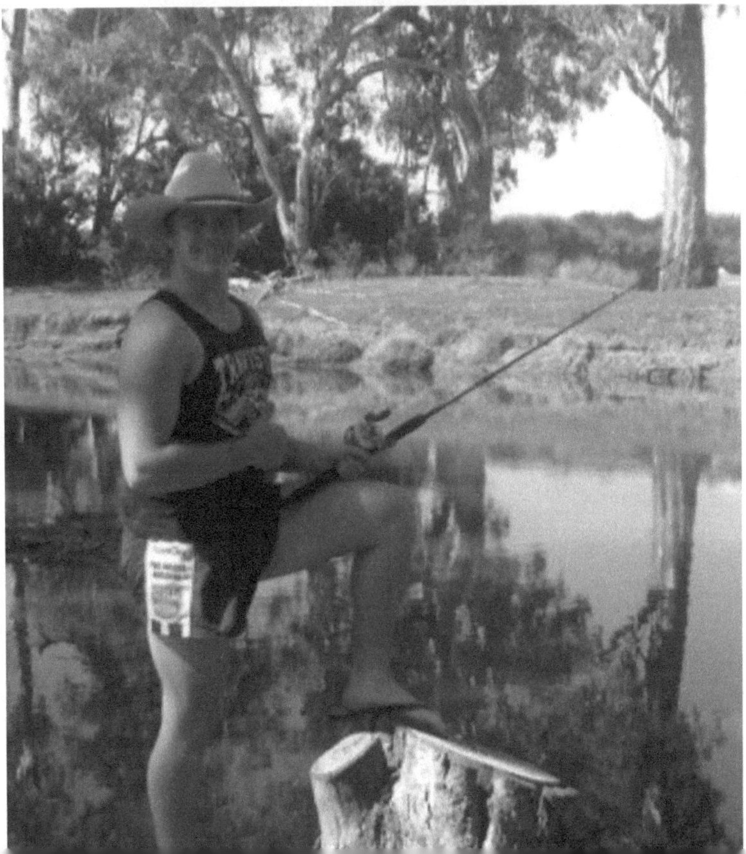

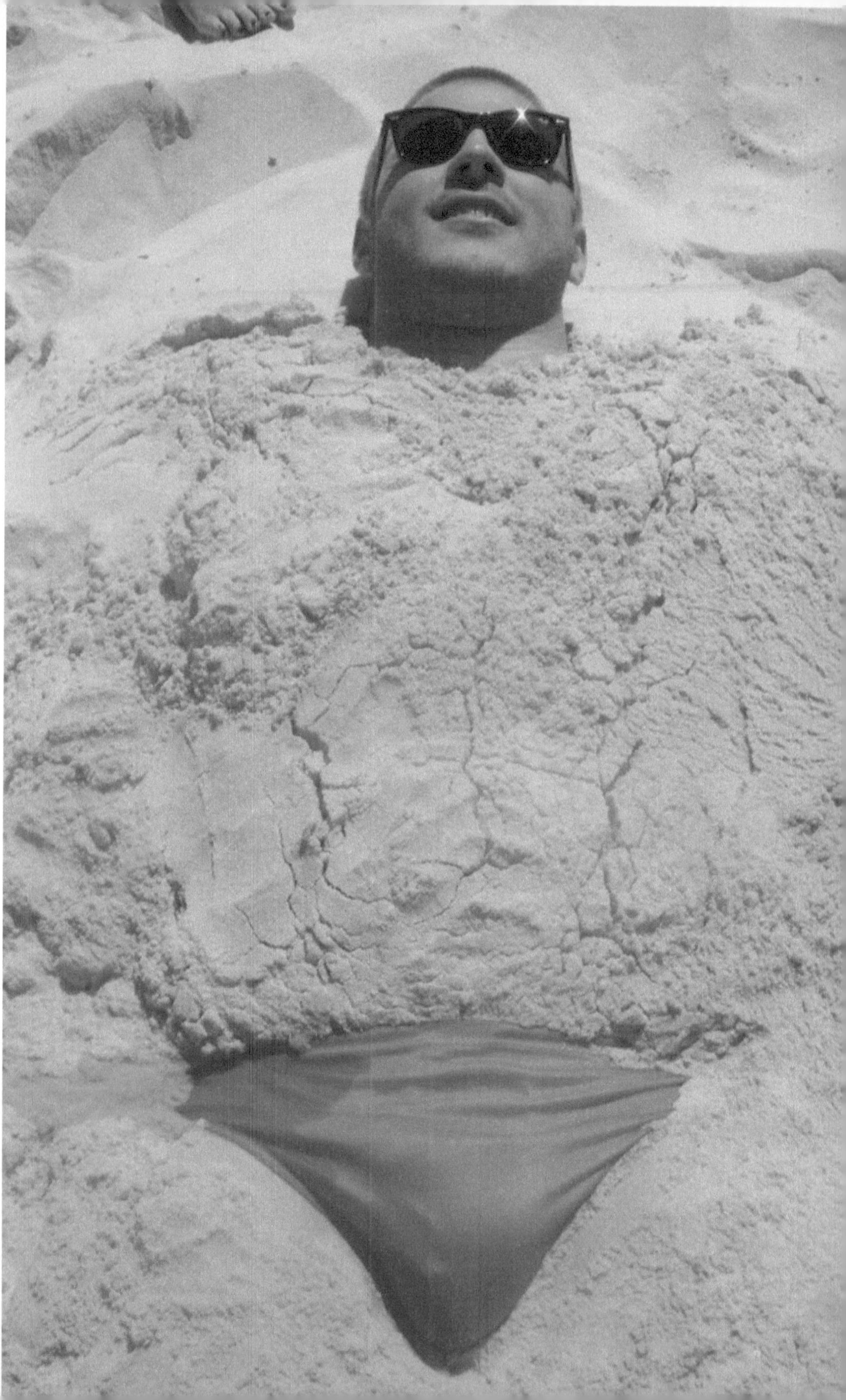

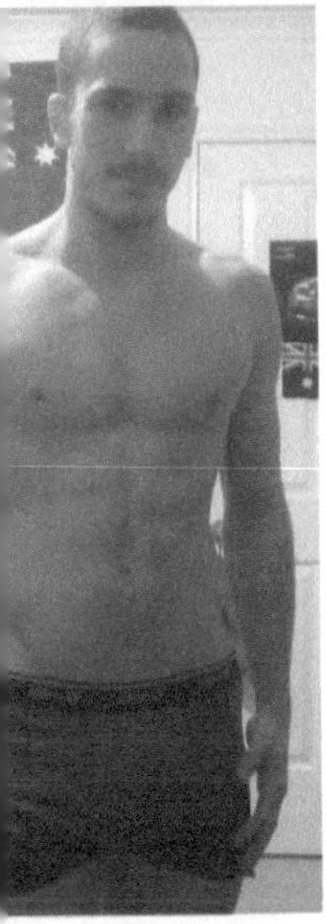

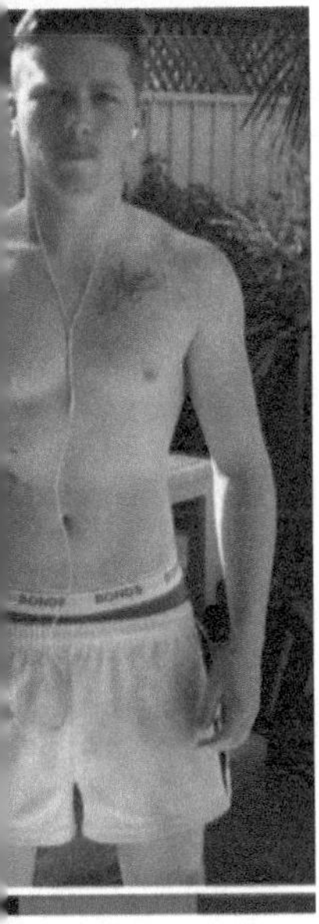
BONDS

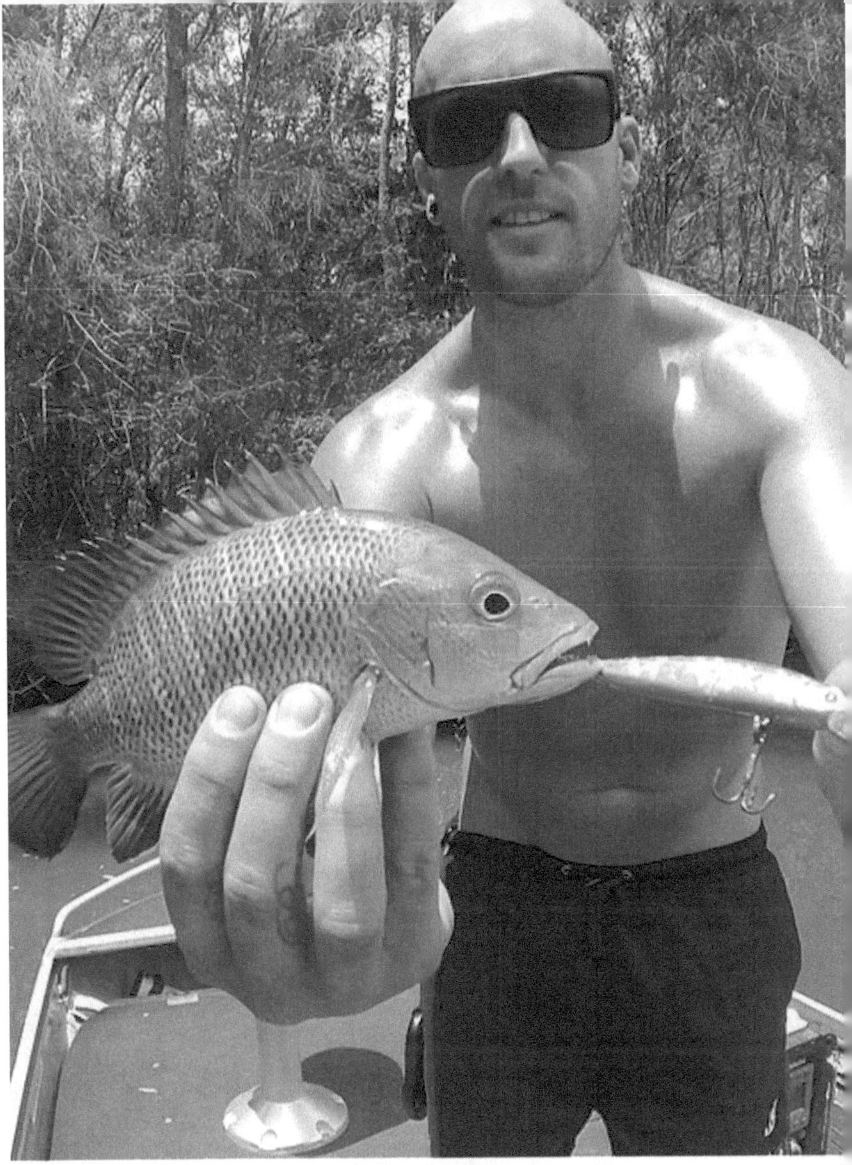

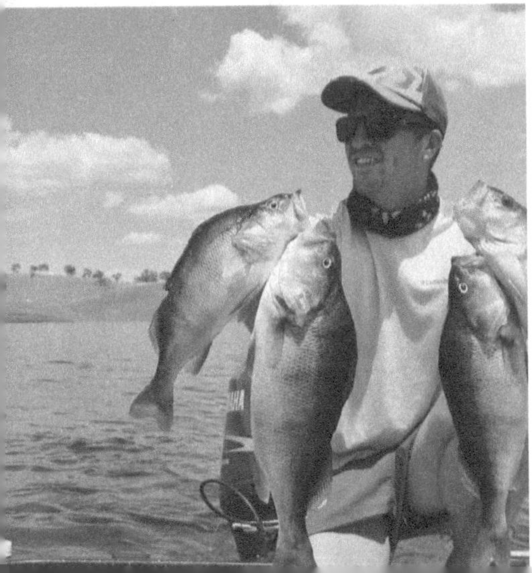

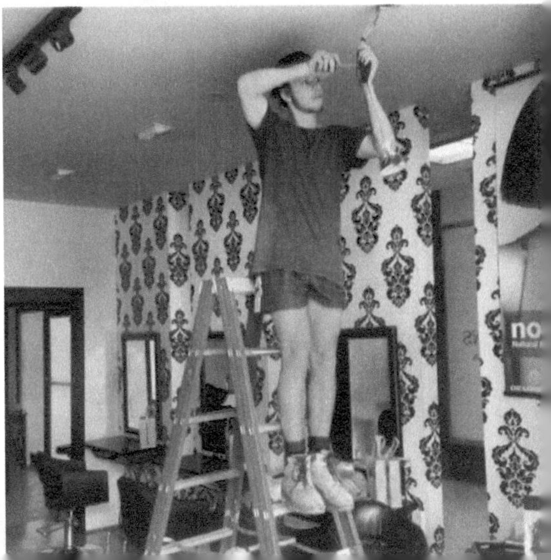
no

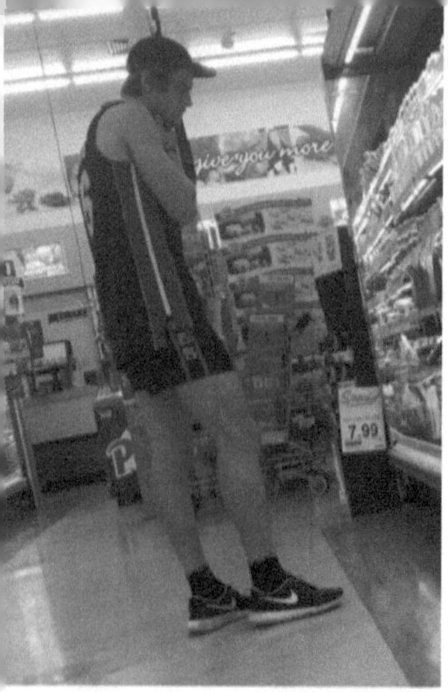
give you more
7.99

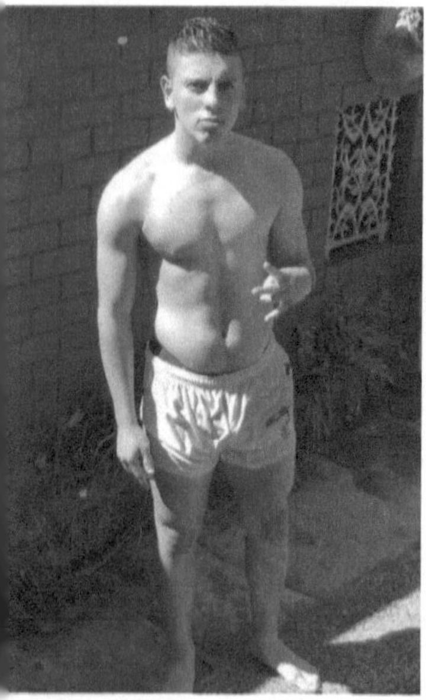

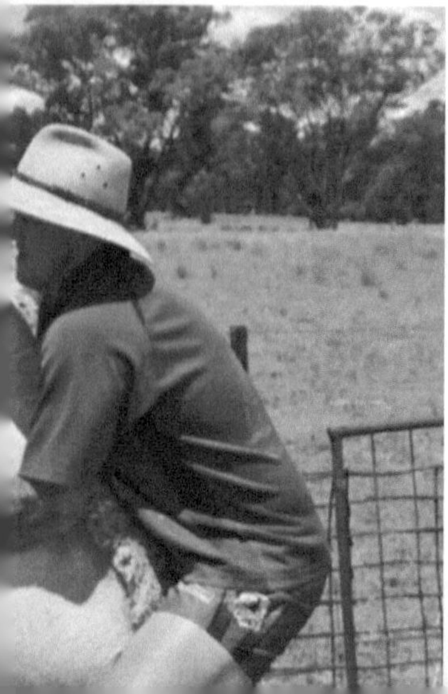

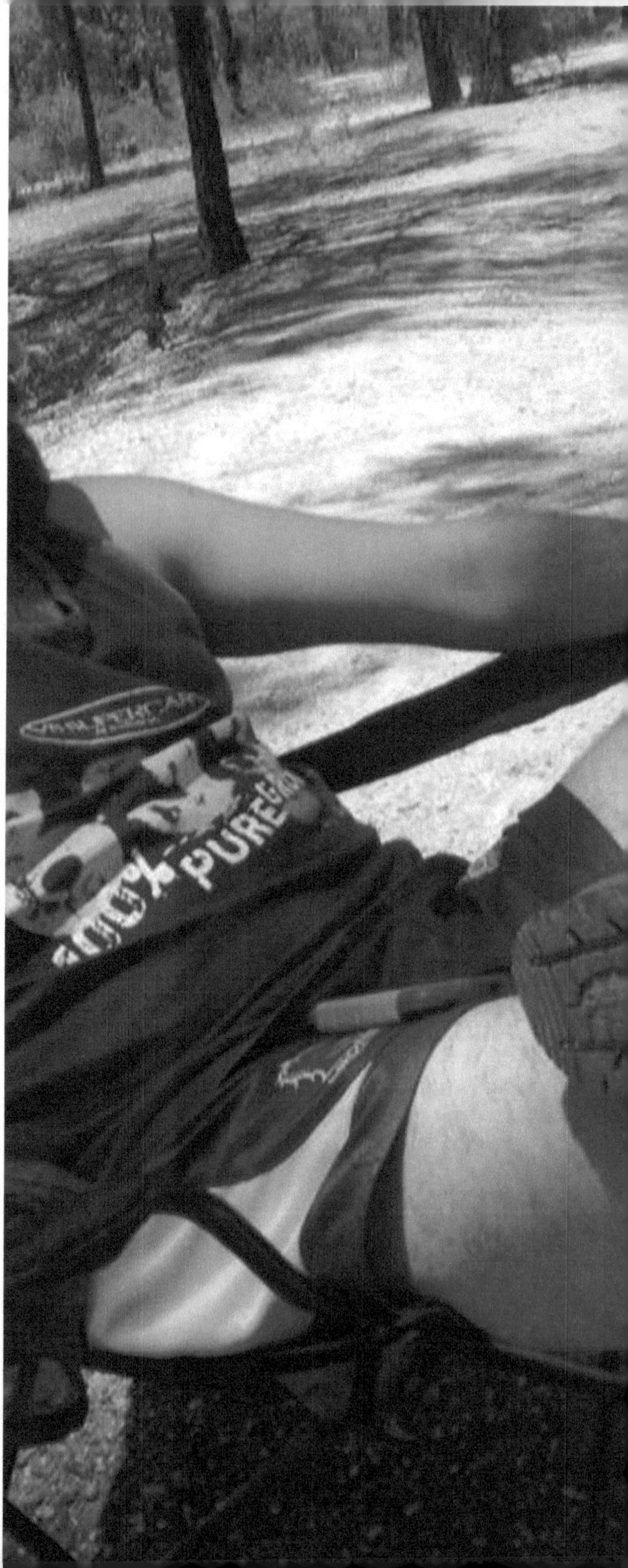

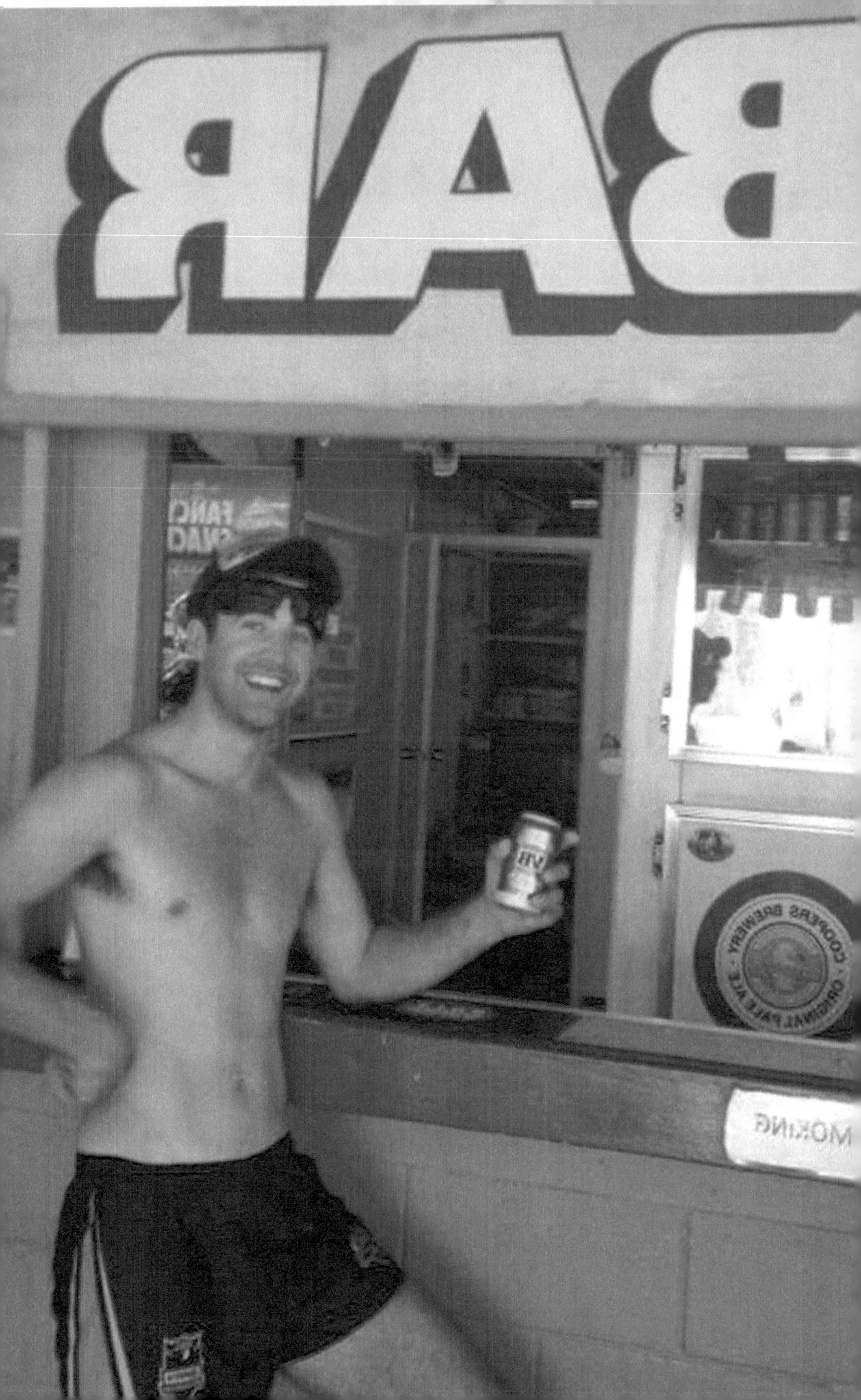
BAR
COOPERS BREWERY
ORIGINAL PALE ALE

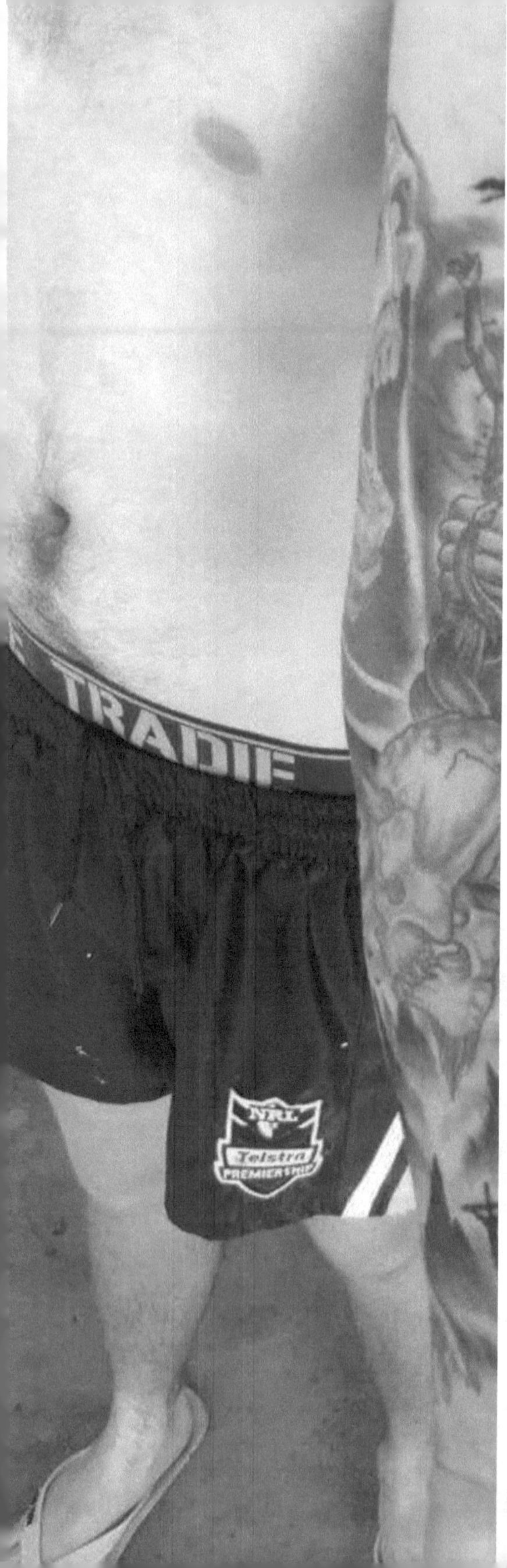
TRADIE
NRL
Telstra
PREMIERSHIP
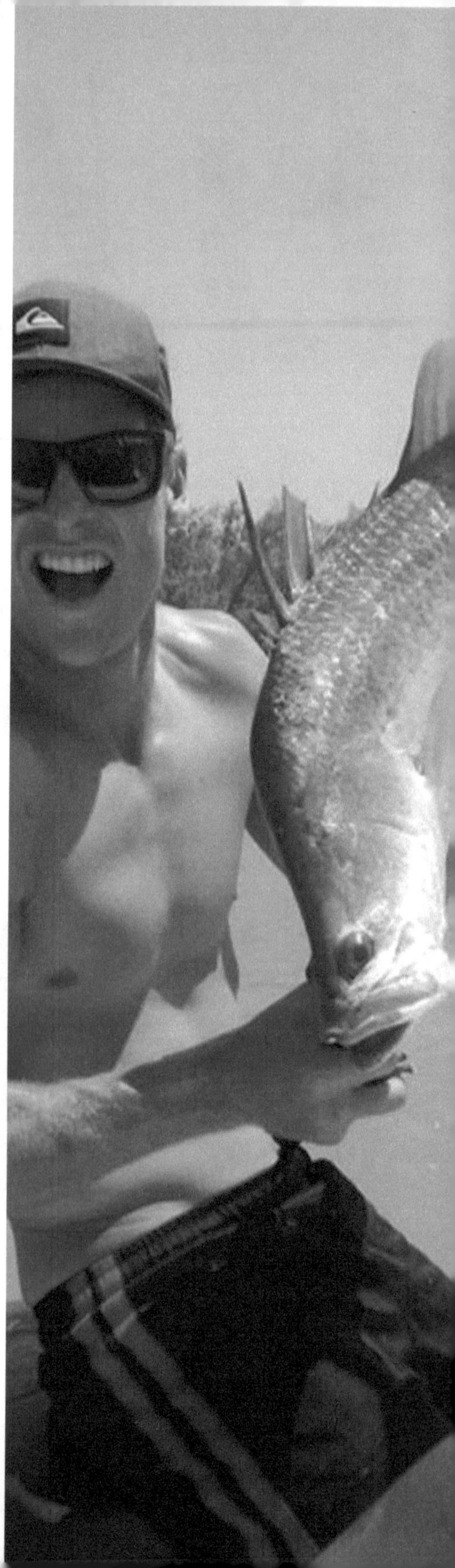

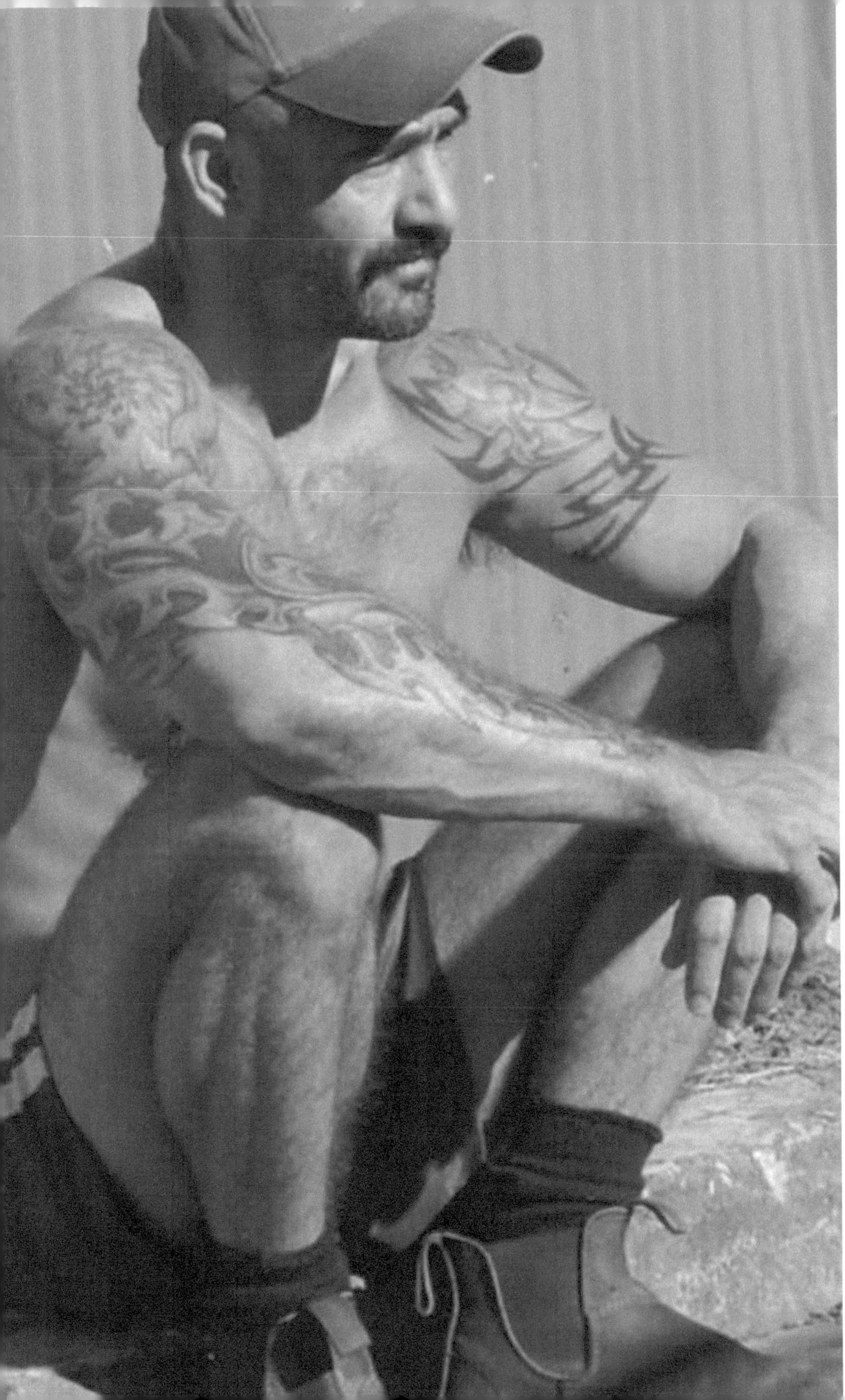

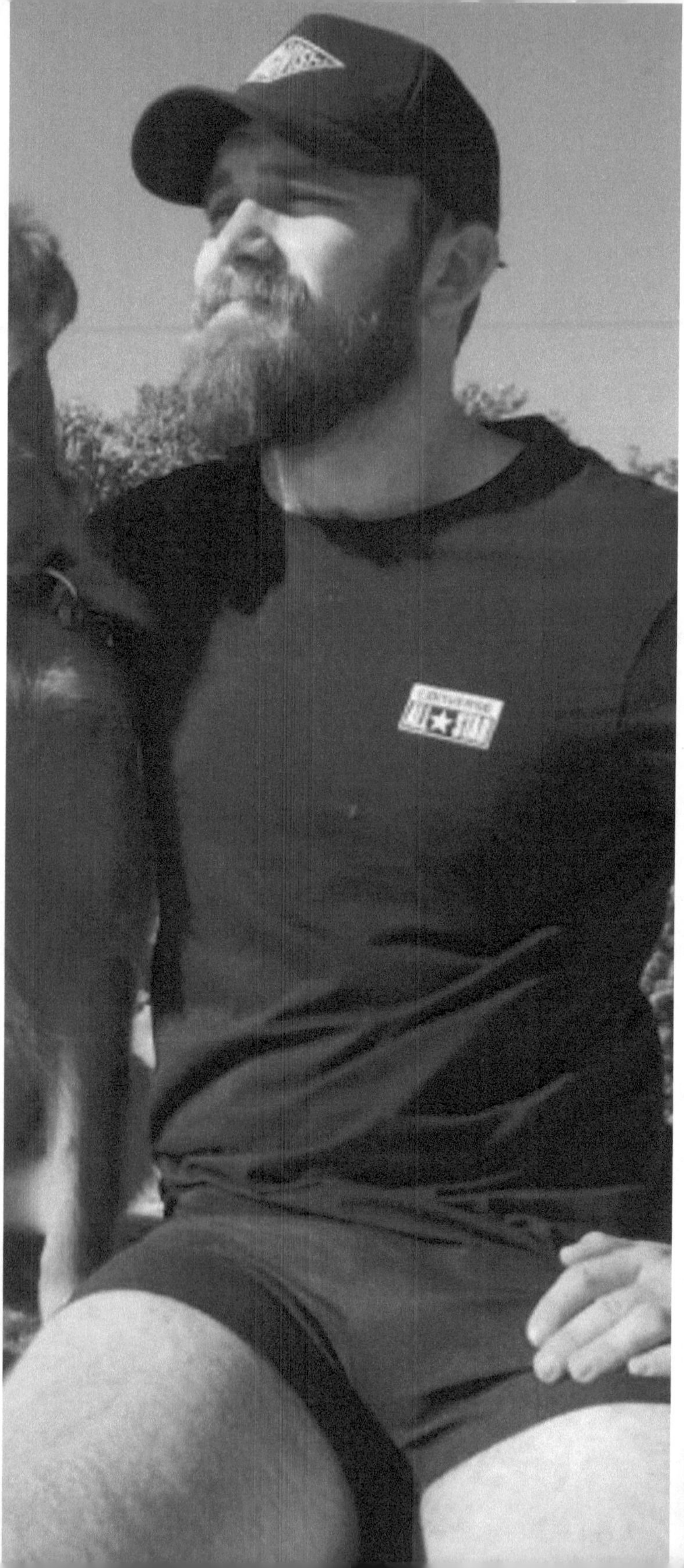

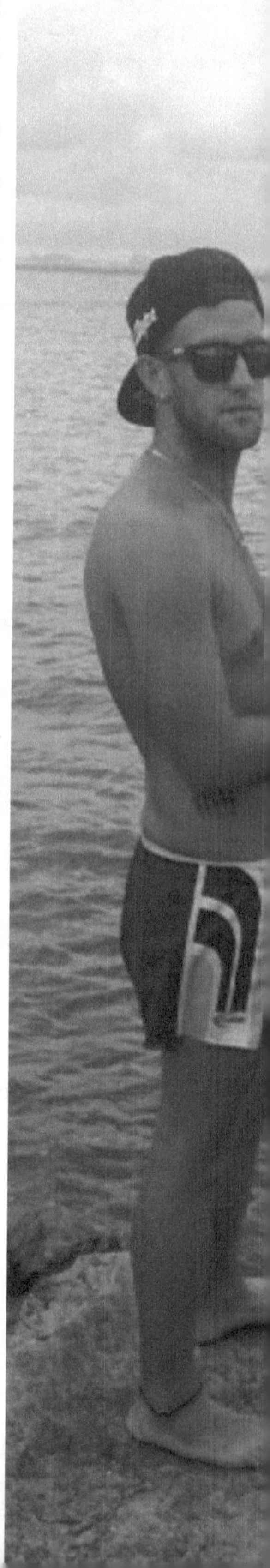

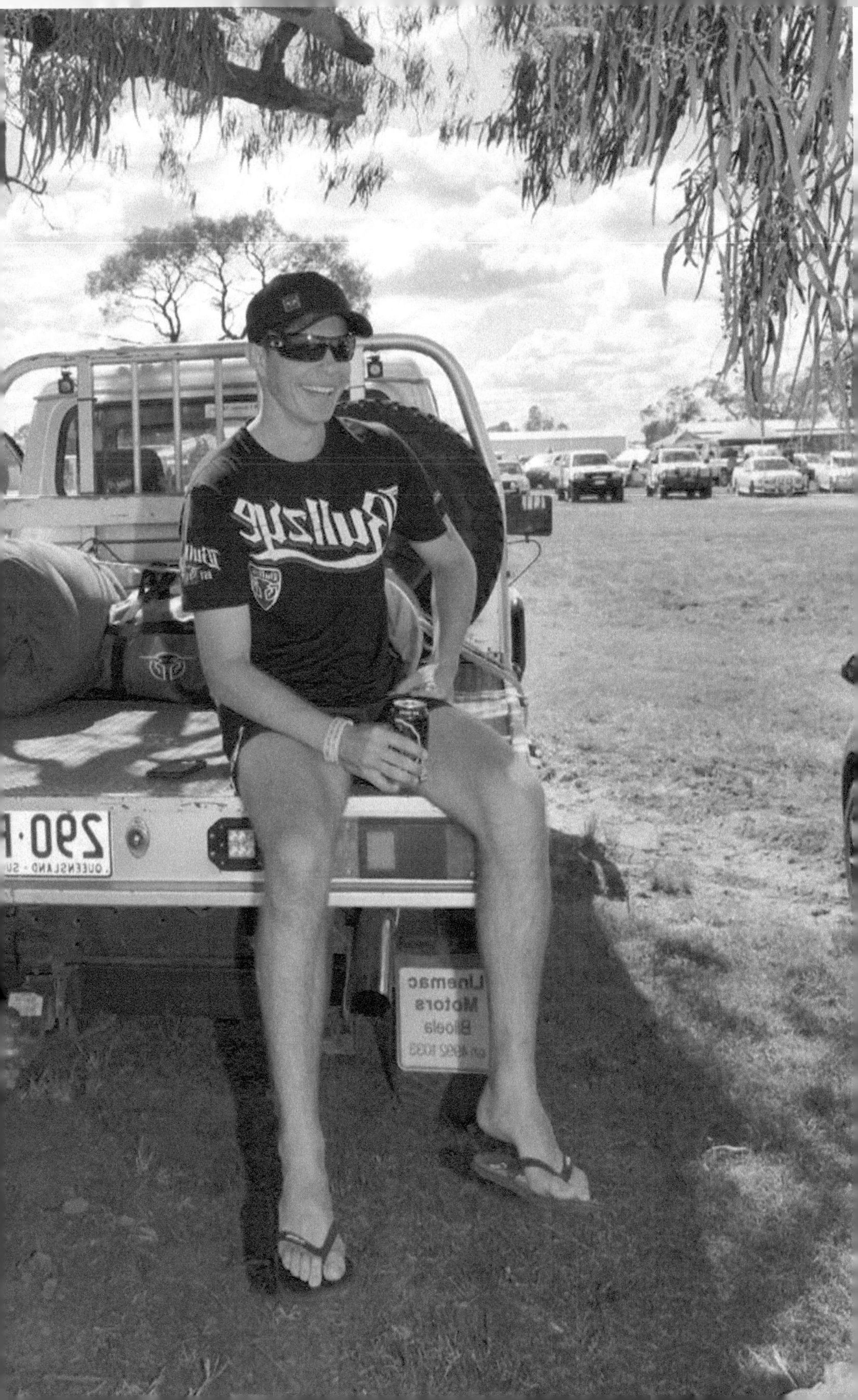
Linemac
Motors
Biloela

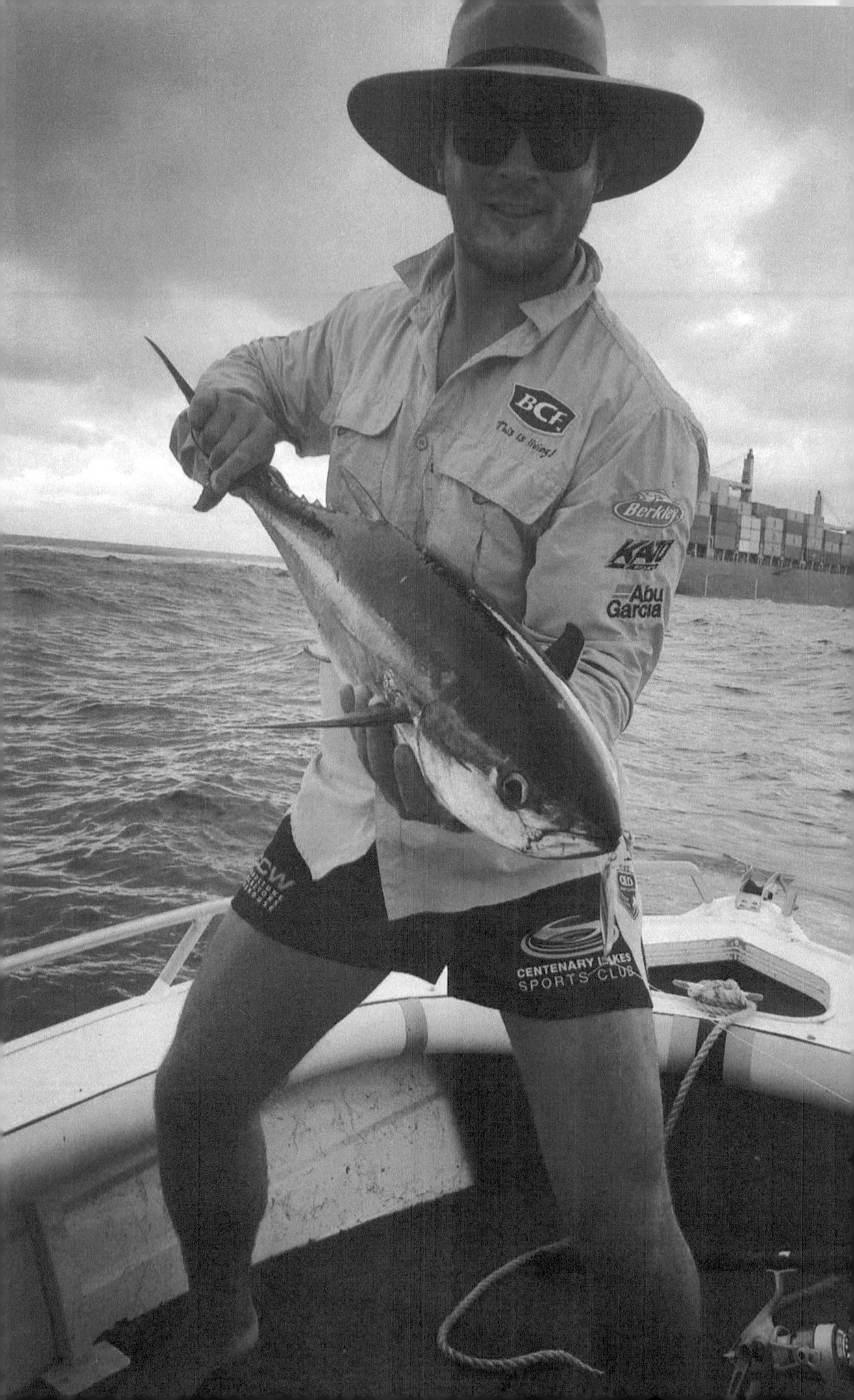
BCF
This is living!
Berkley
Abu Garcia
CENTENARY LAKES
SPORTS CLUB

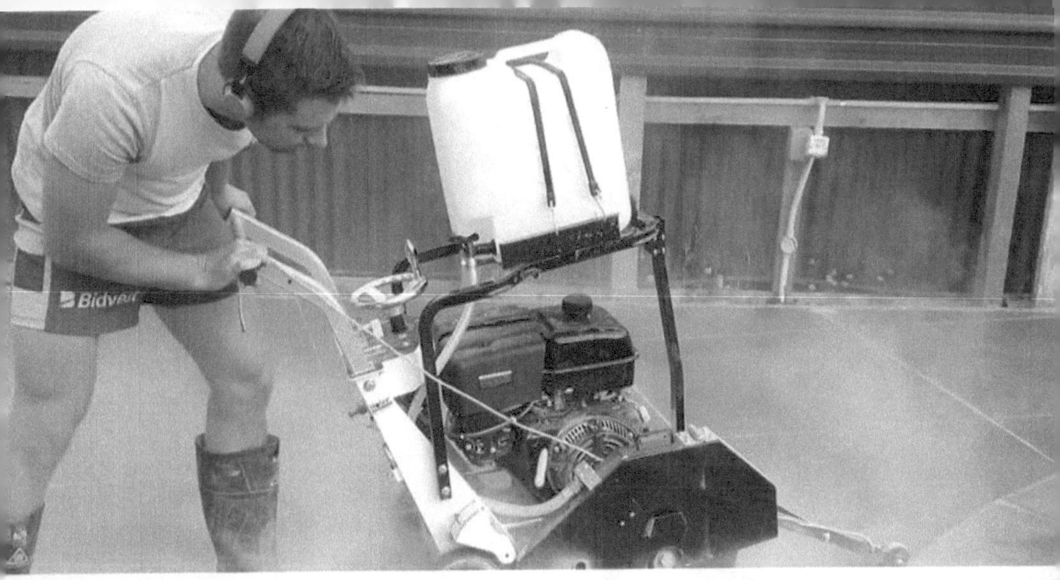
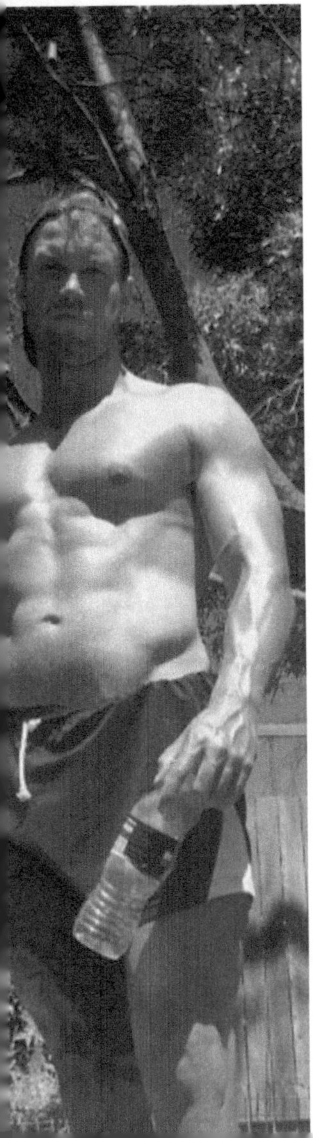
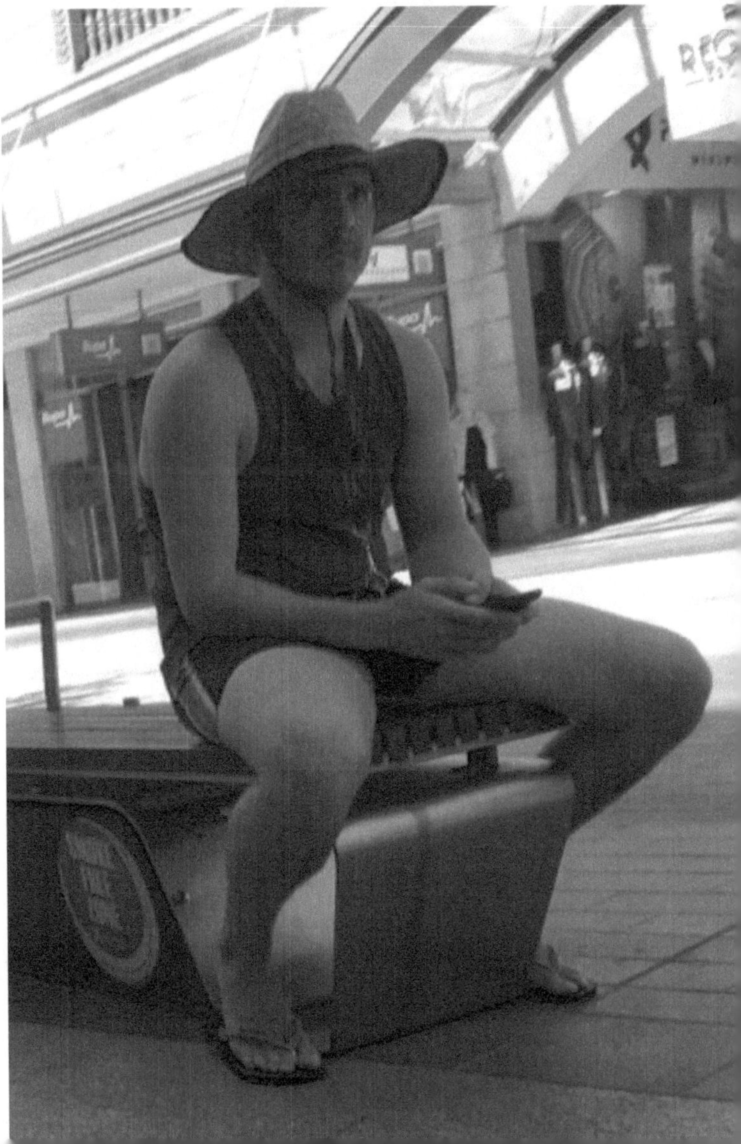

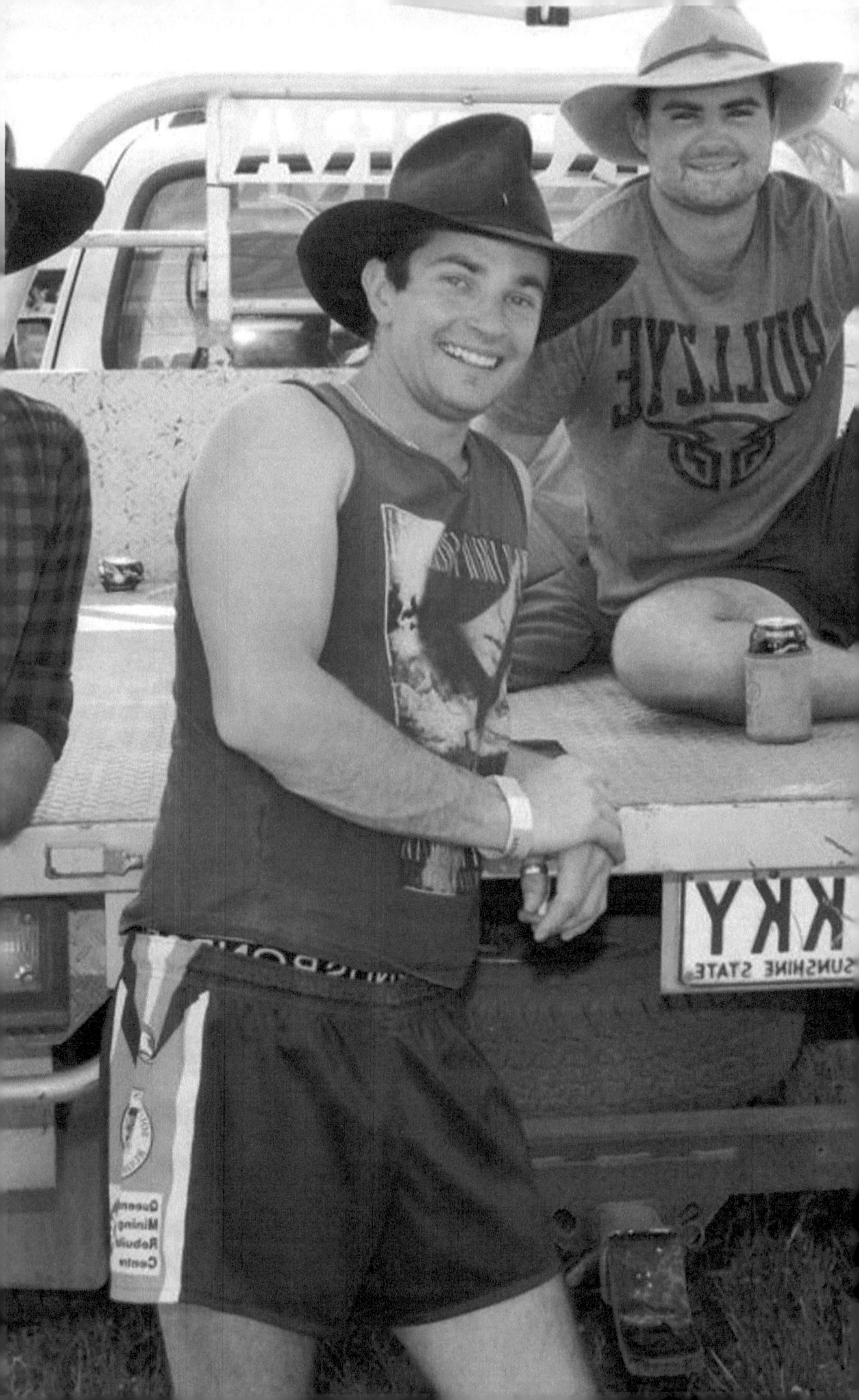
Mining
Centre

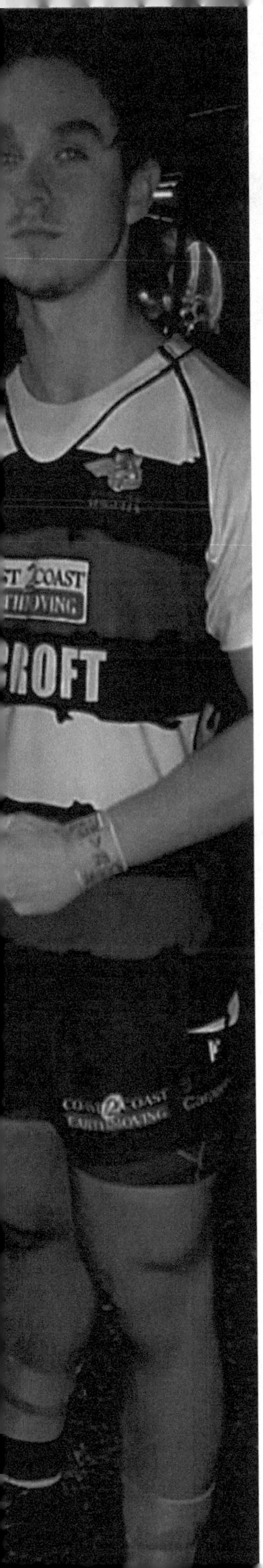

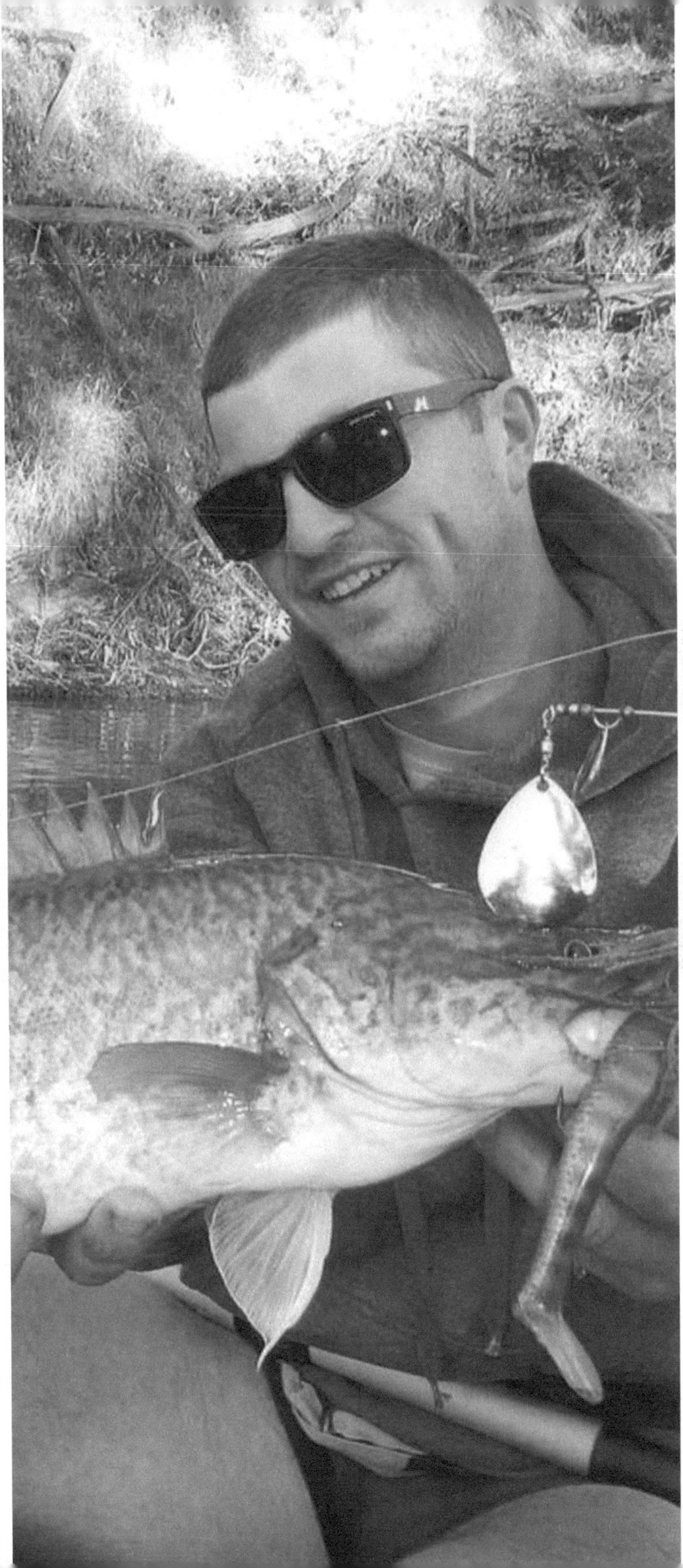

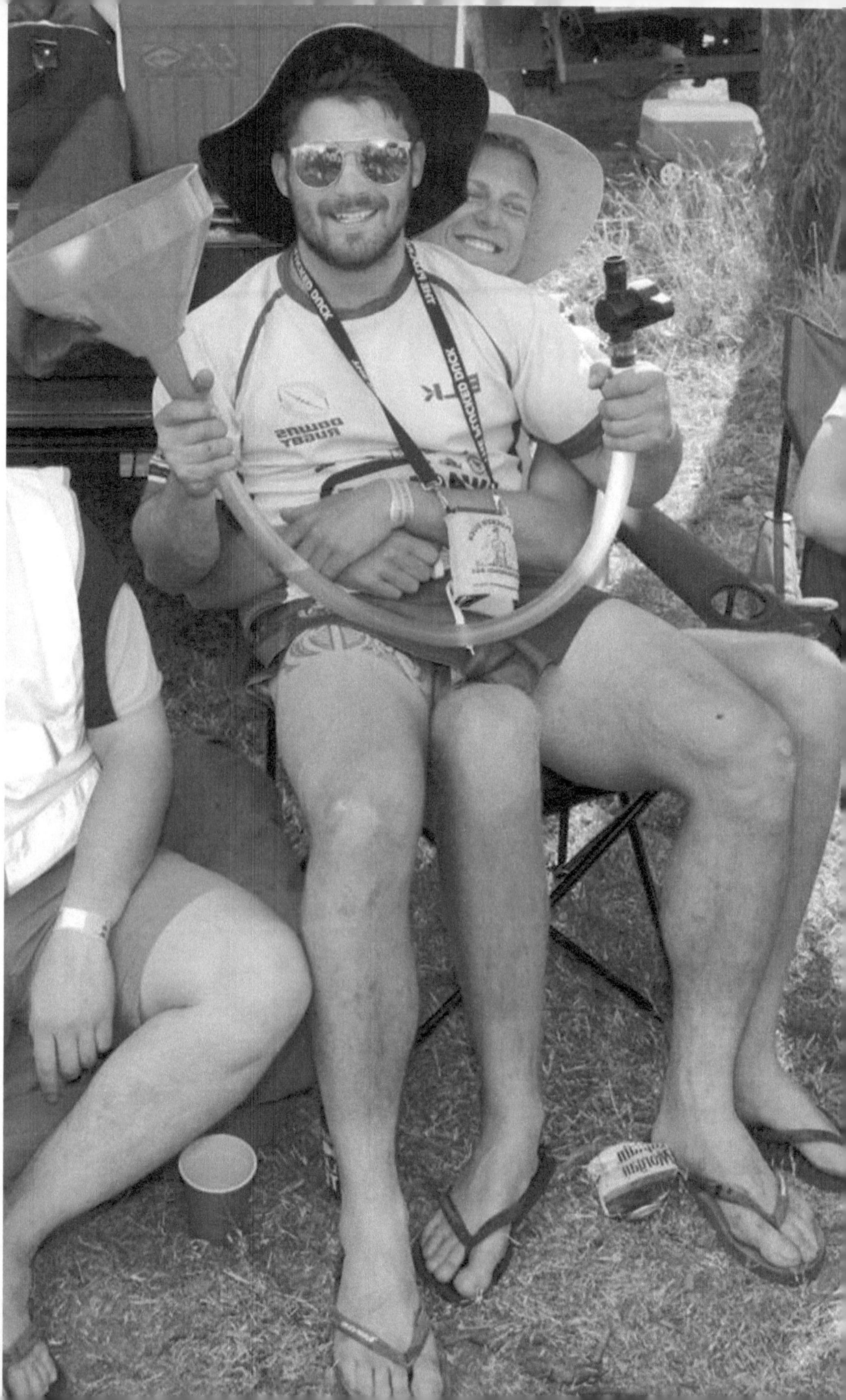

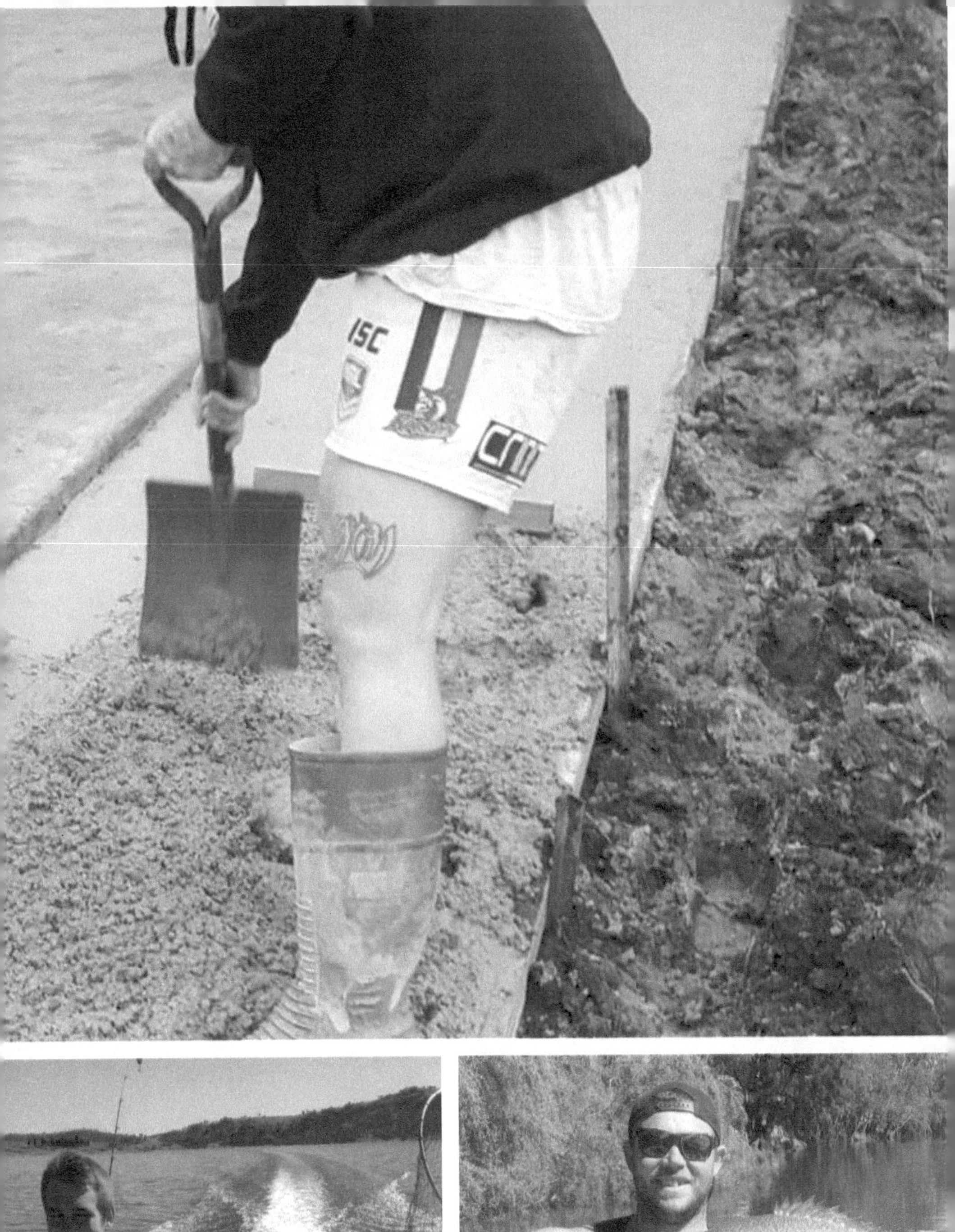

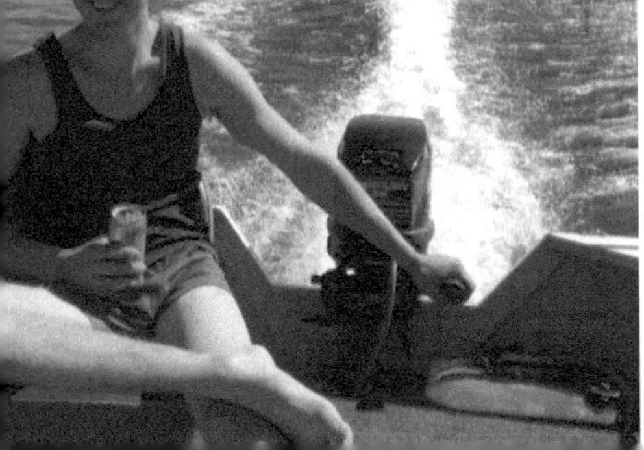

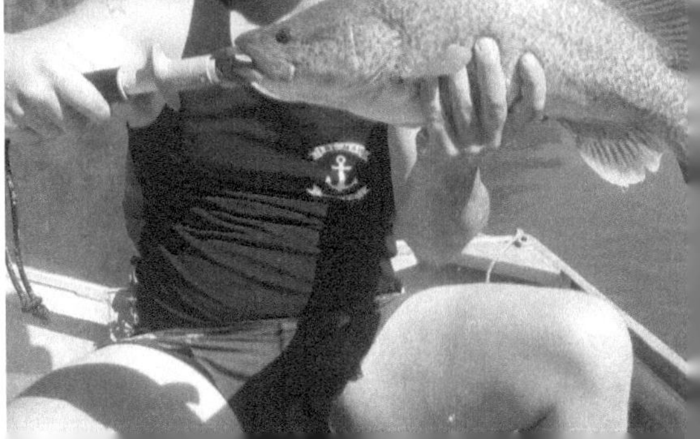

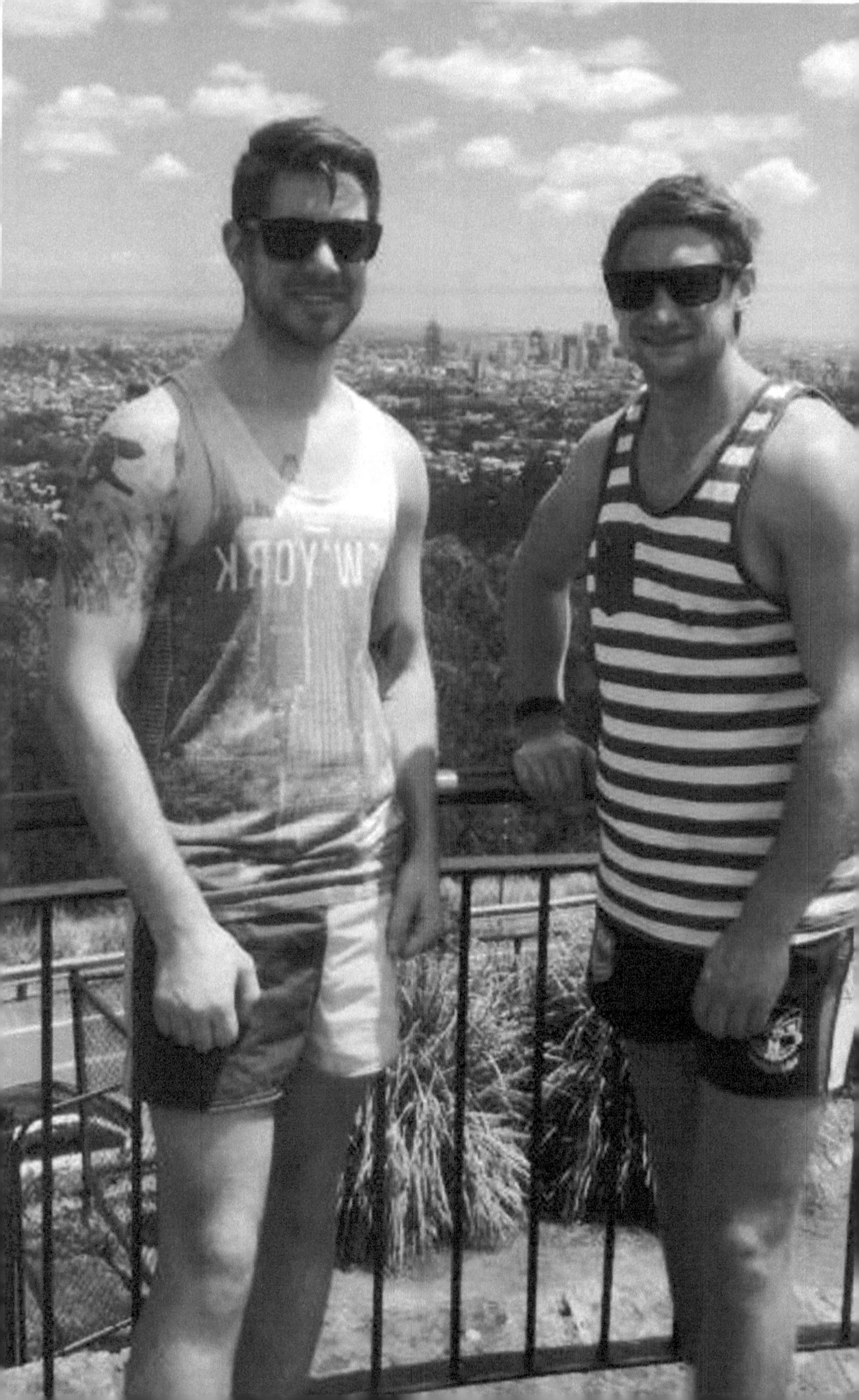

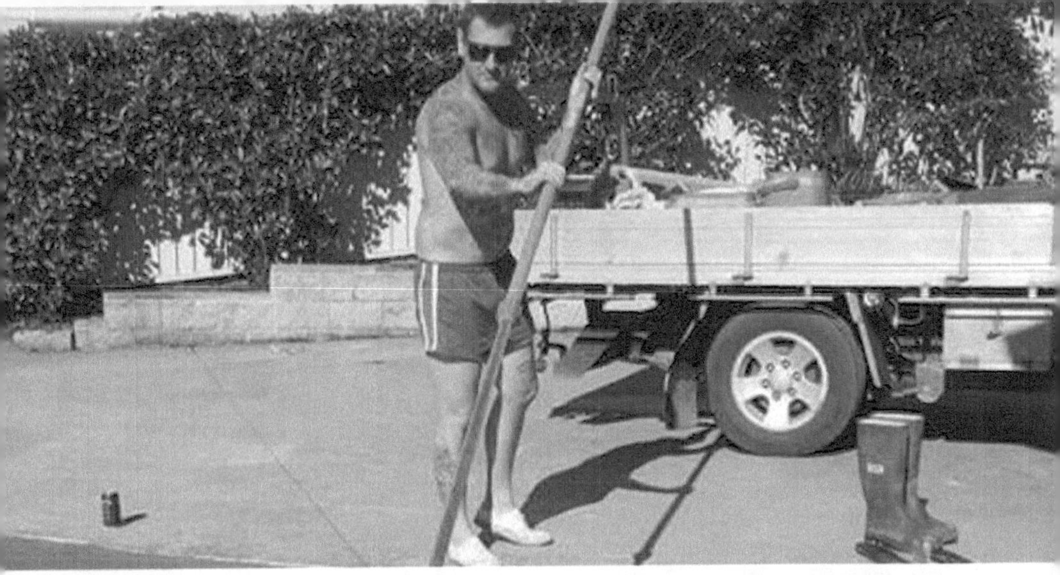

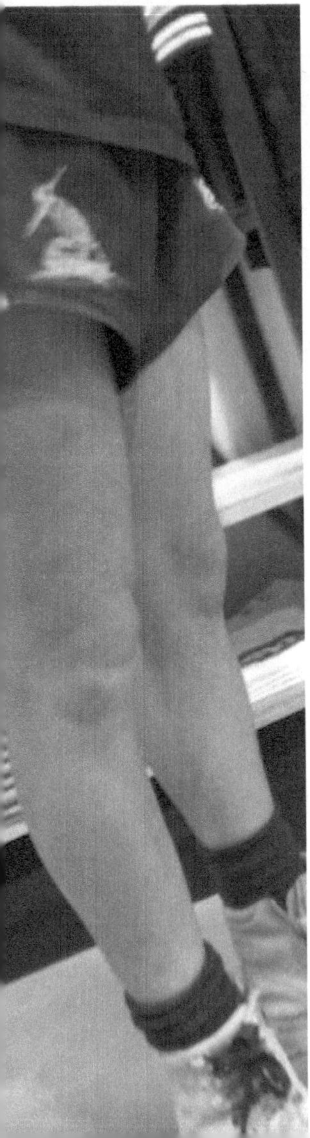

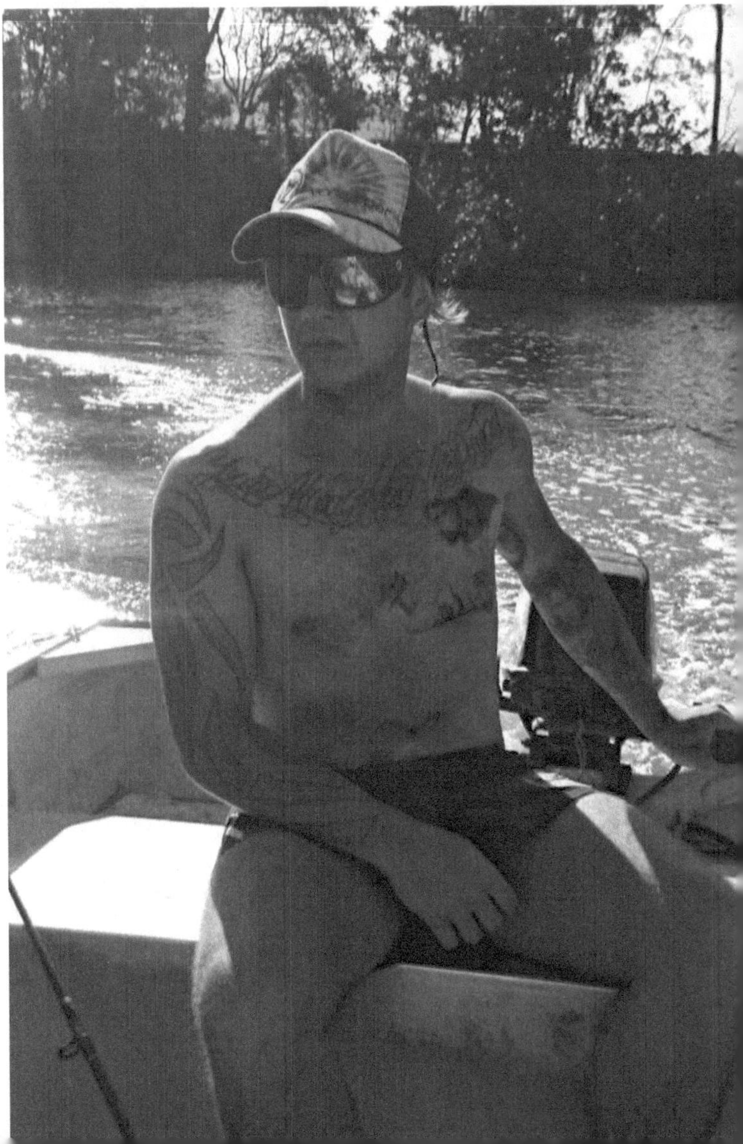

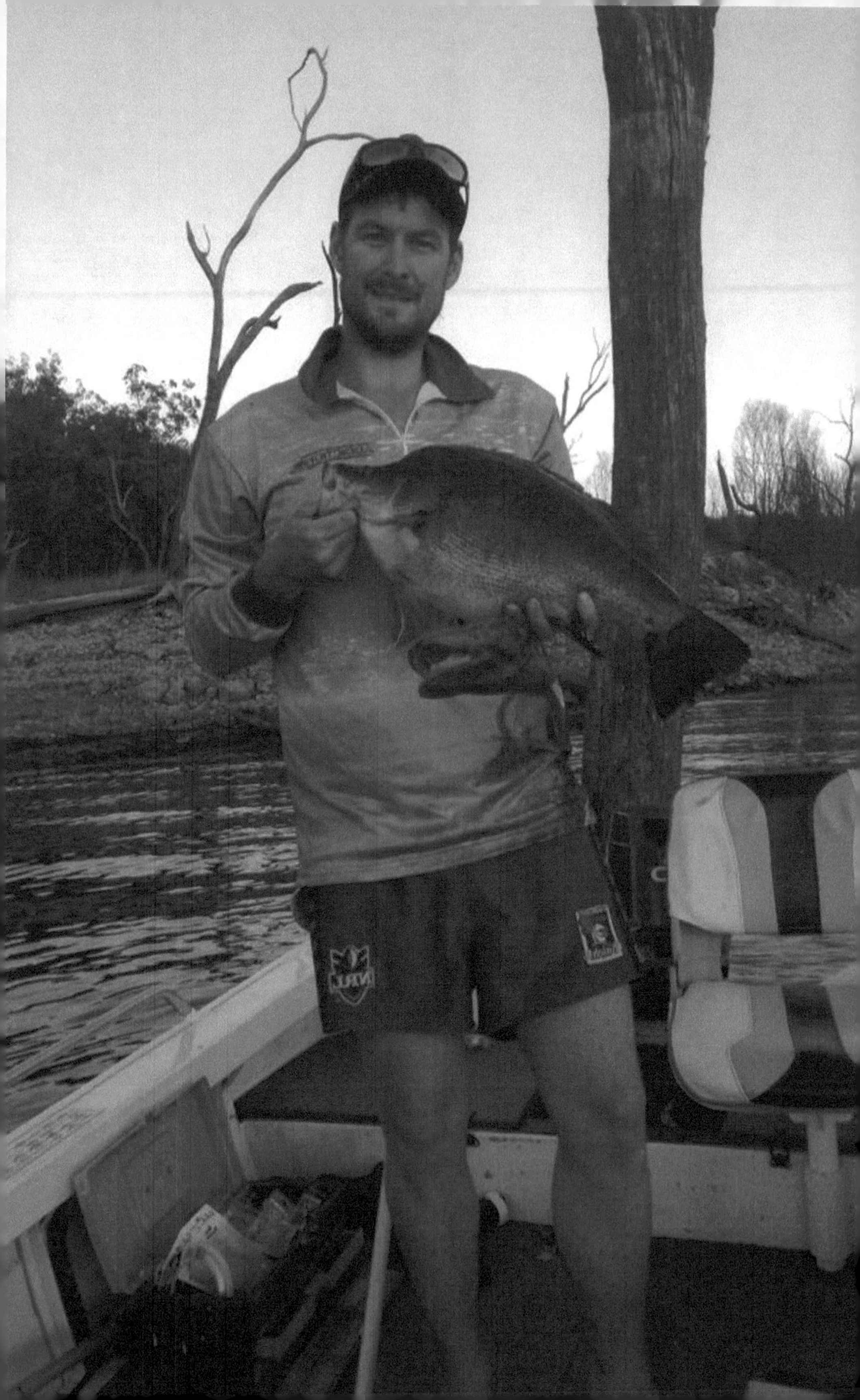

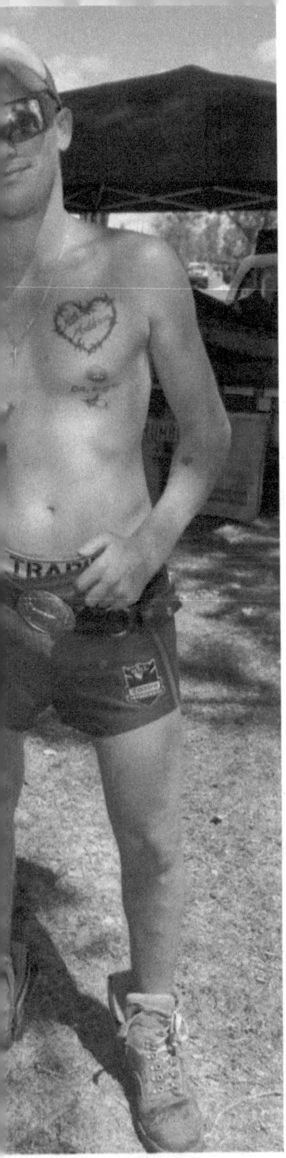

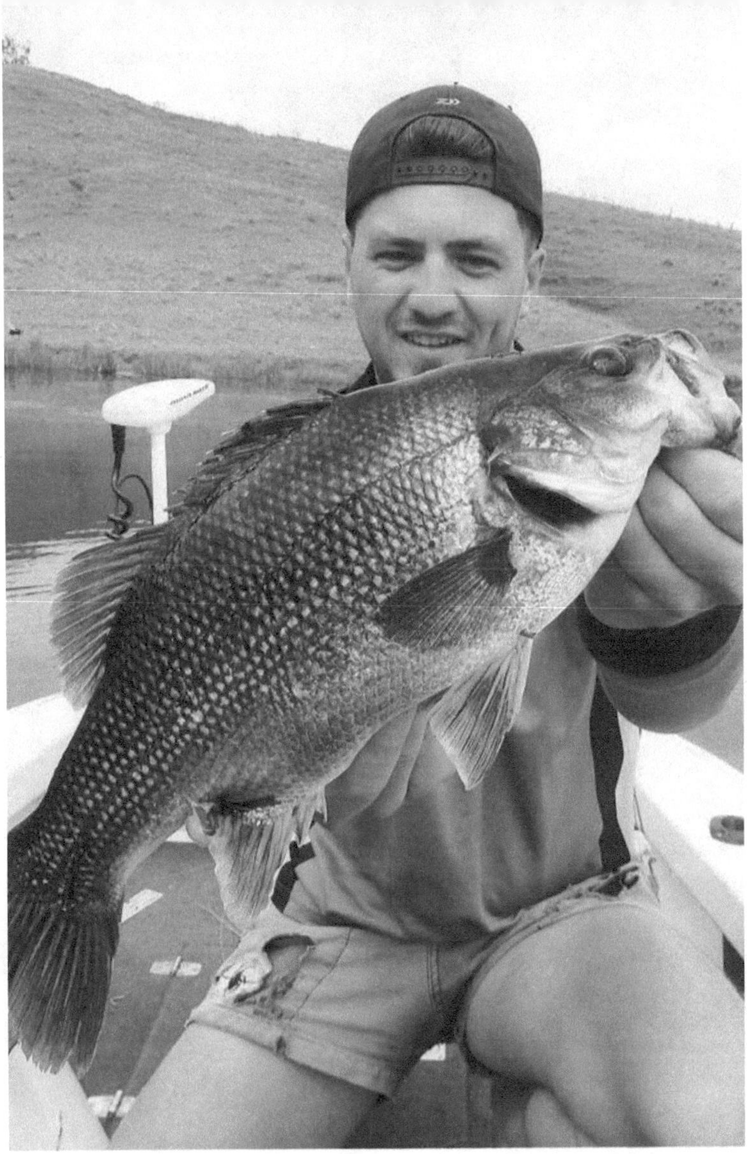

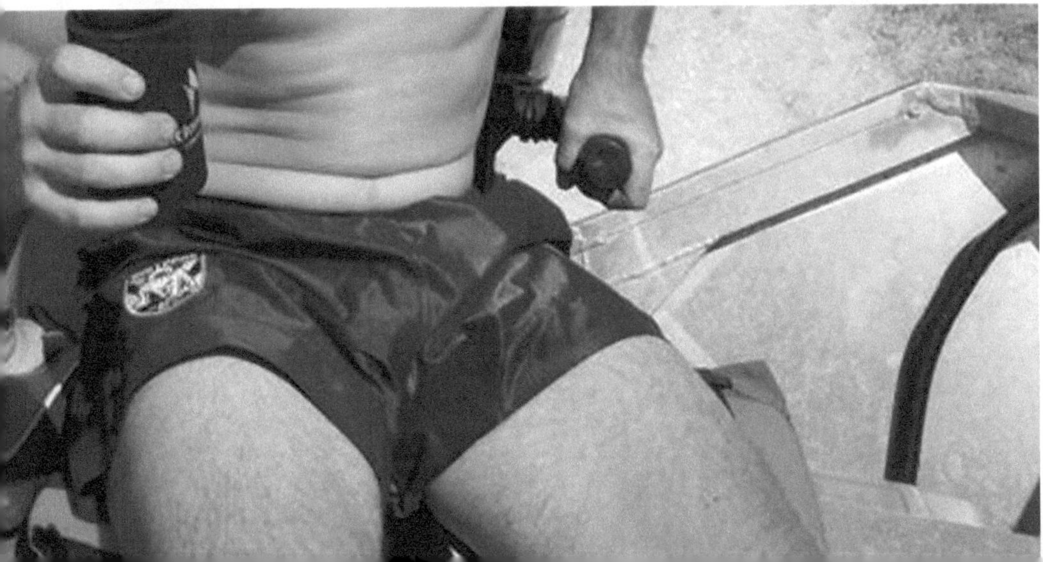

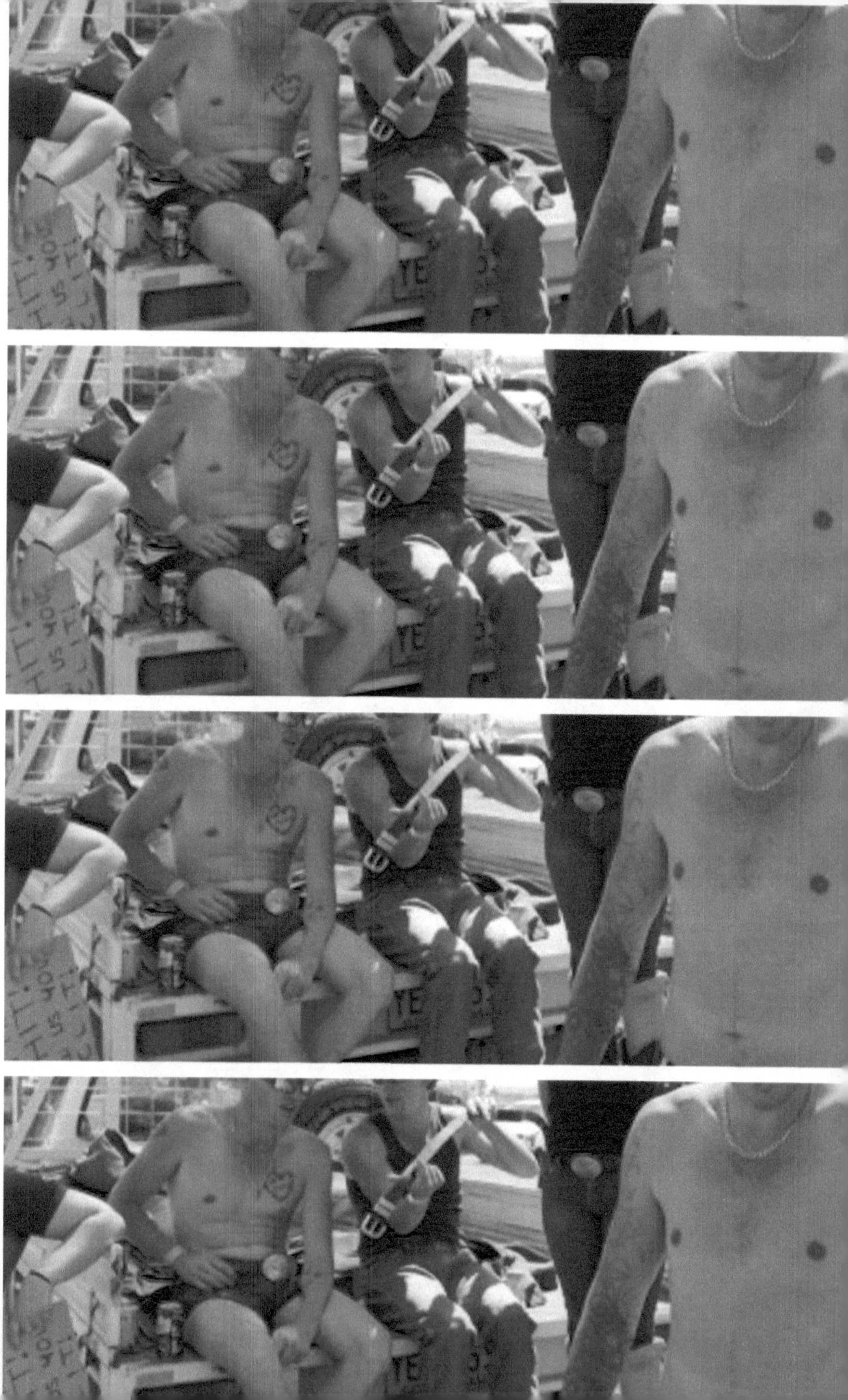

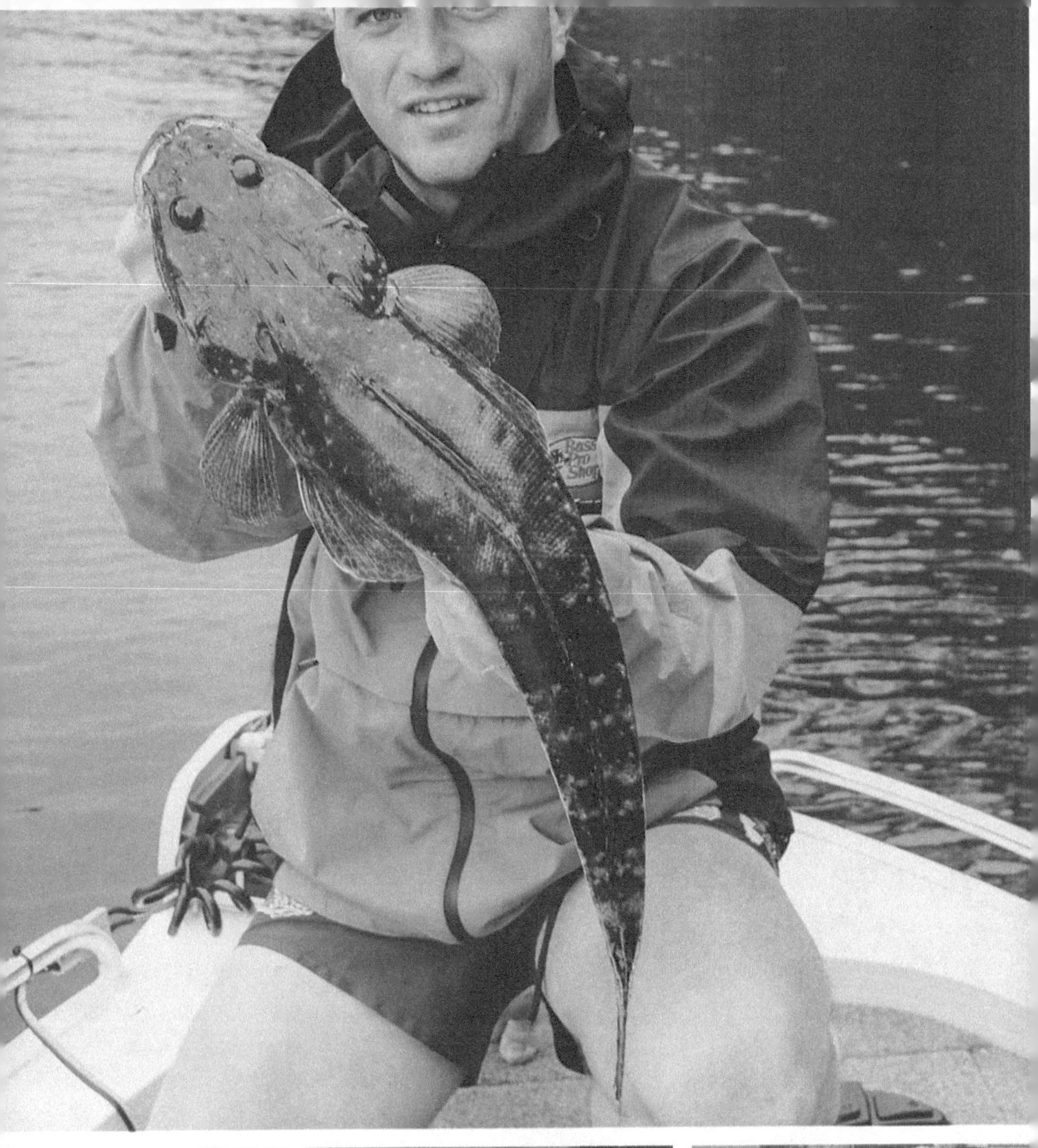

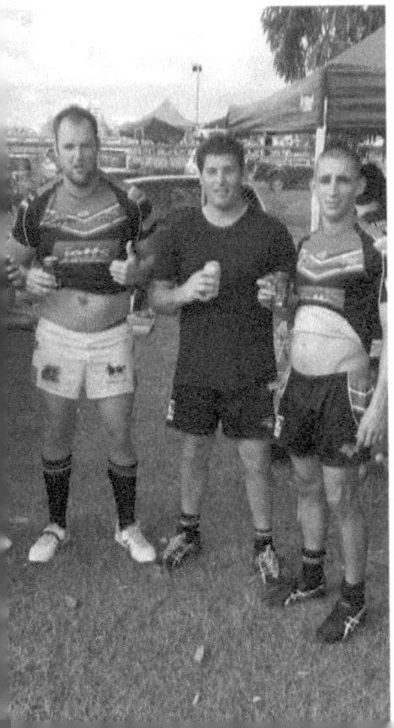

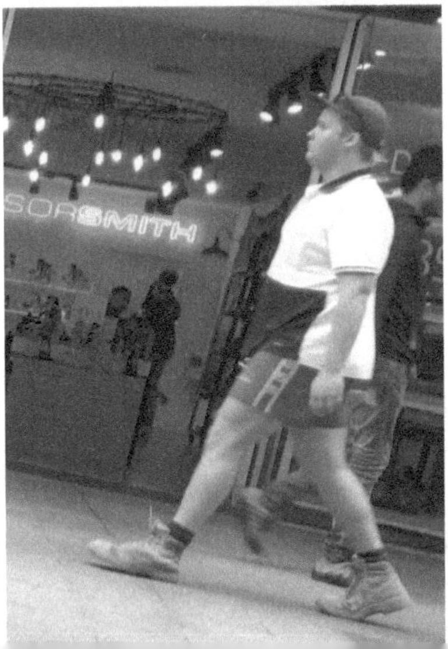

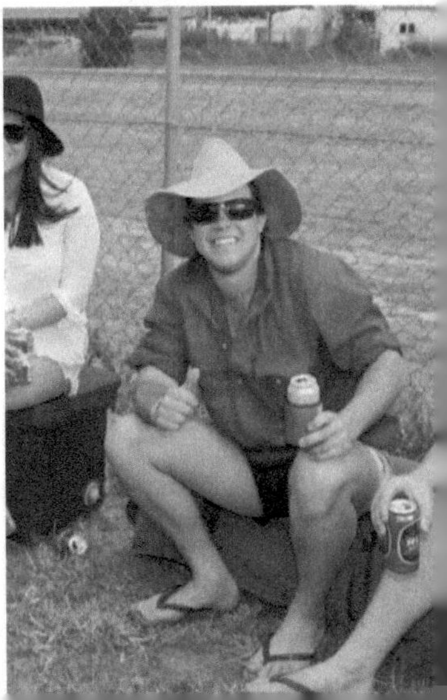

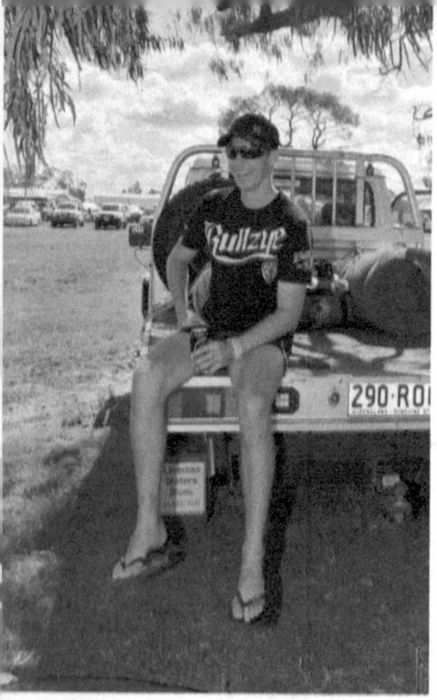
Bullzye
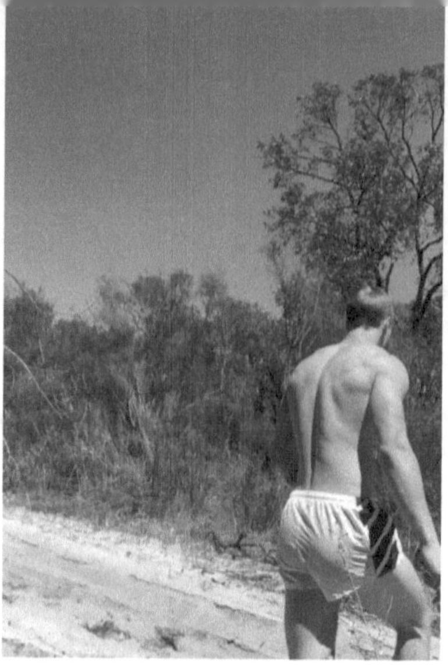
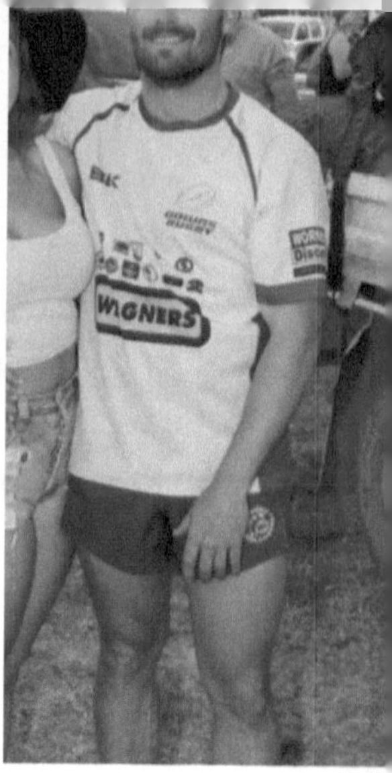
WAGNERS
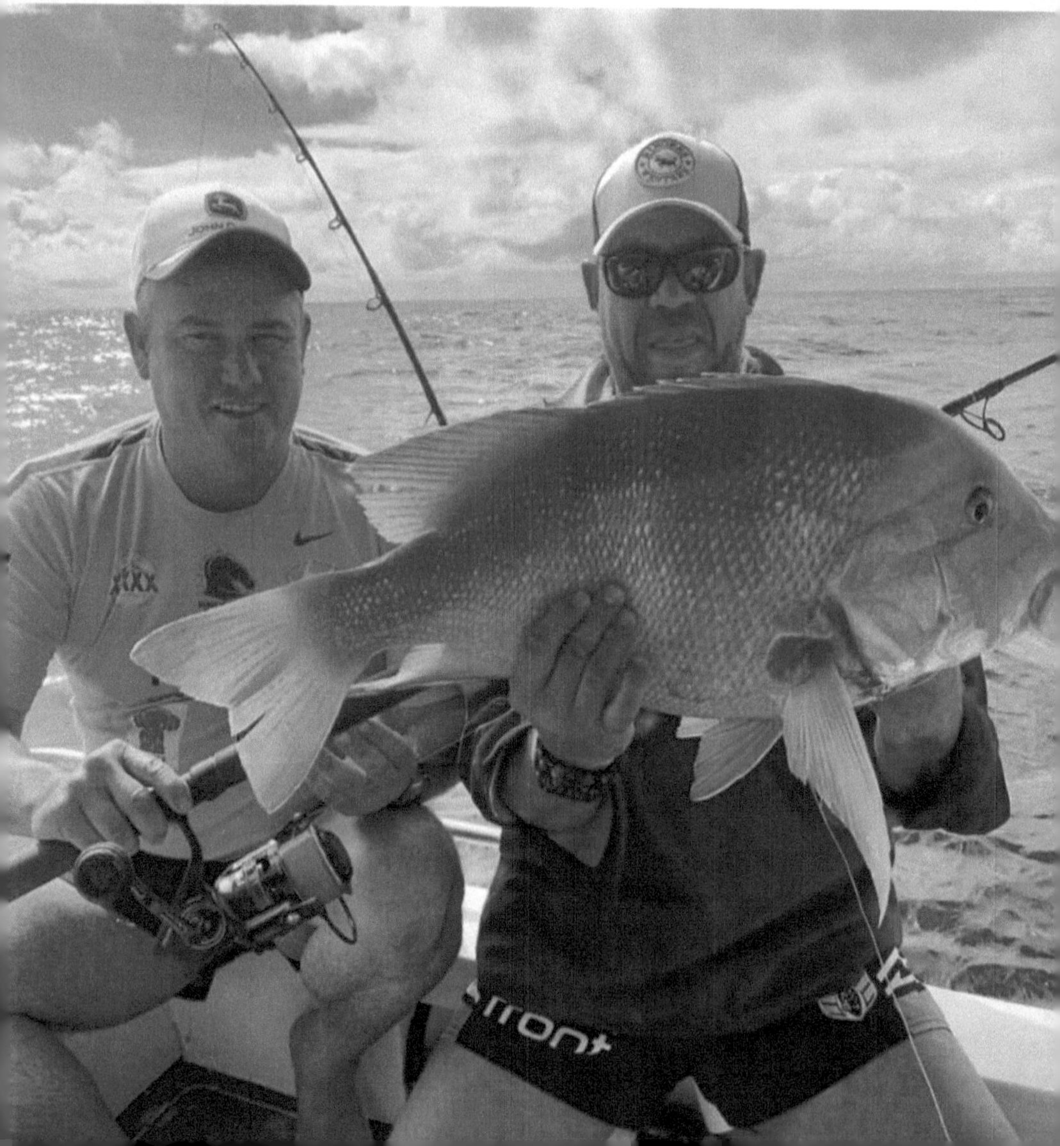

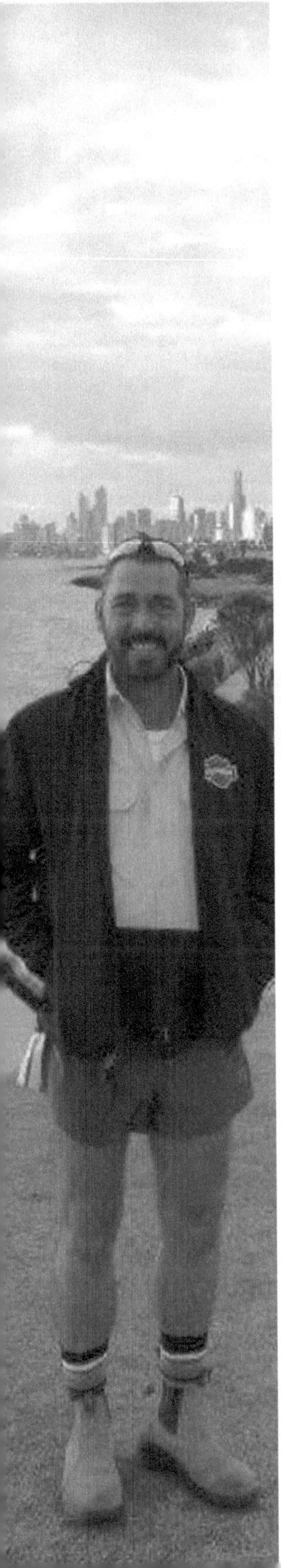

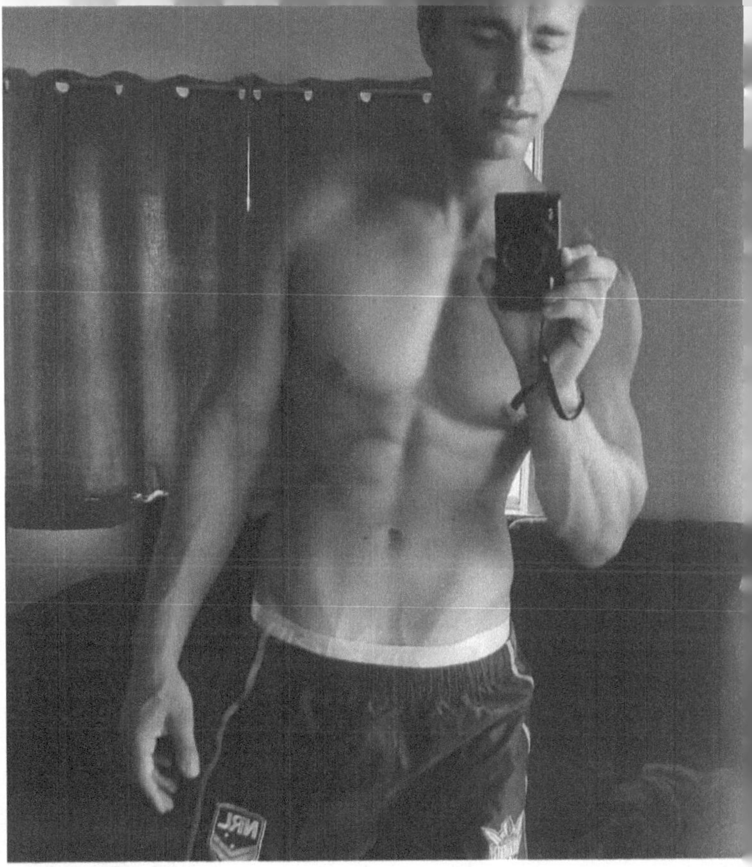
NRL

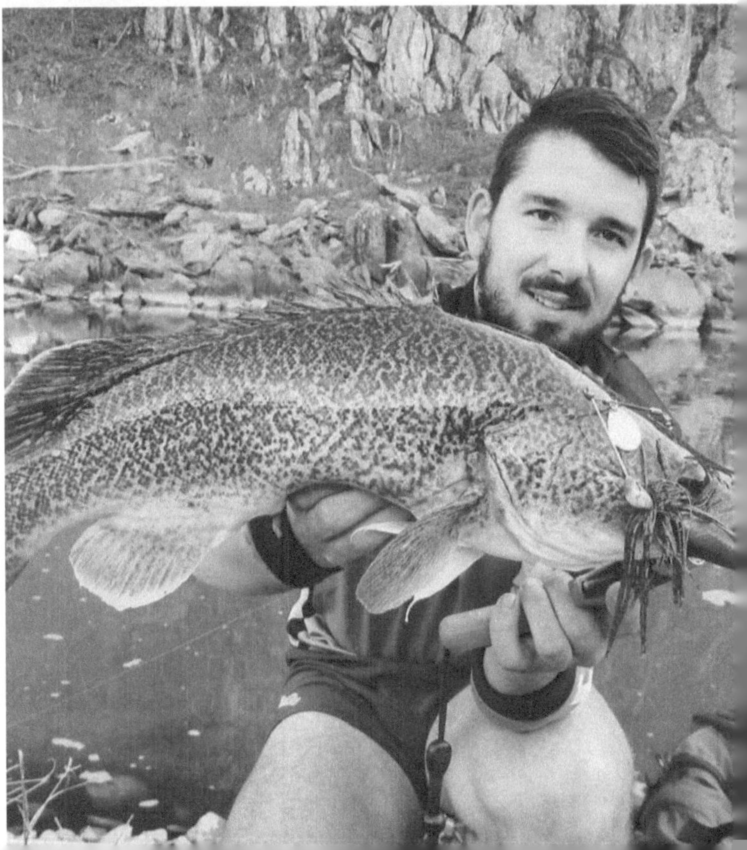

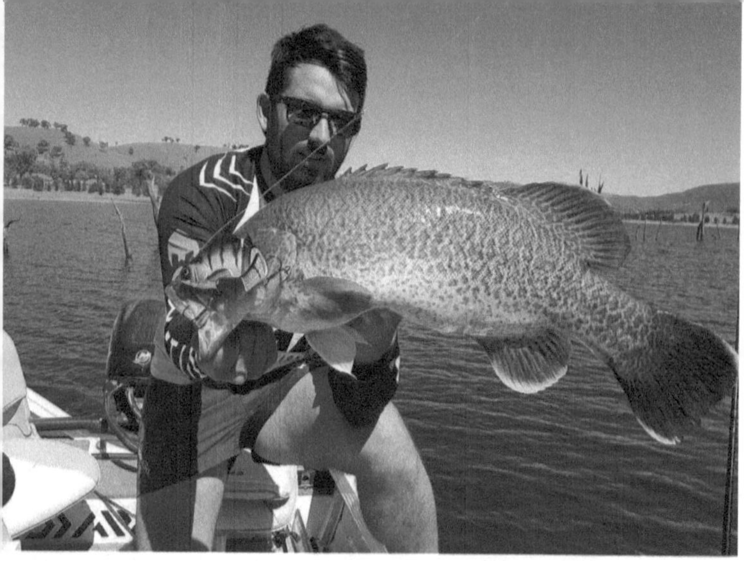

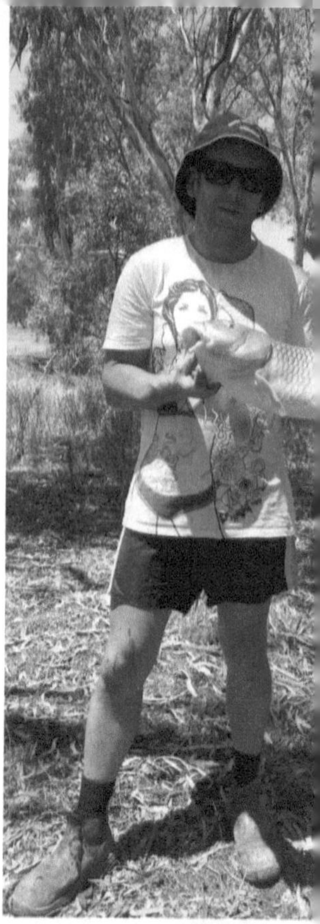

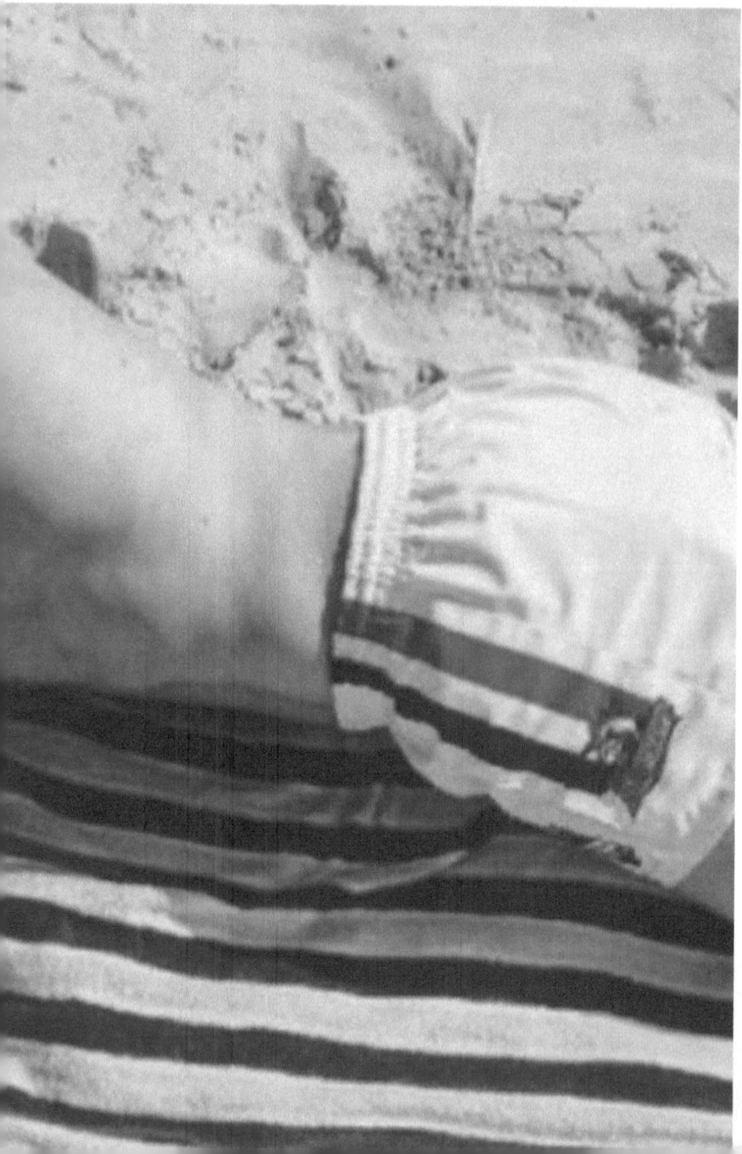

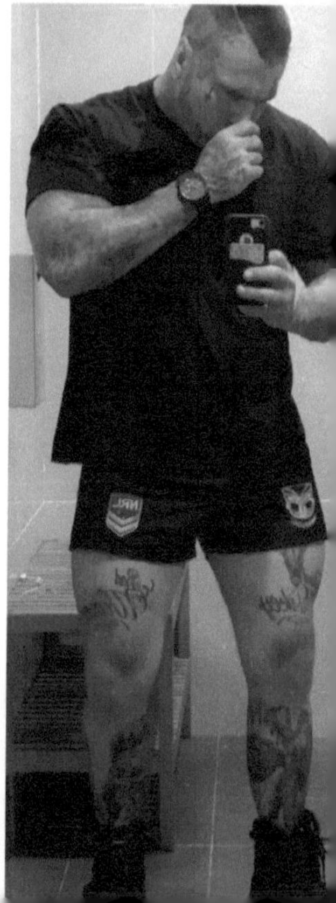

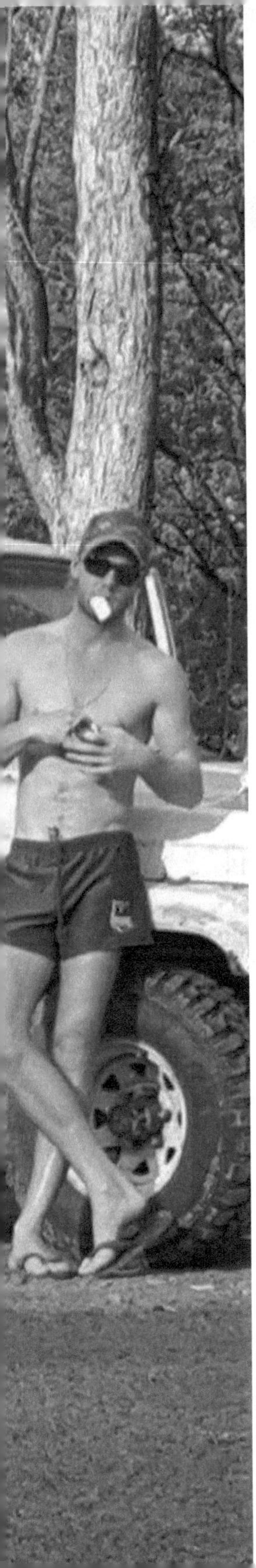
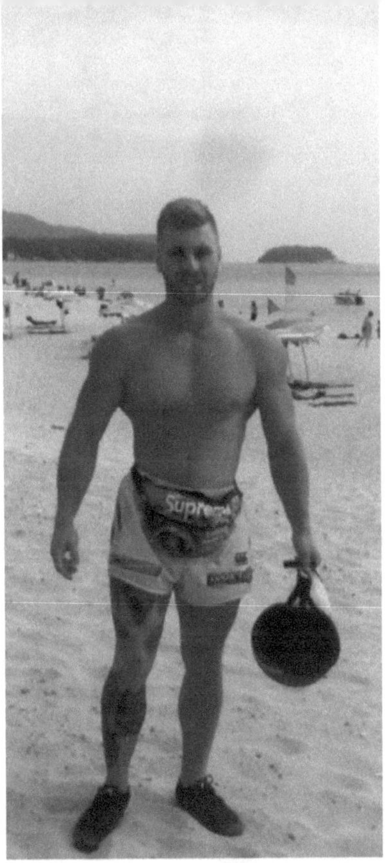
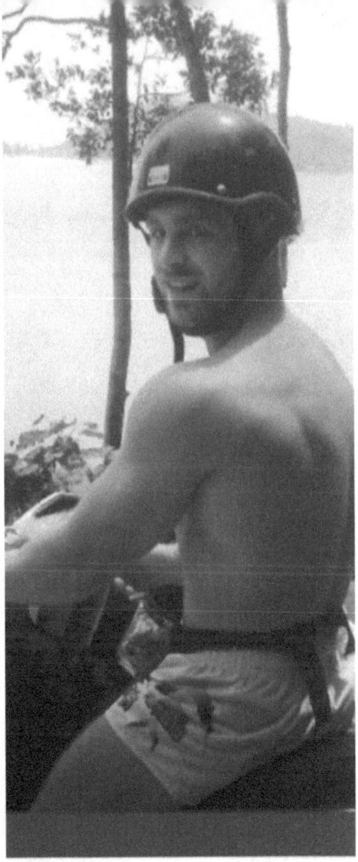
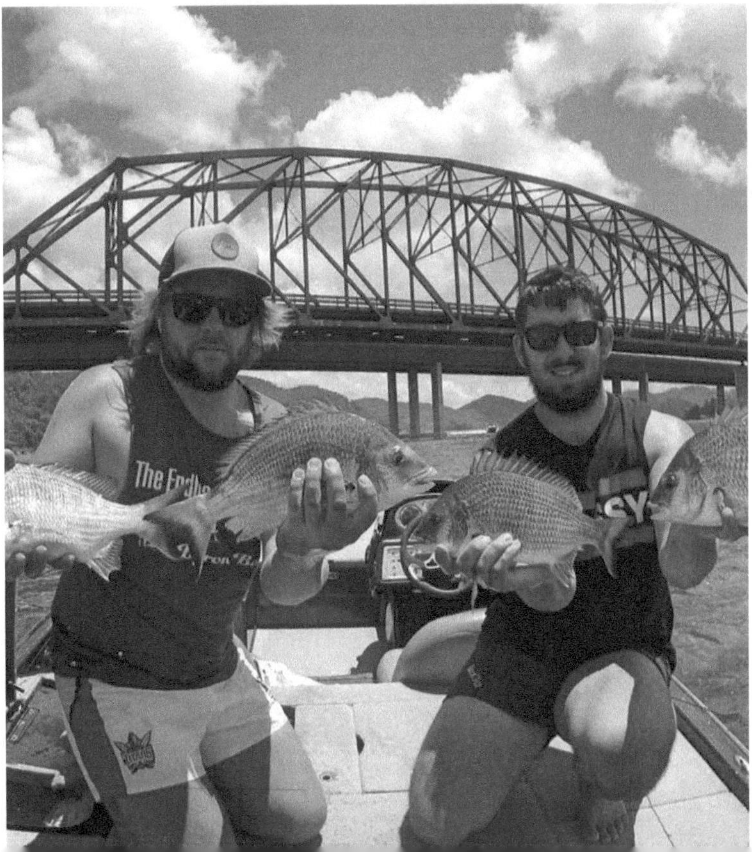

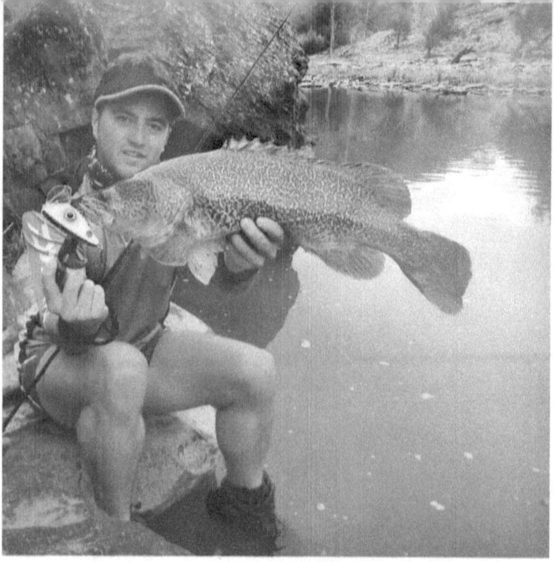

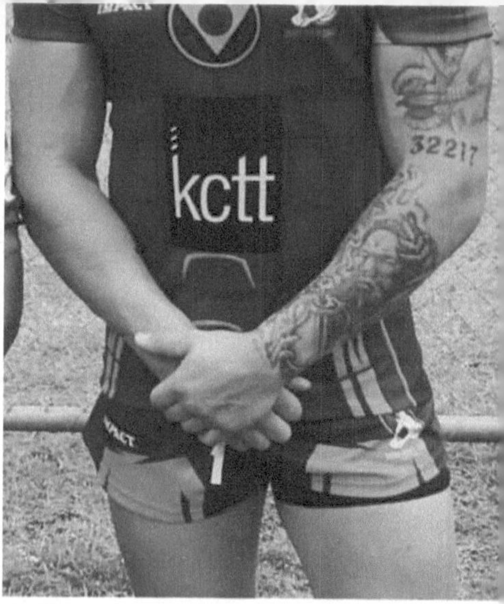
kctt
32217

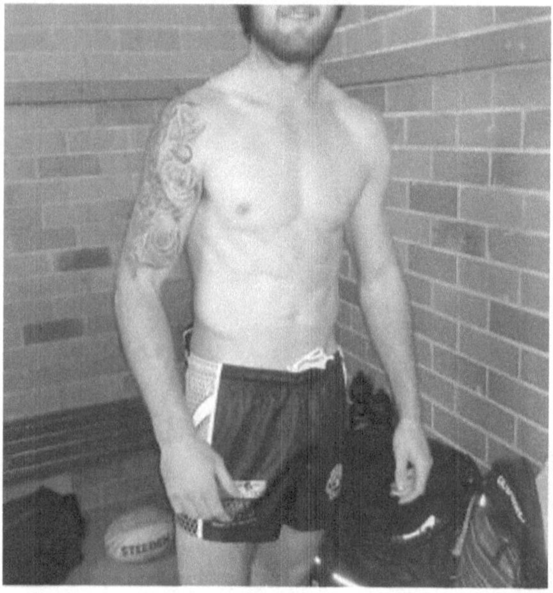

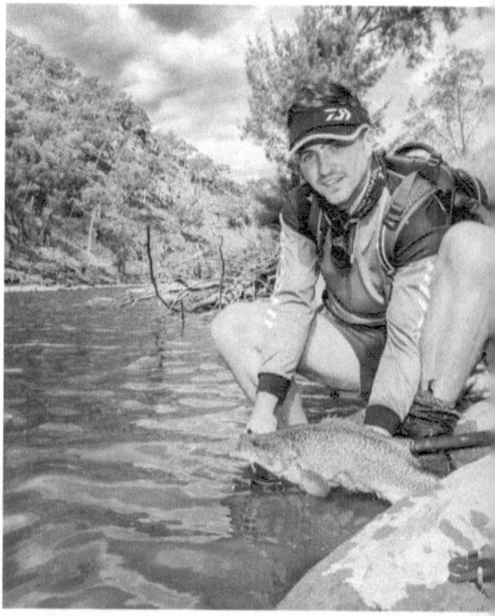

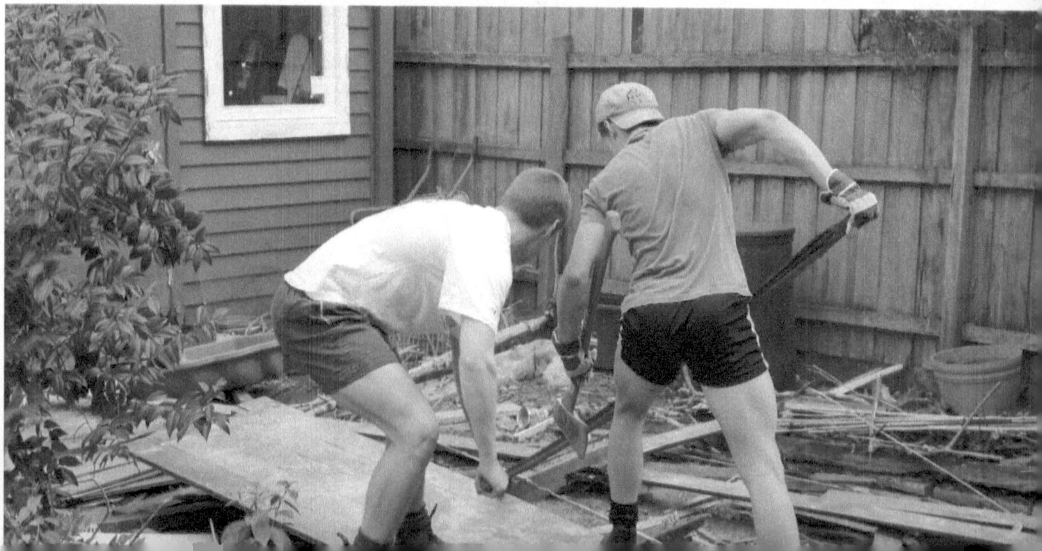

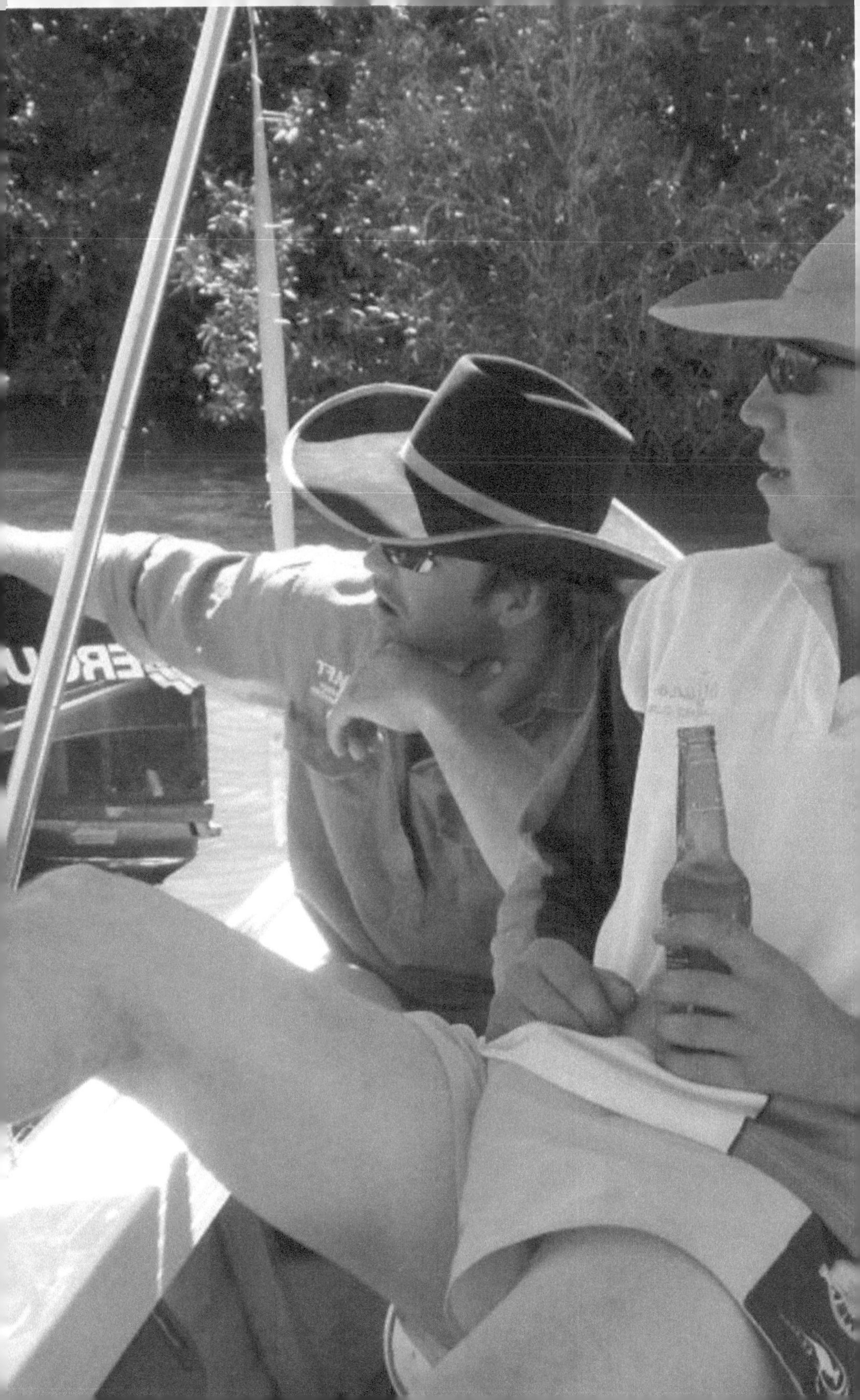

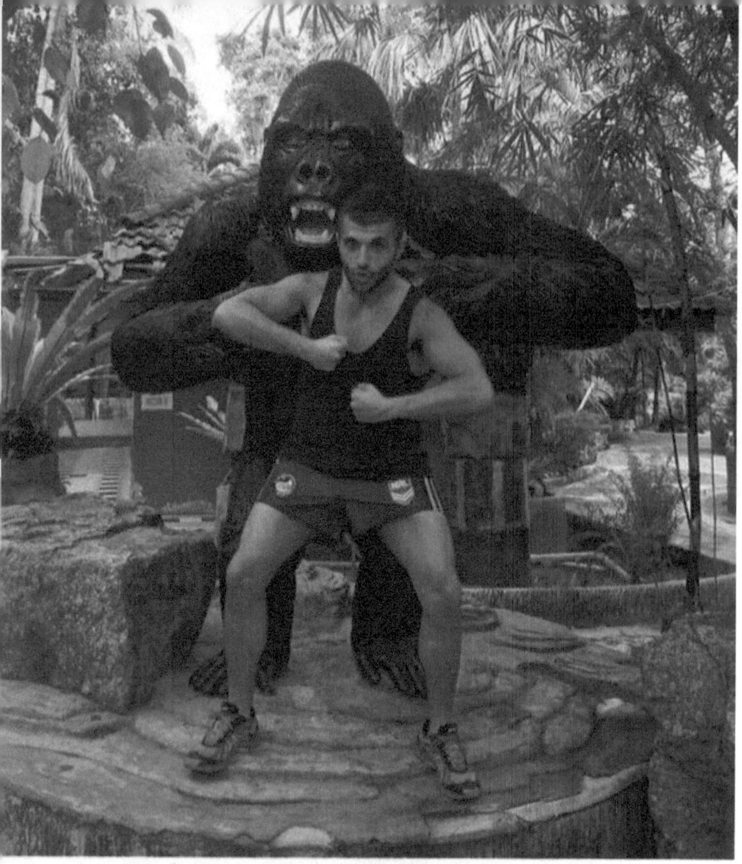

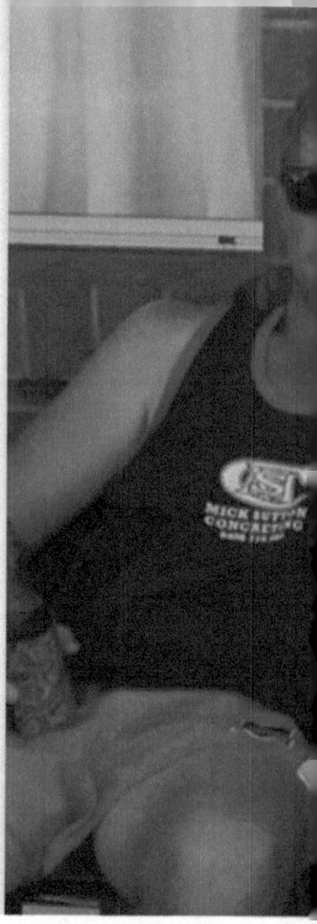

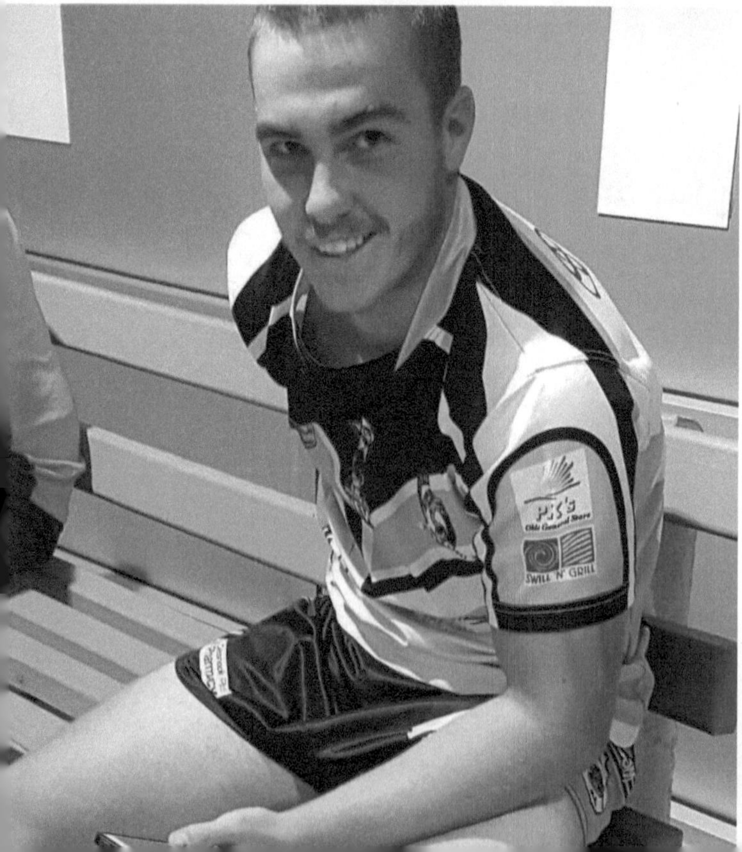
SWILL 'N' GRILL

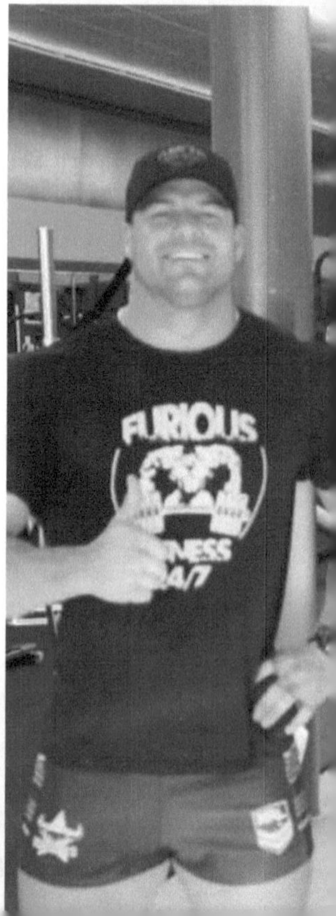
FURIOUS

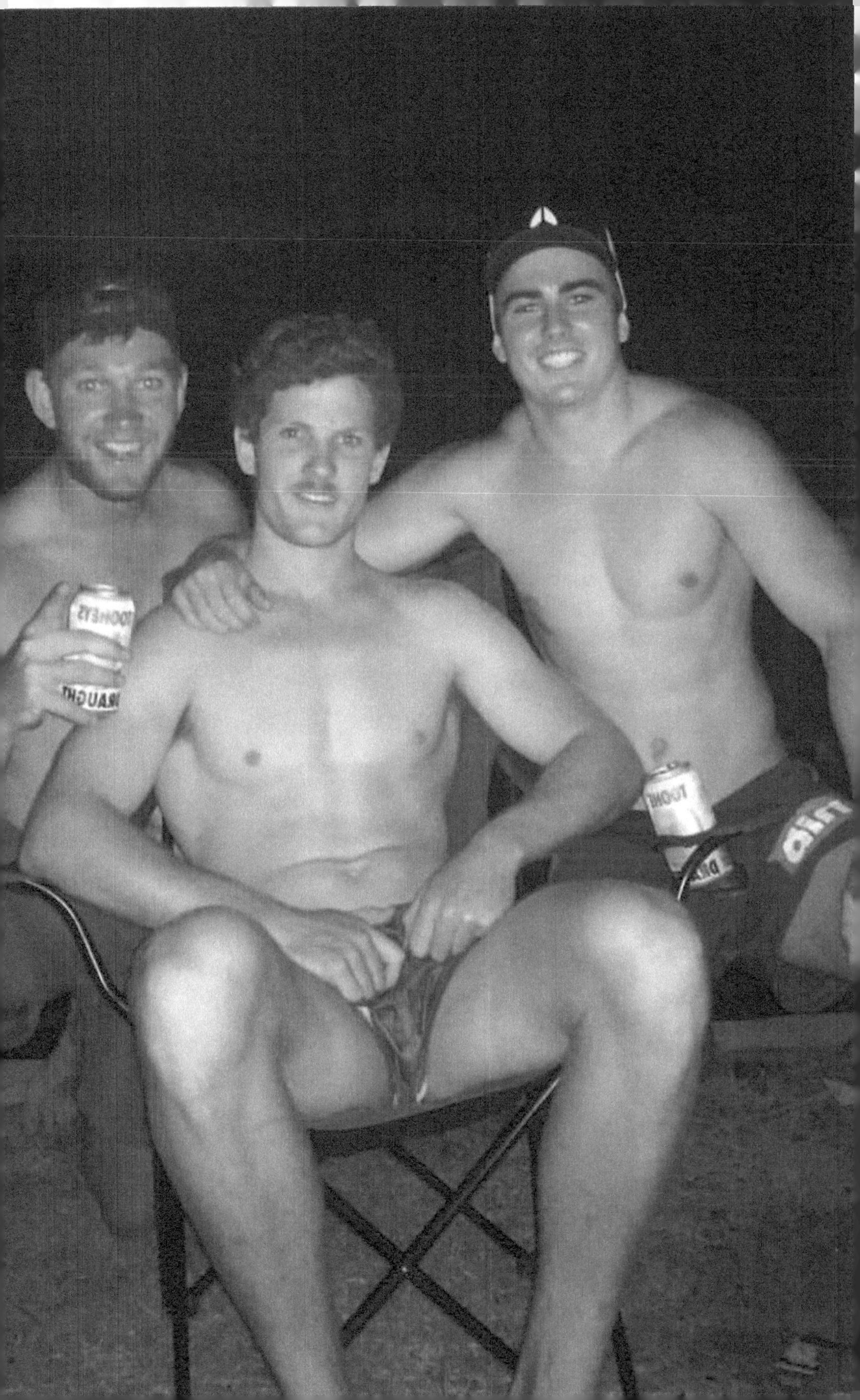
TOOHEYS
DRAUGHT

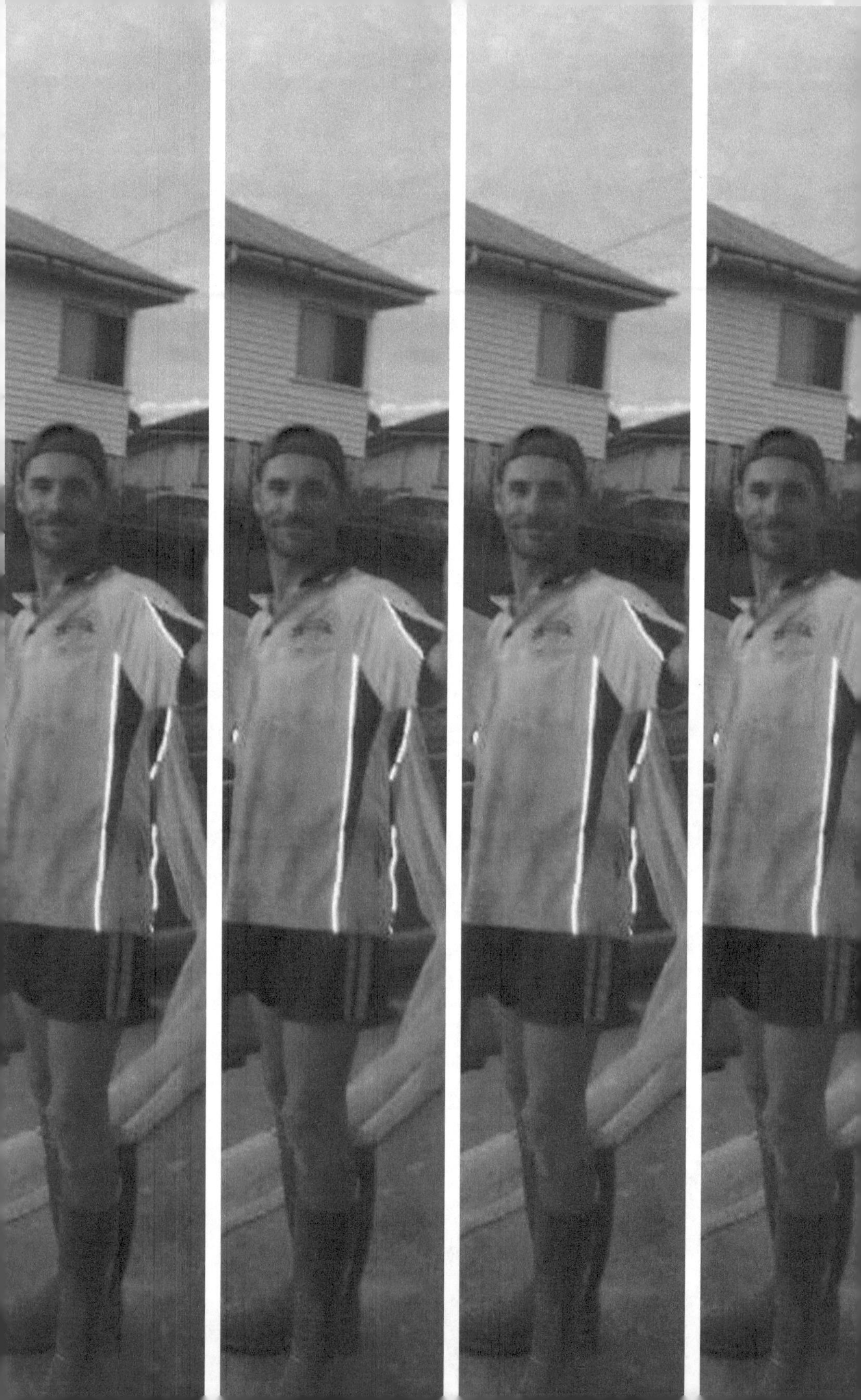

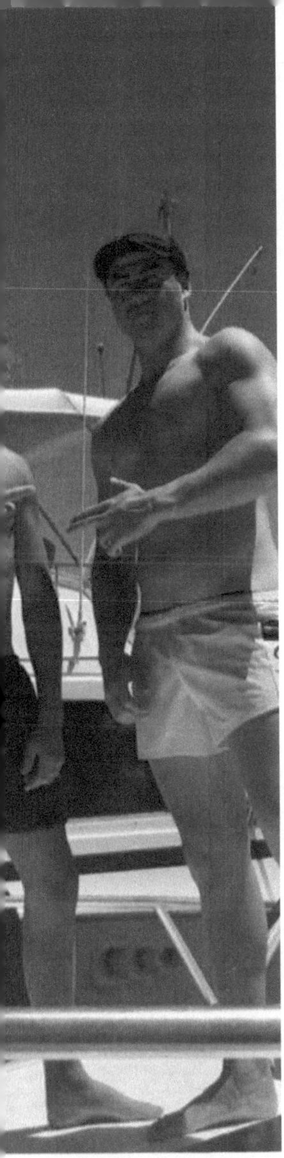

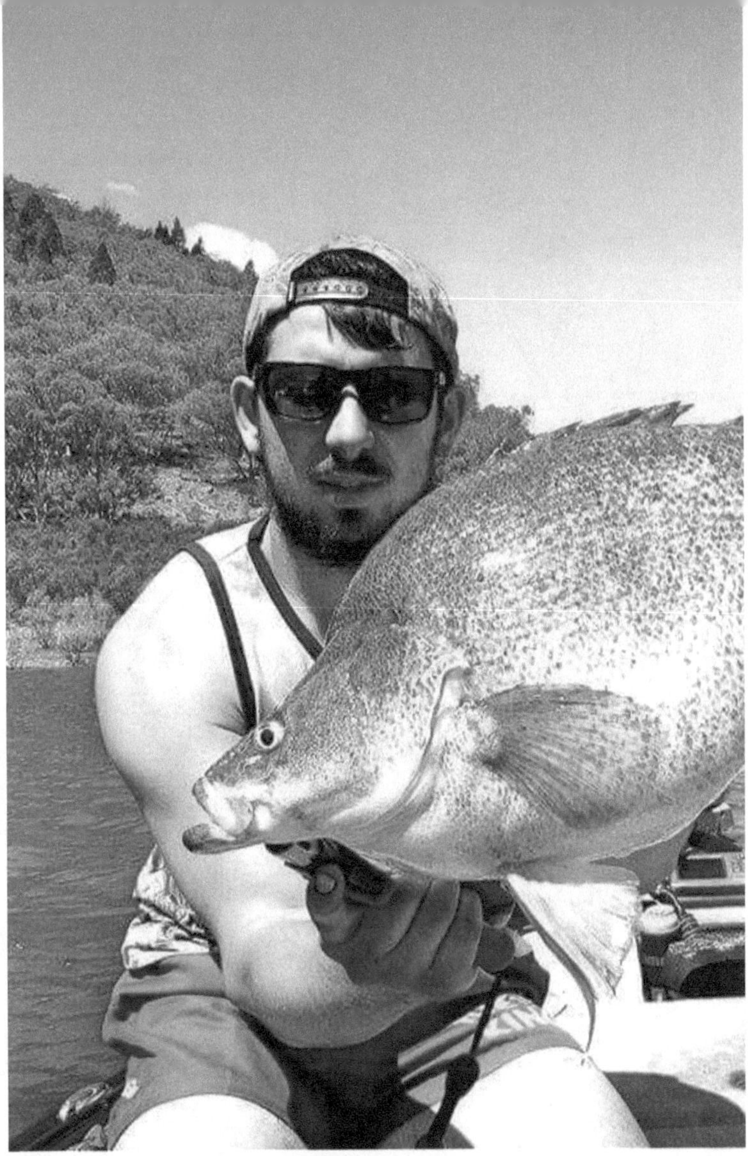

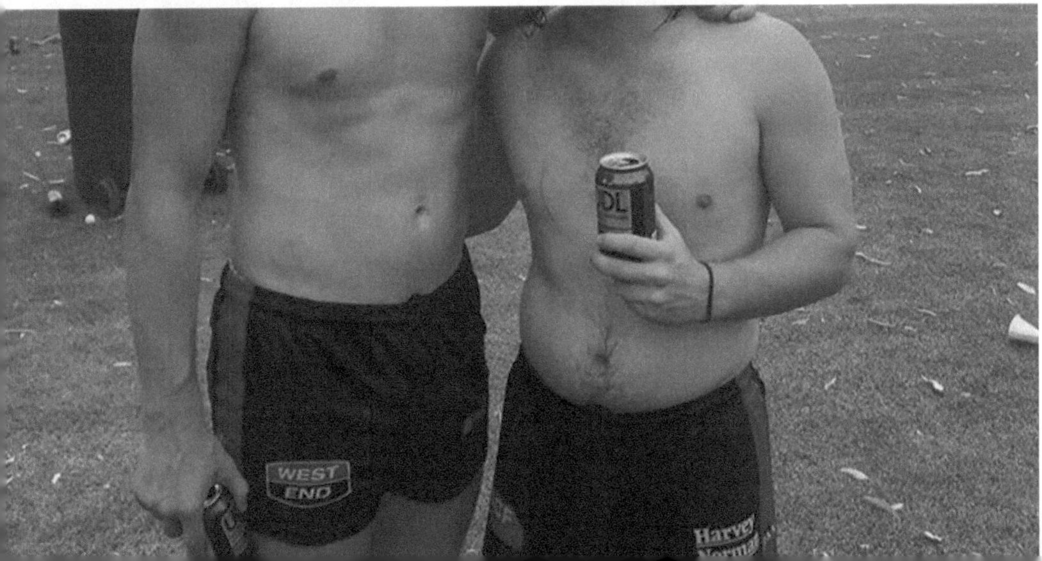
WEST
END
Harvey

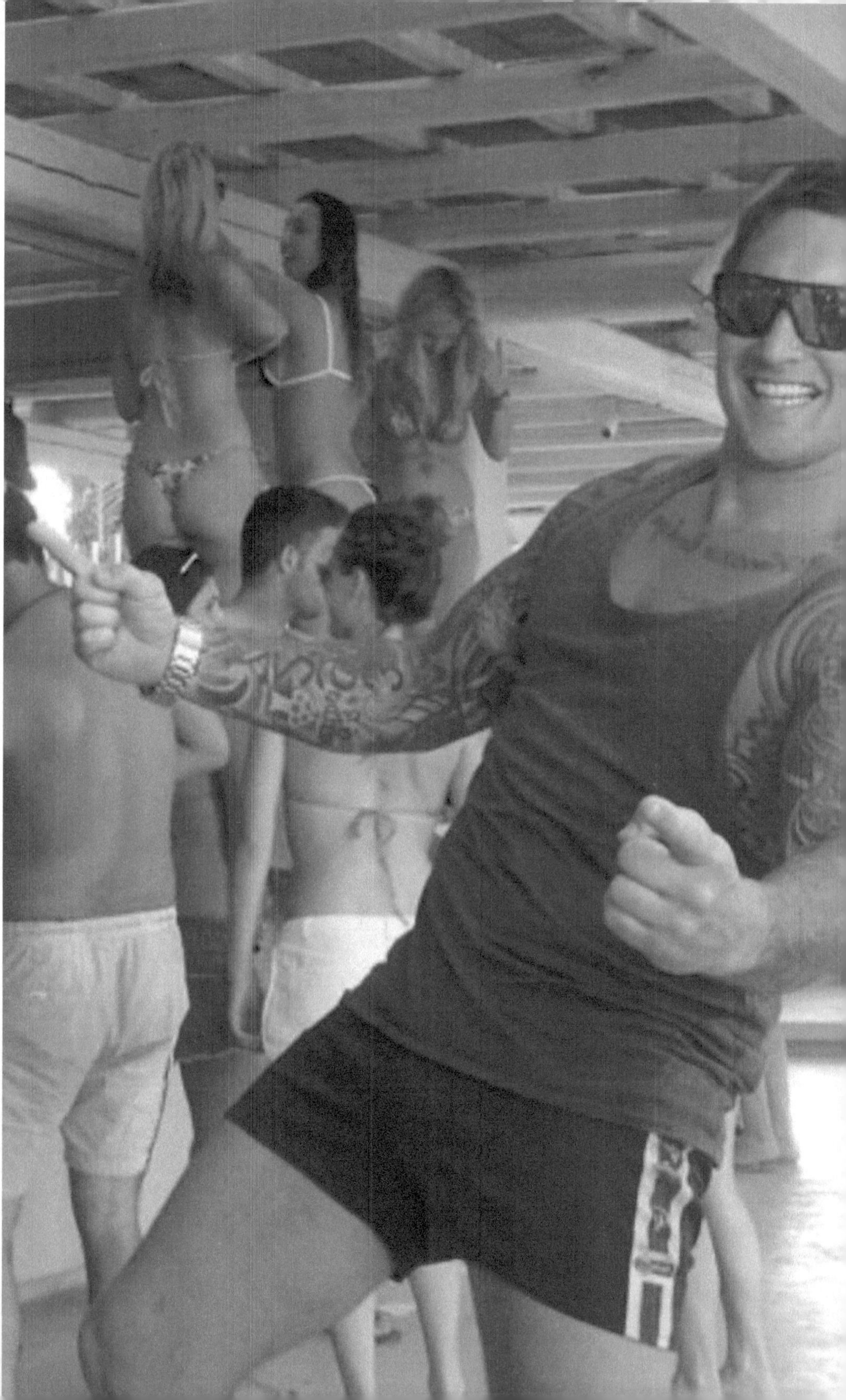

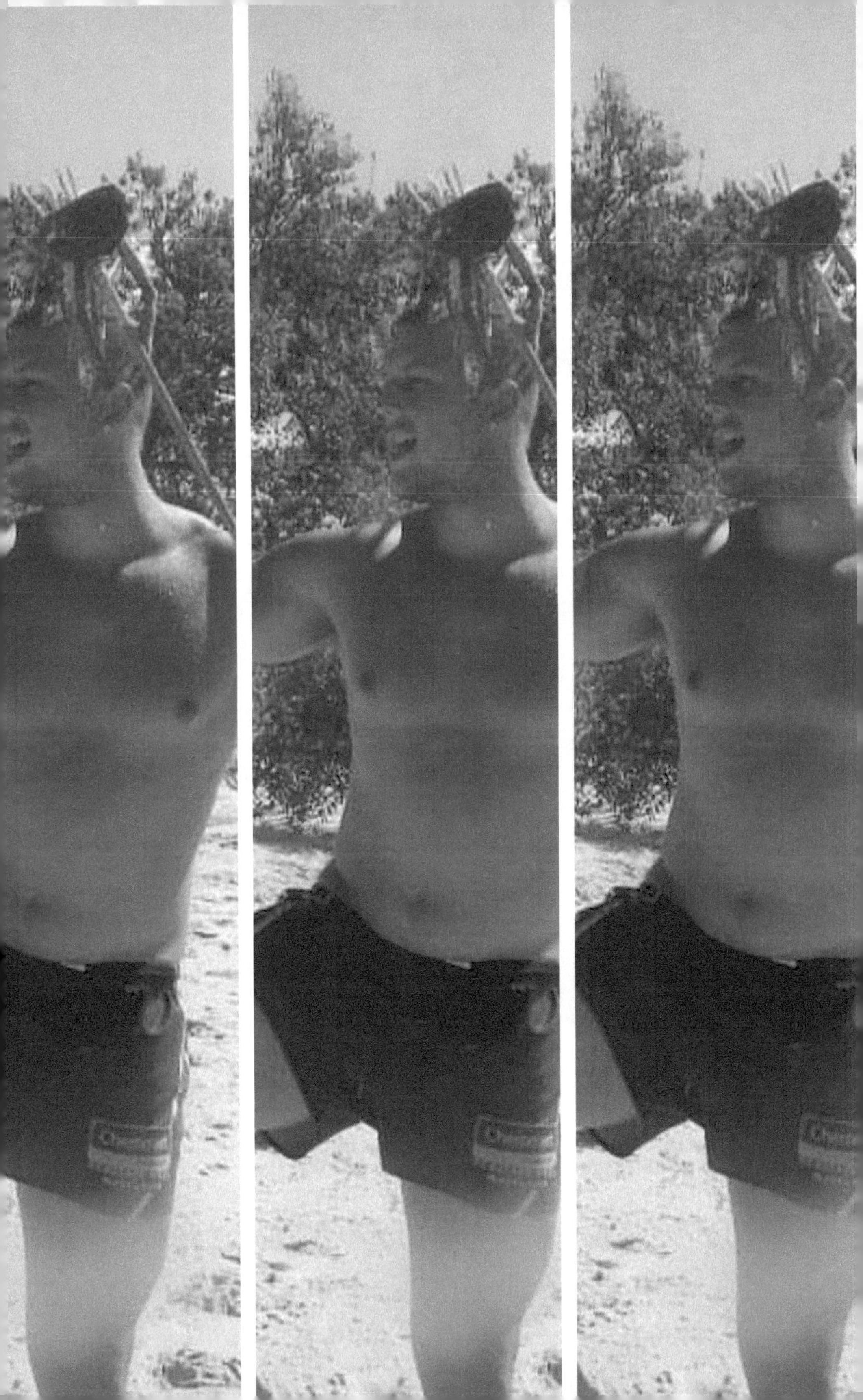

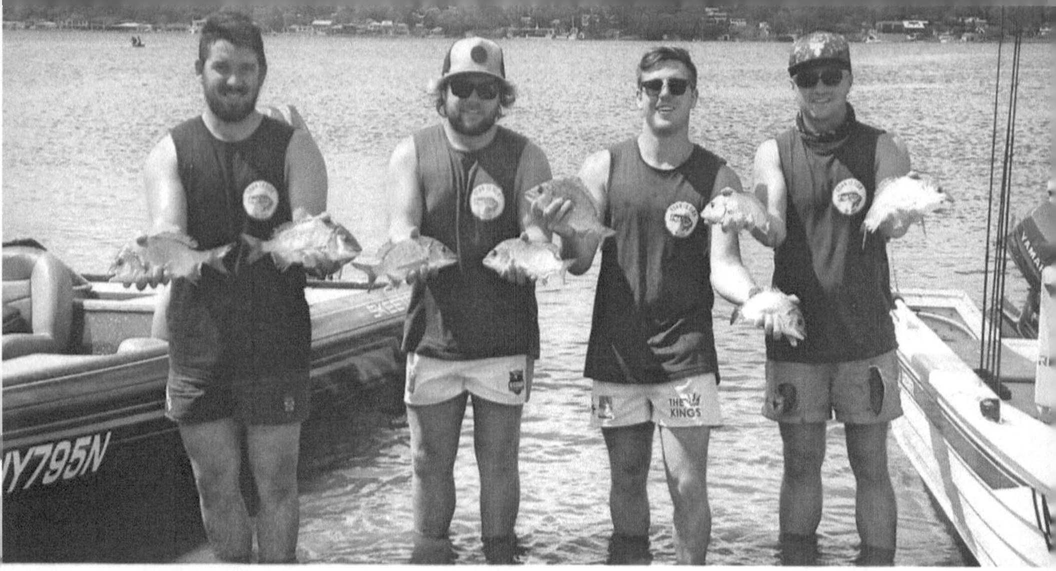
Y795N
THE KINGS

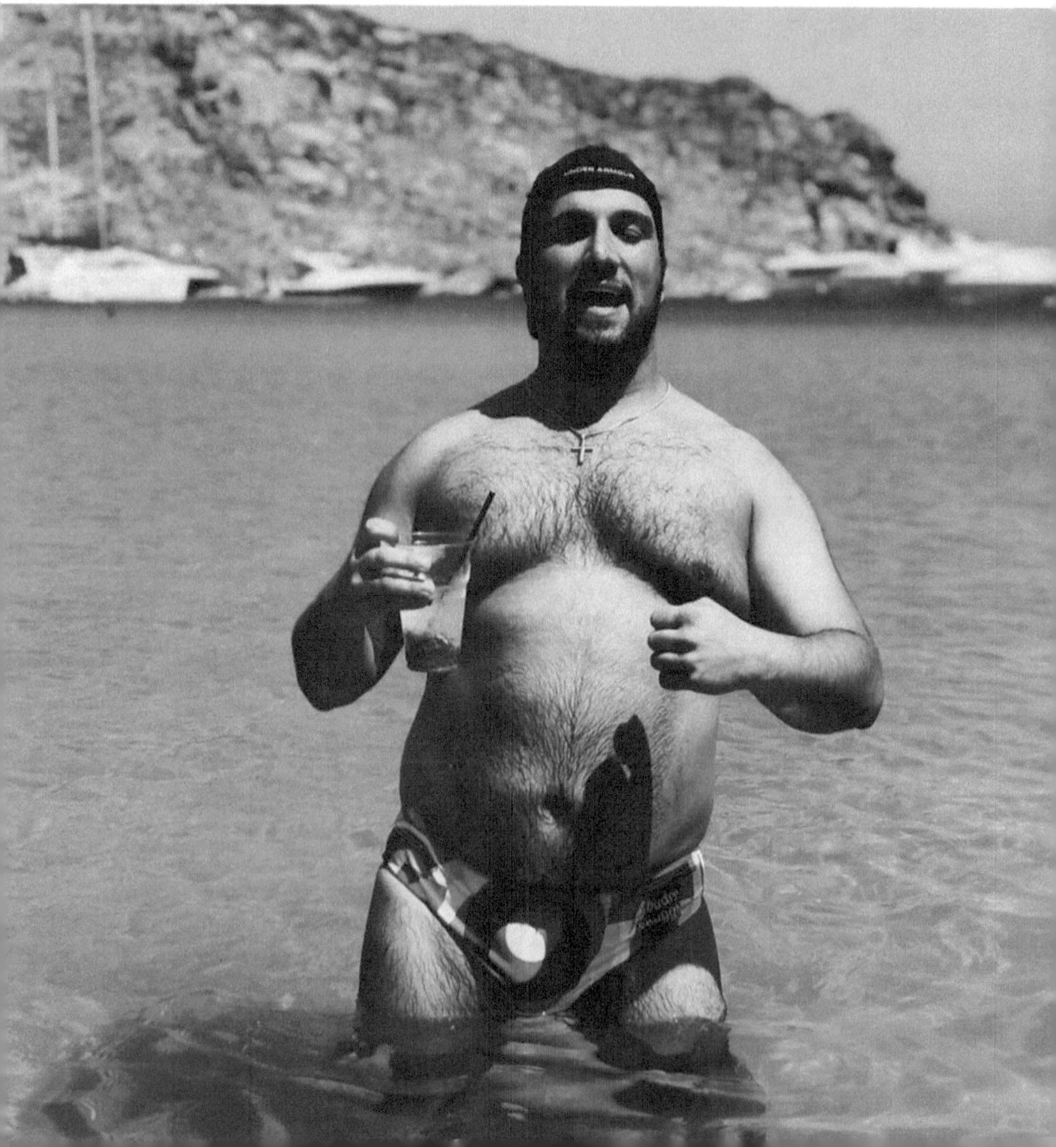

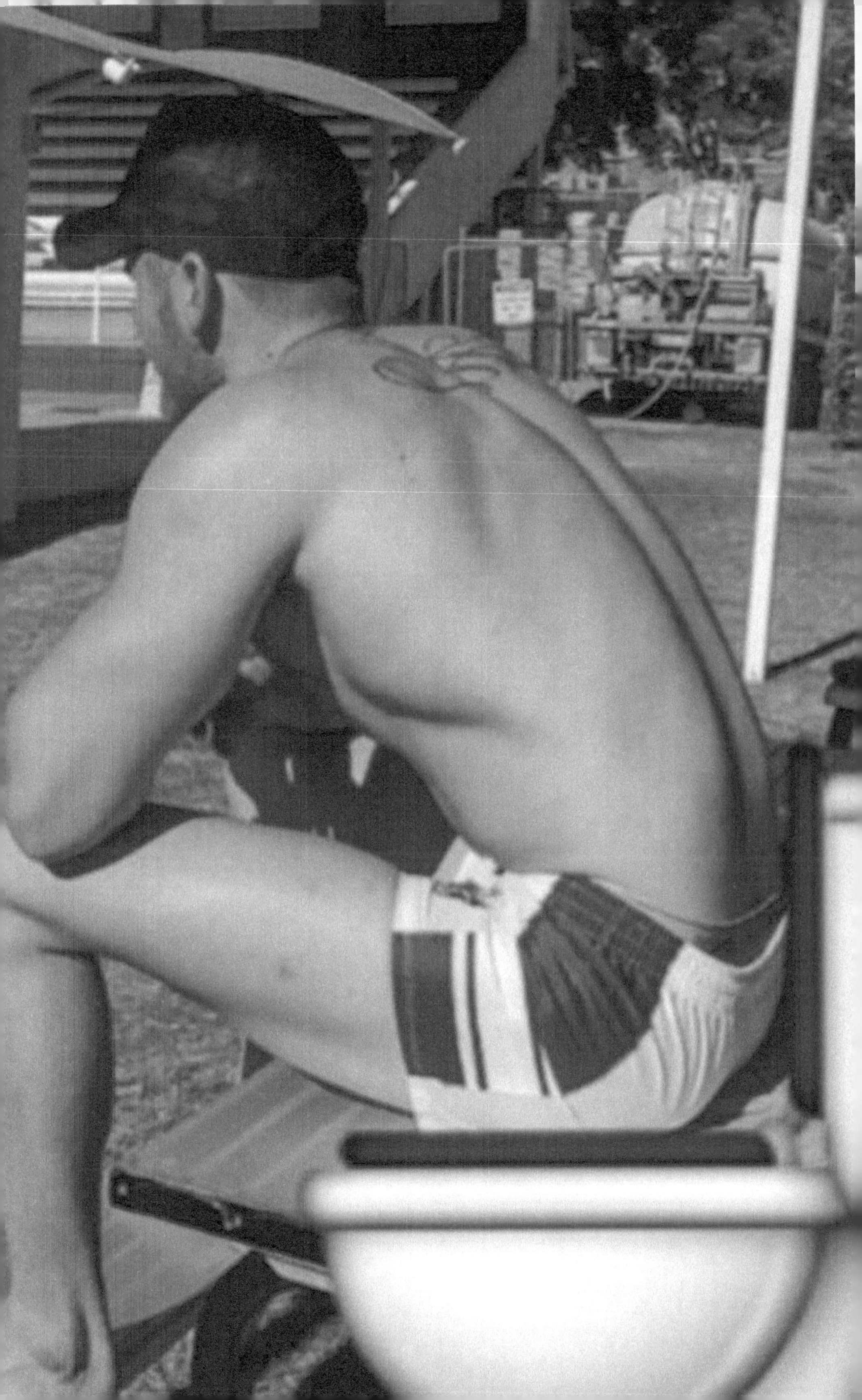

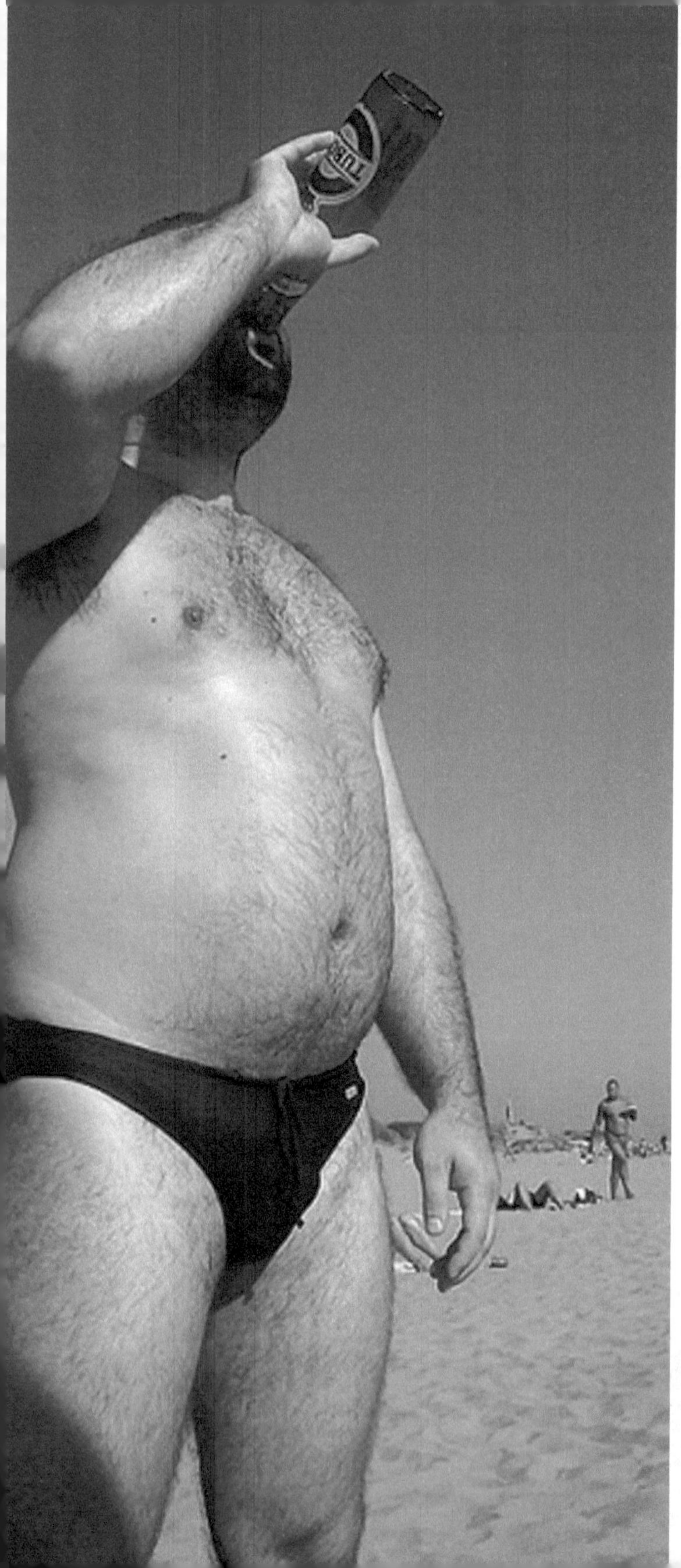

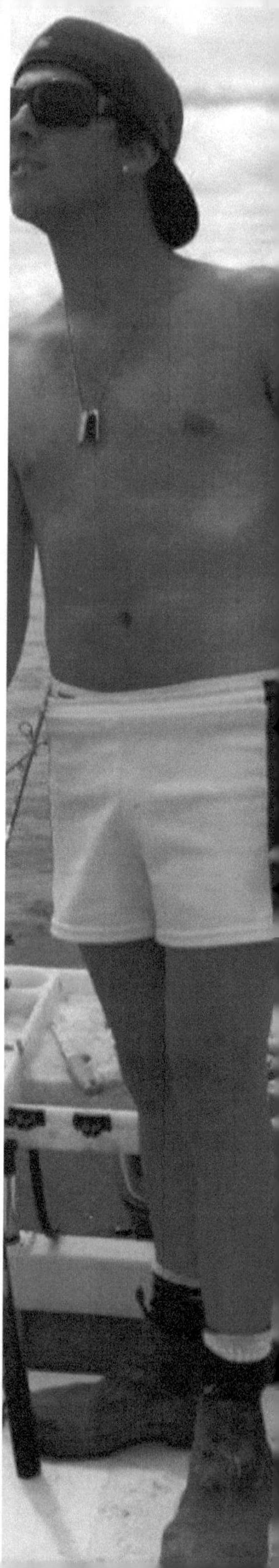

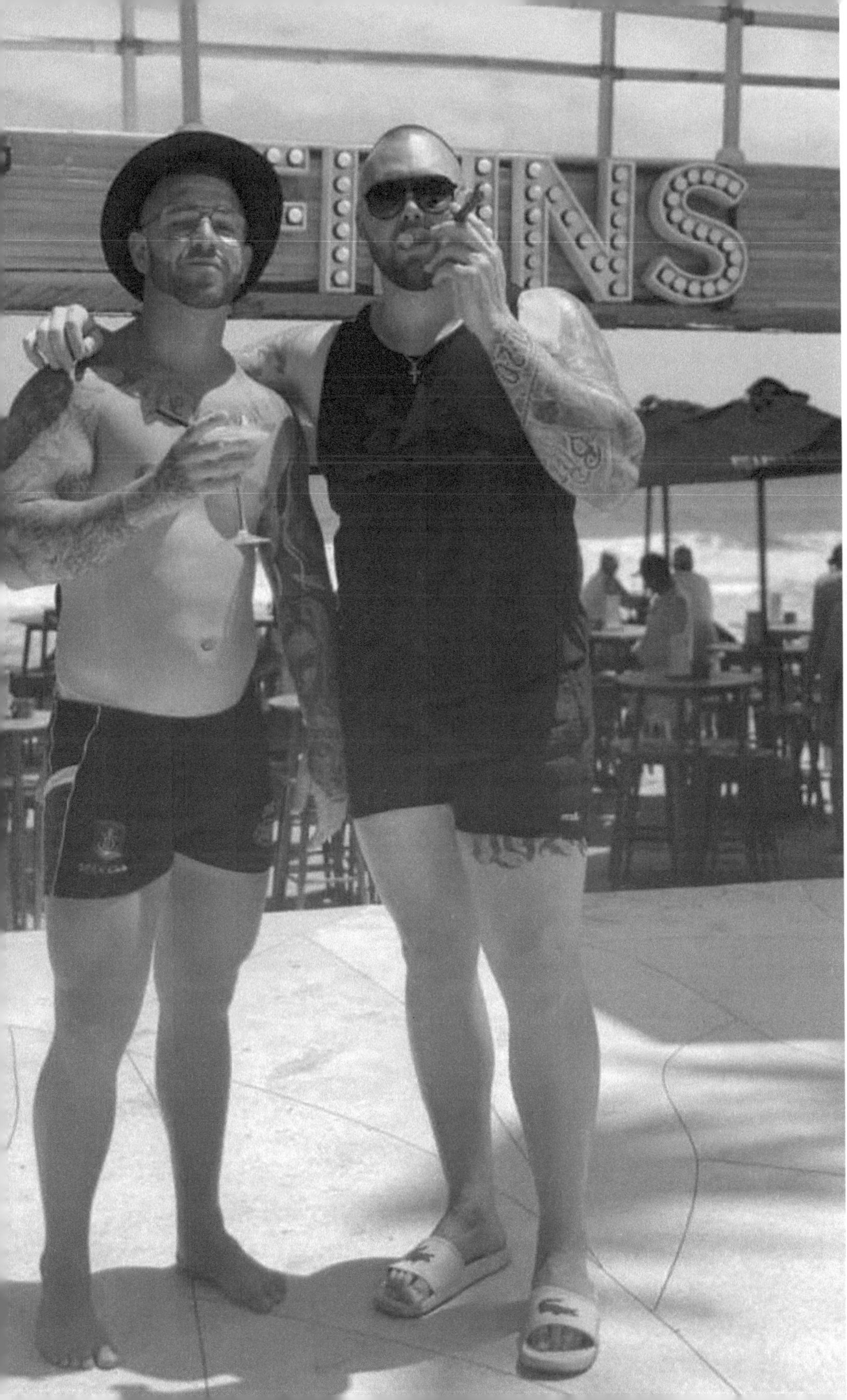

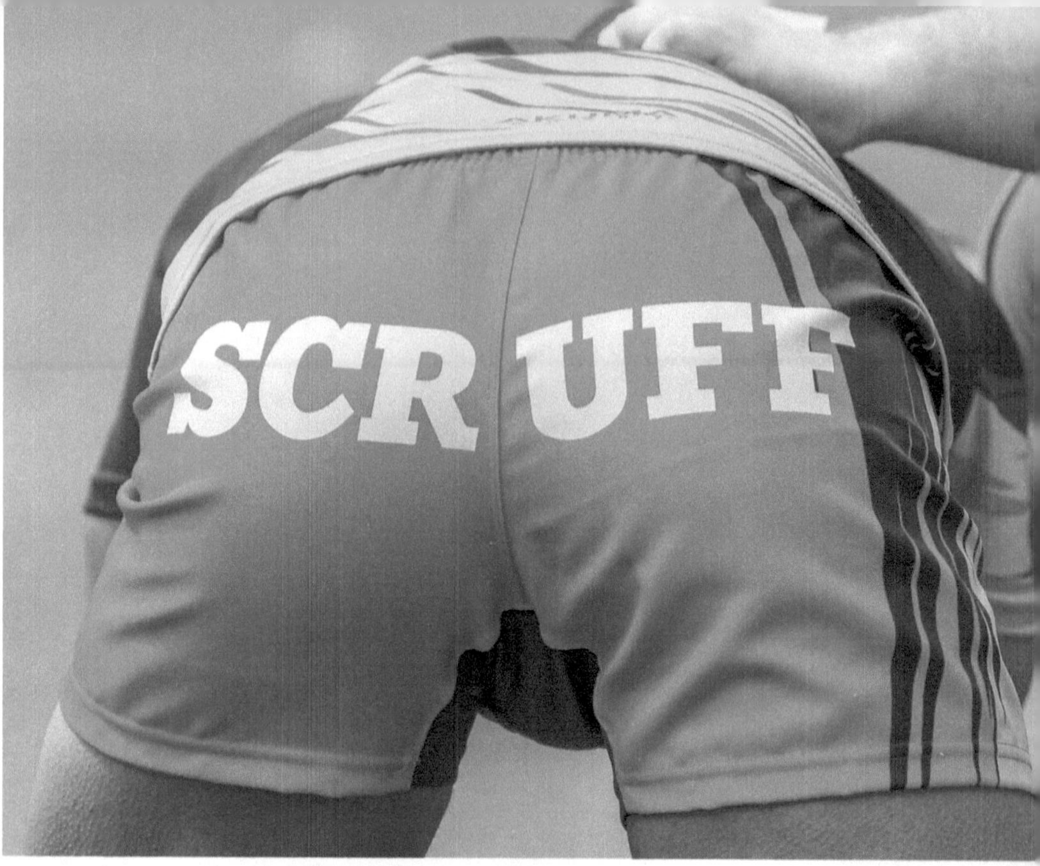
SCRUFF

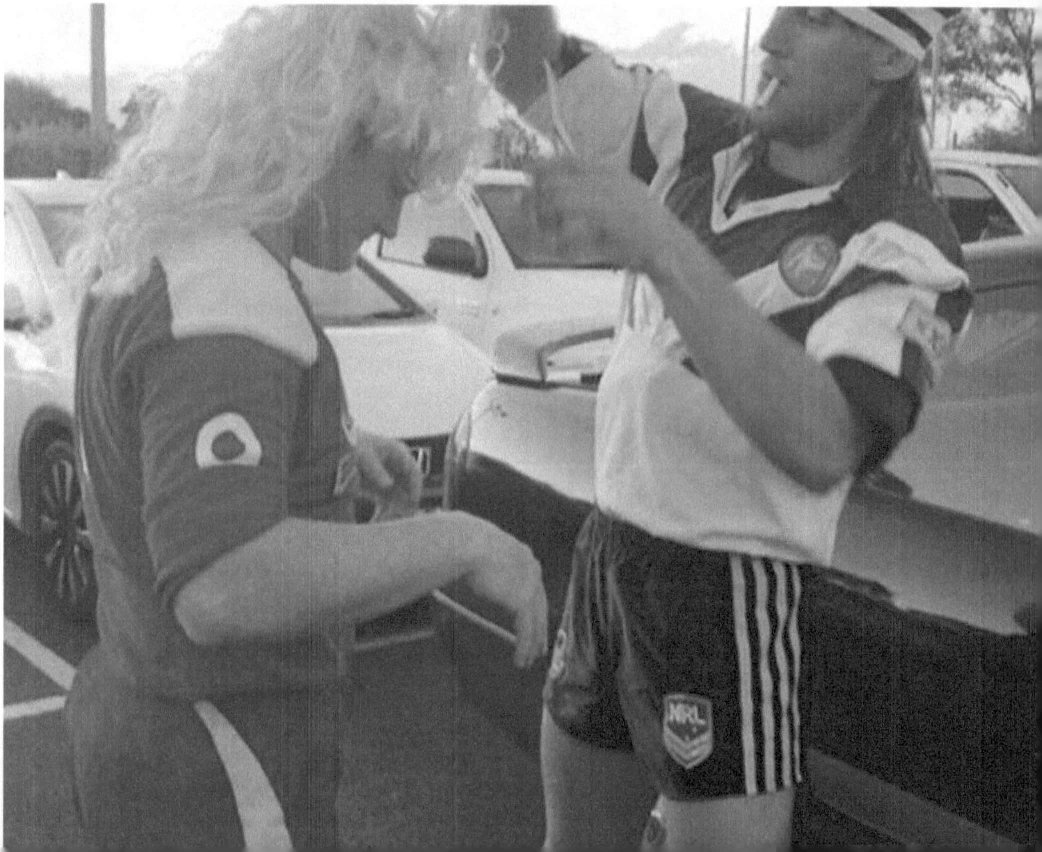

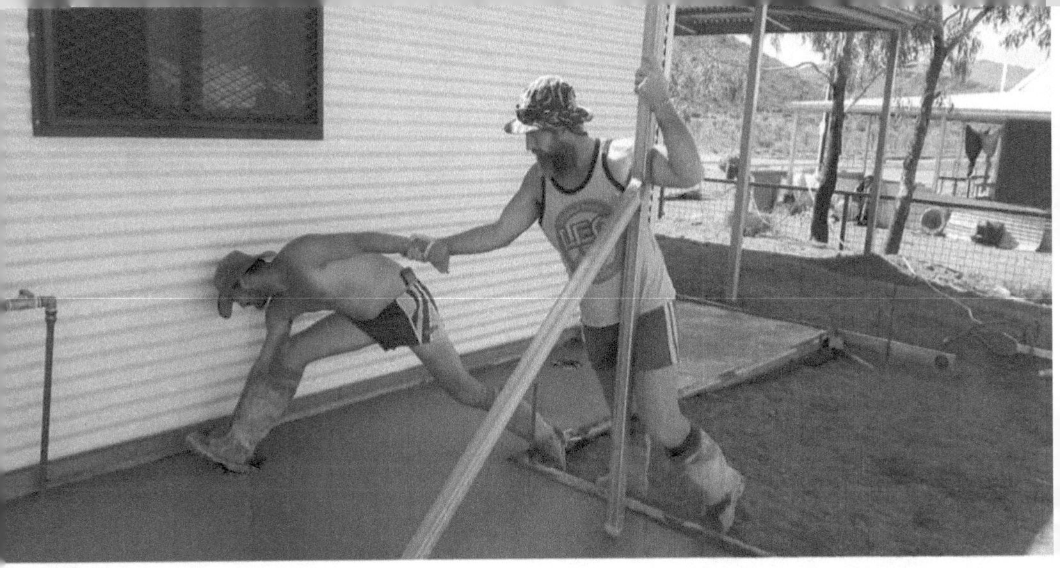

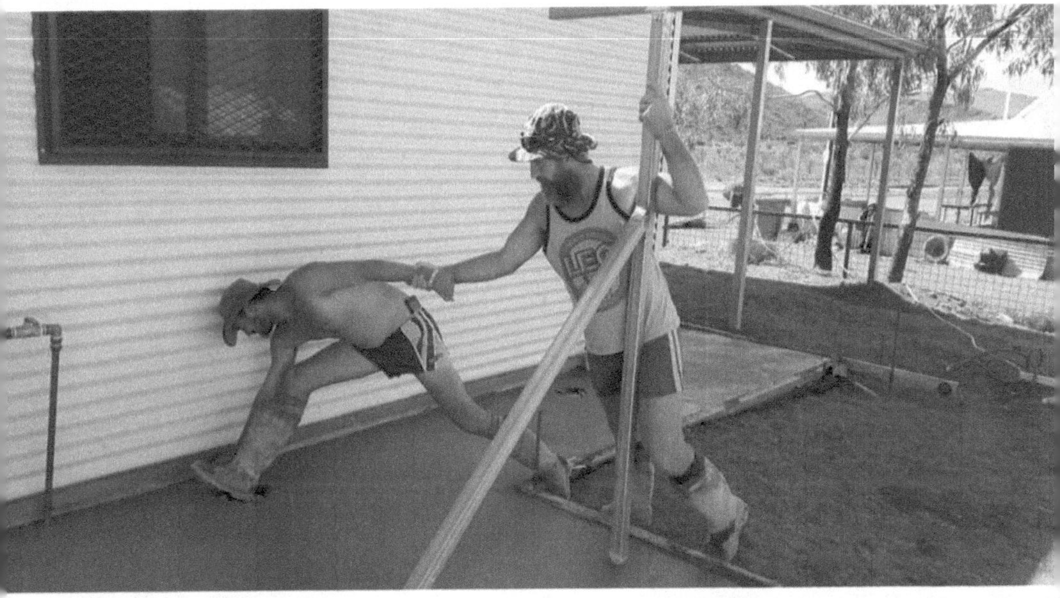

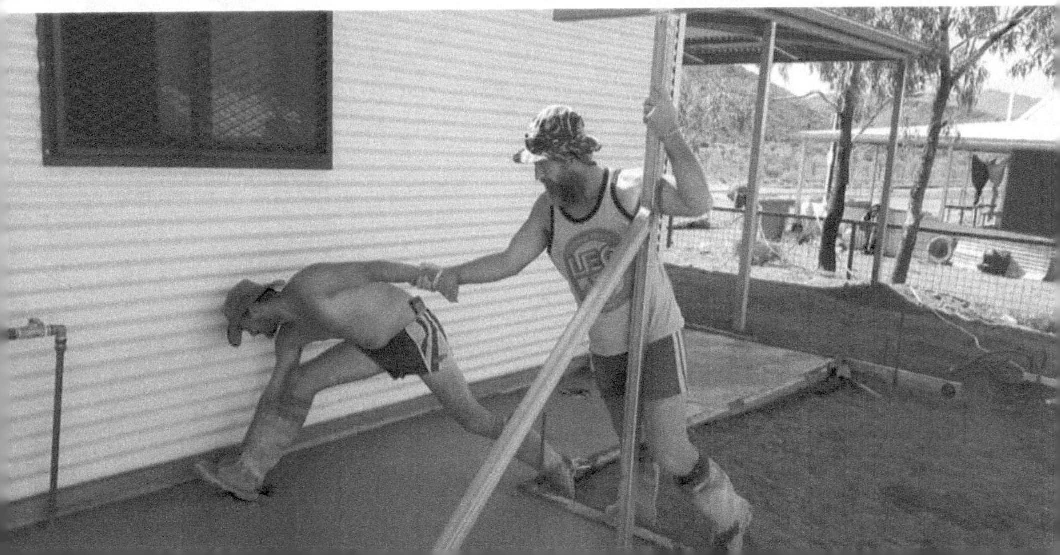

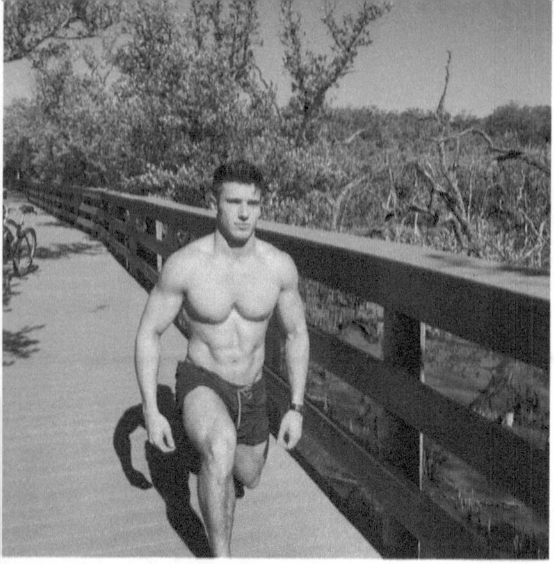

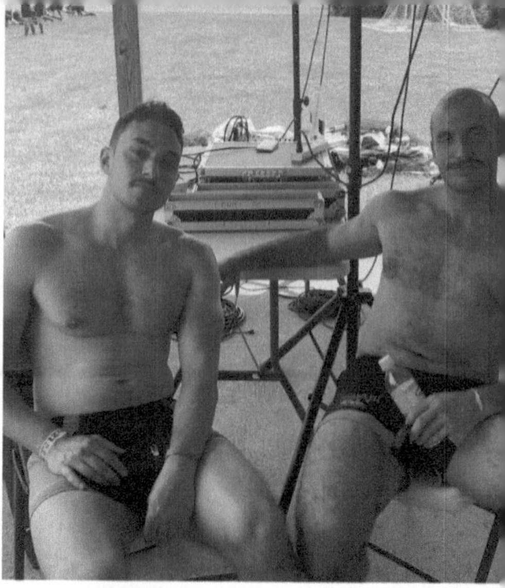

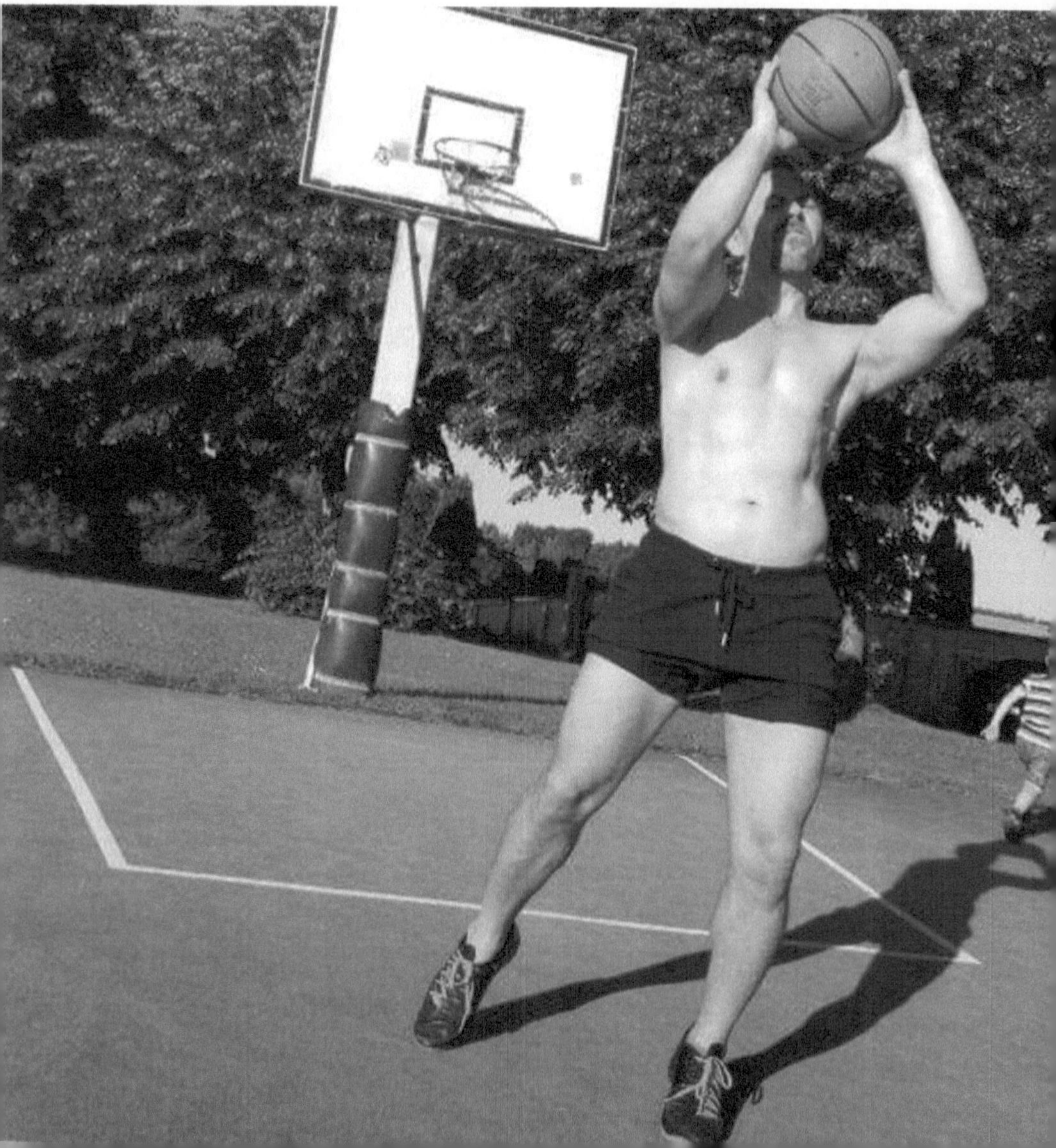

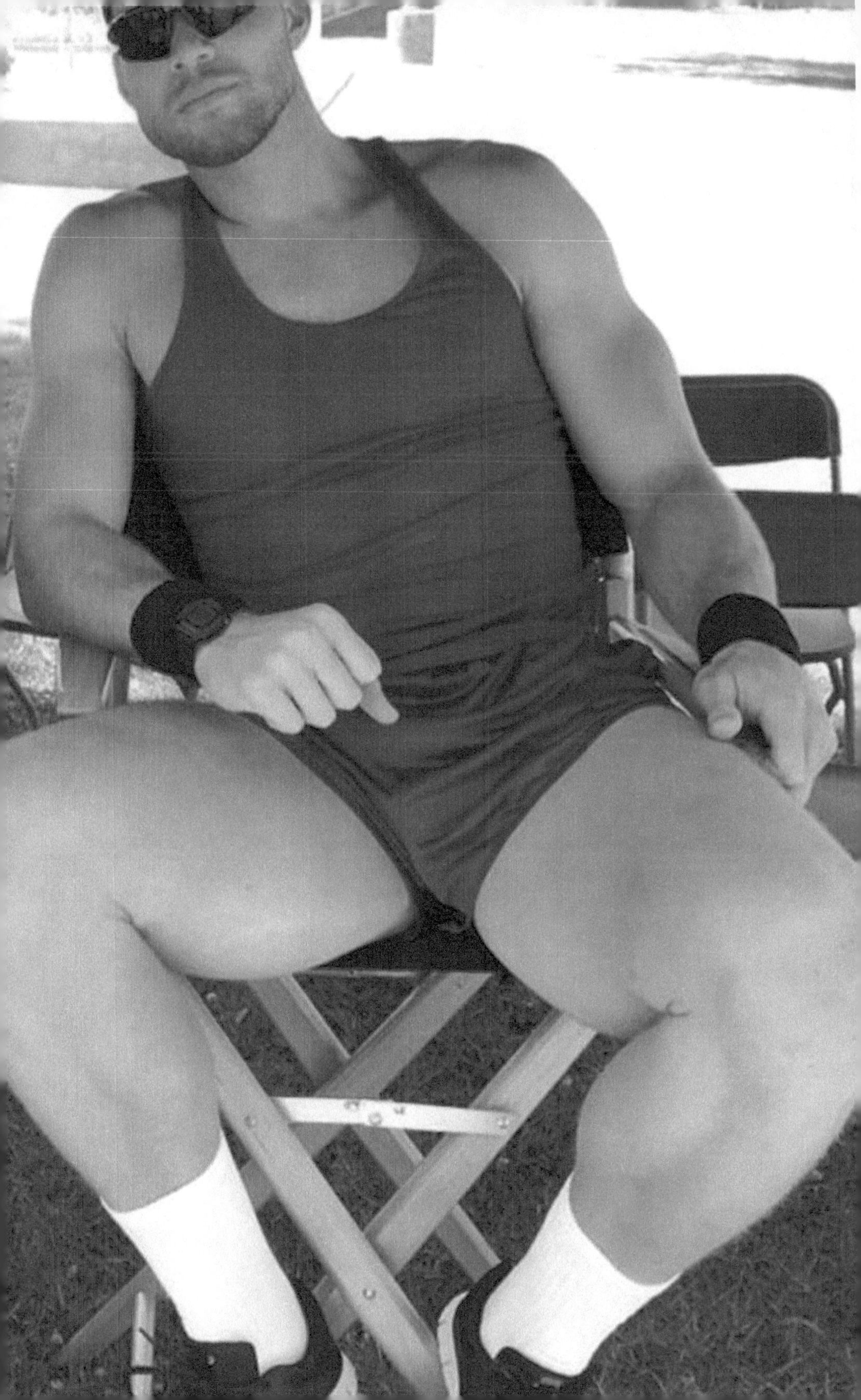

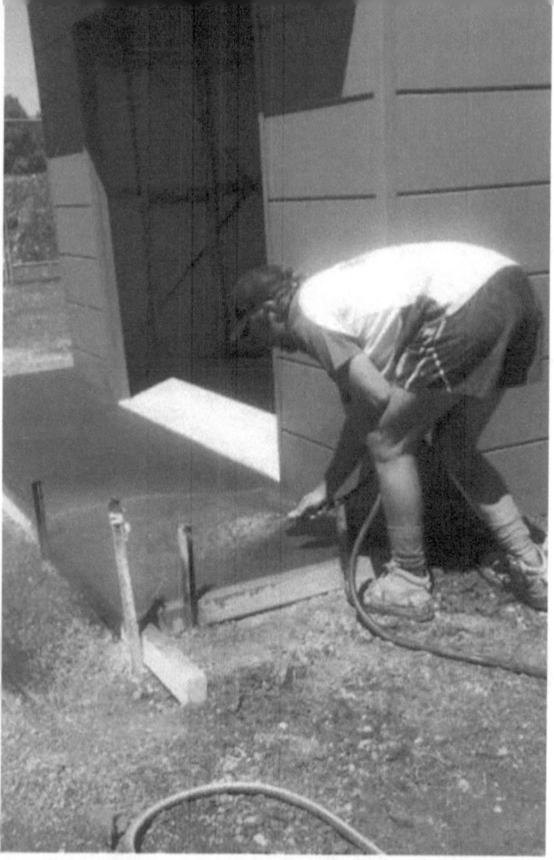

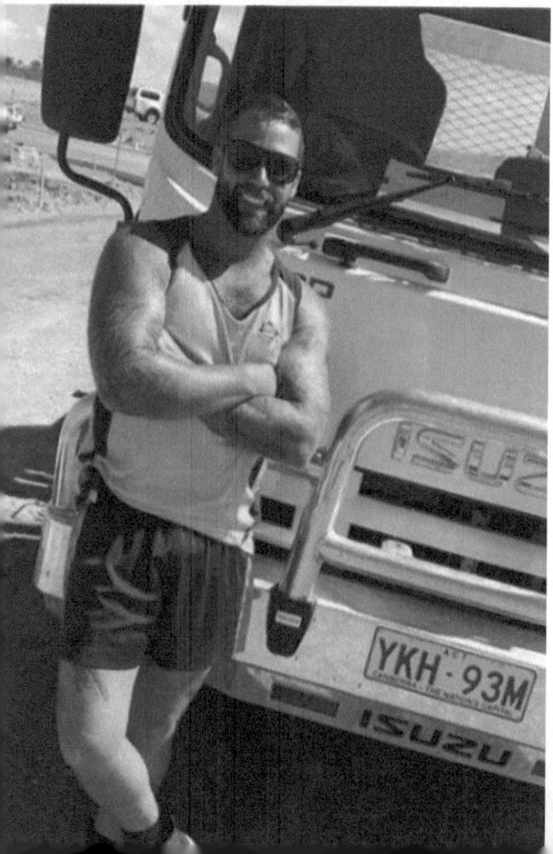
ISUZU
YKH·93M
ISUZU

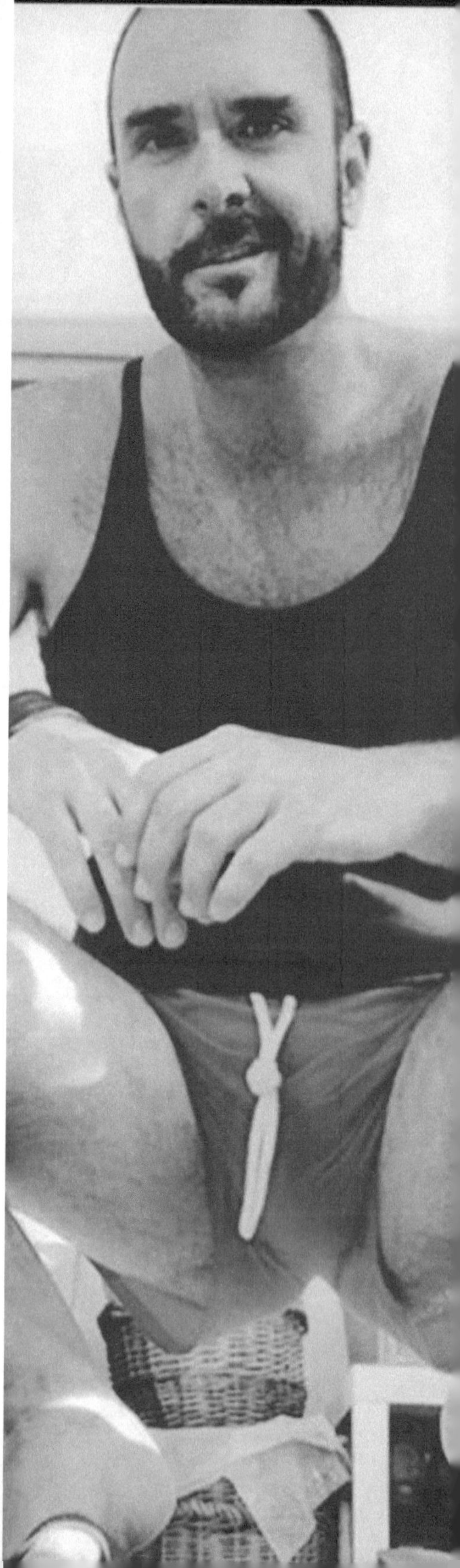

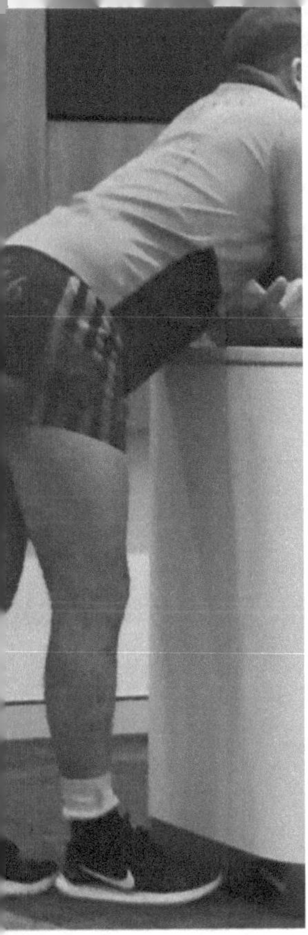
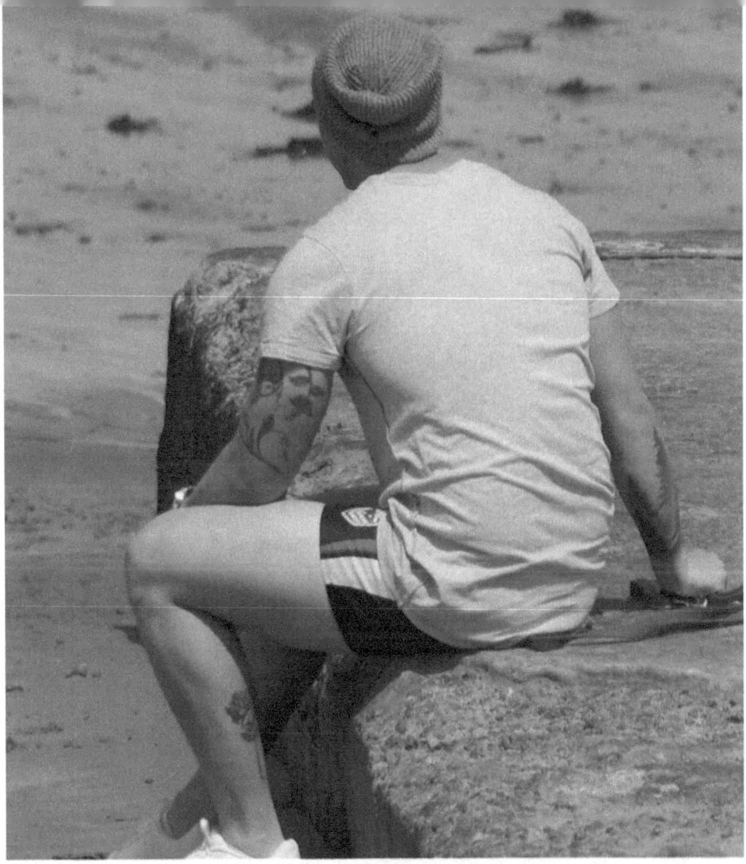
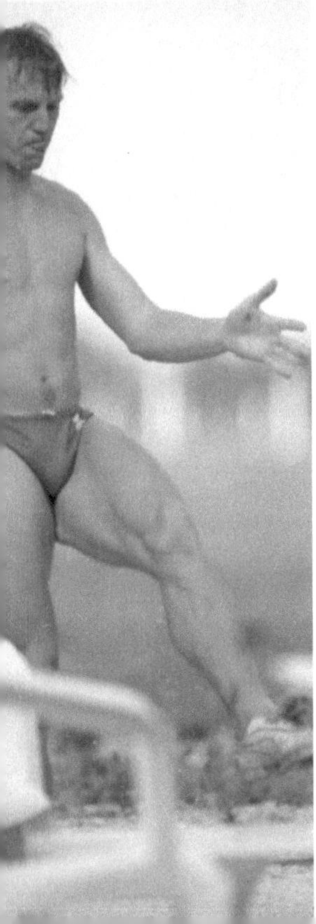
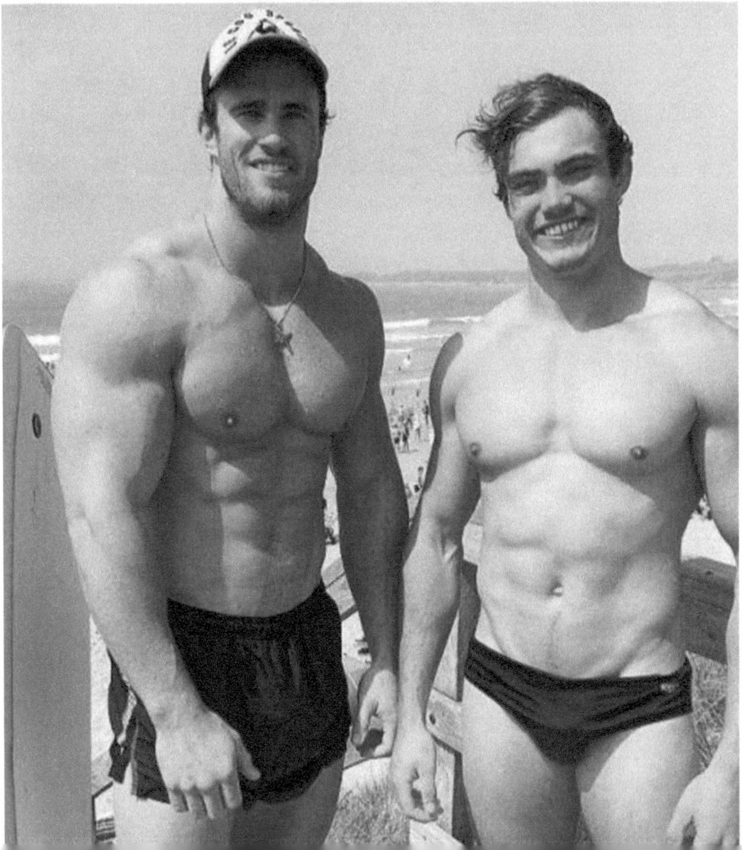

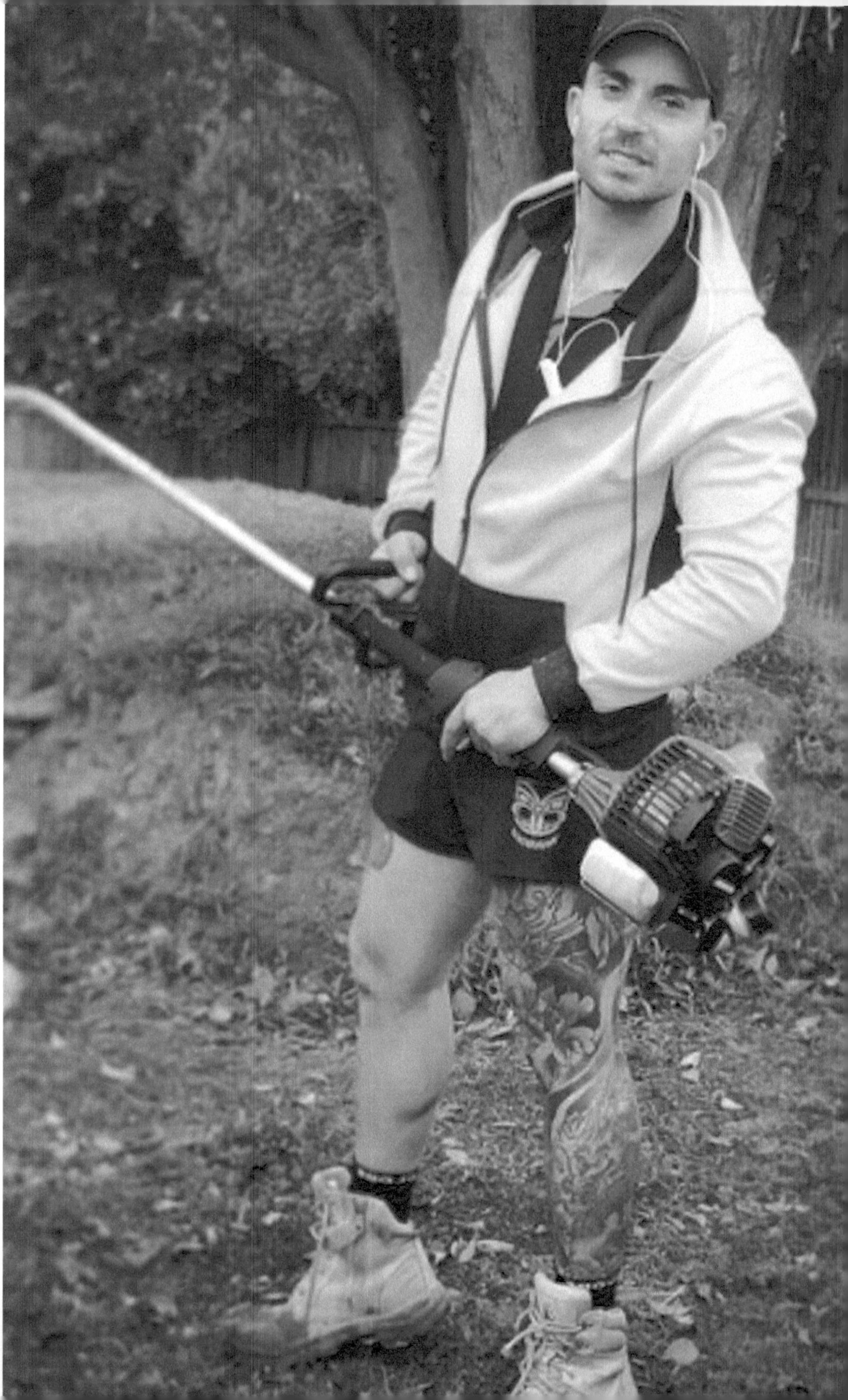

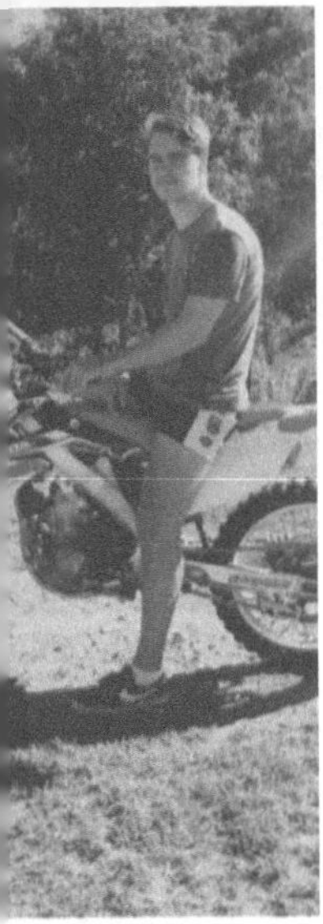

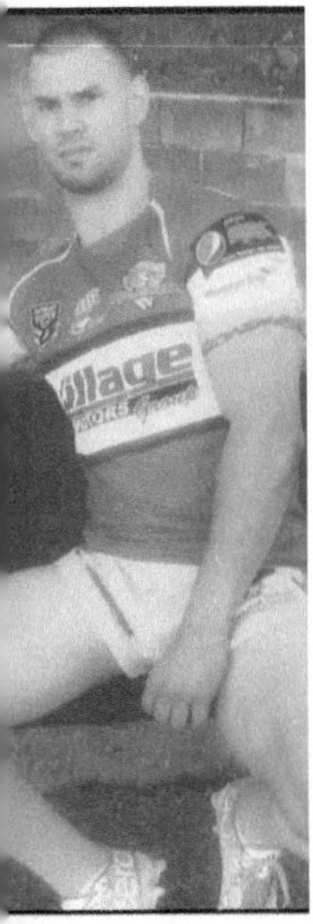
Village

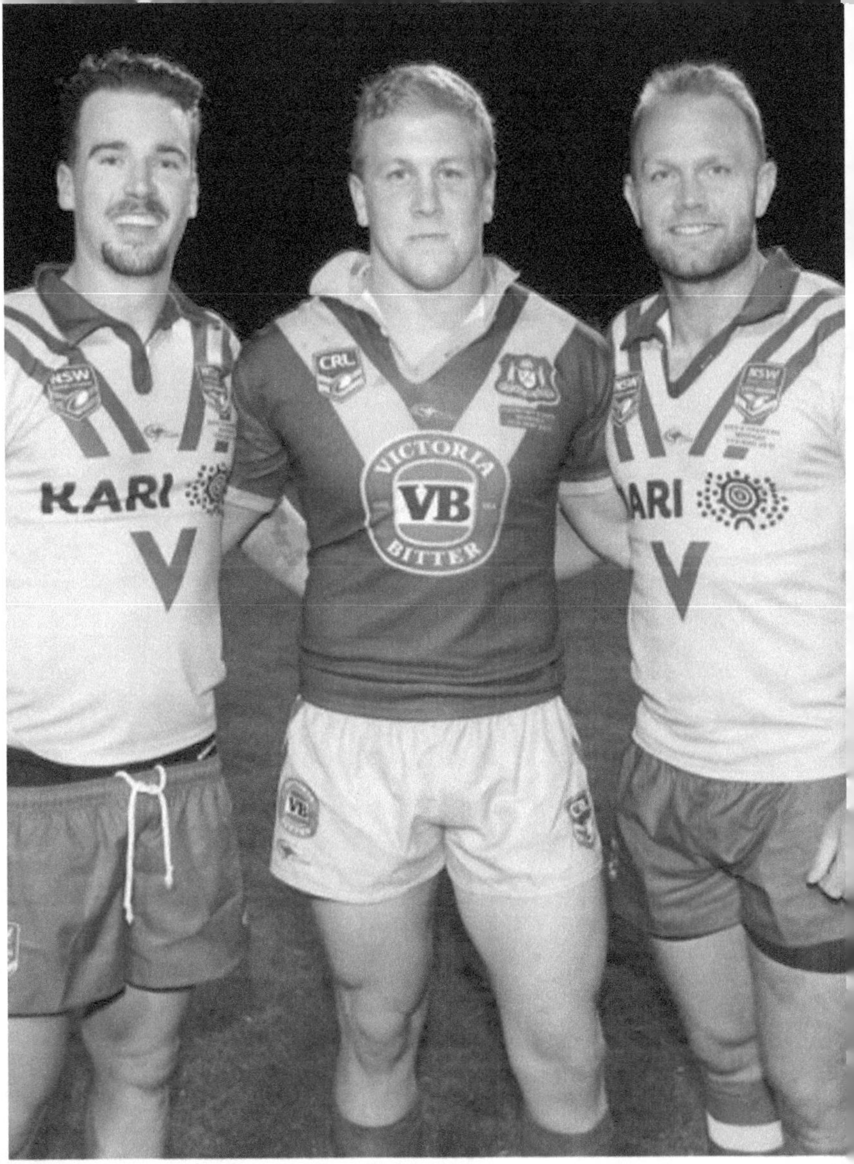
KARI
VICTORIA
VB
BITTER
KARI

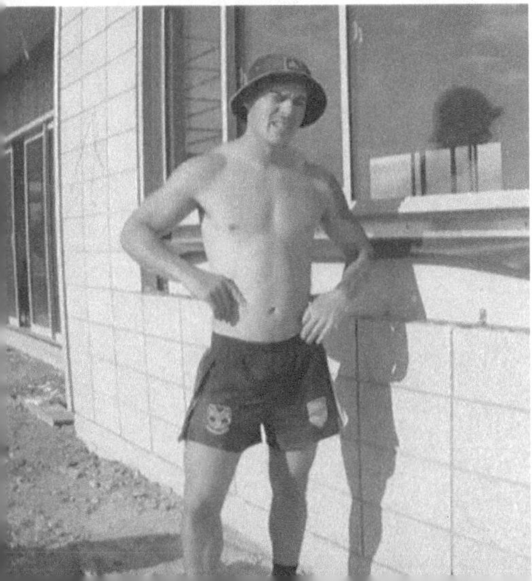

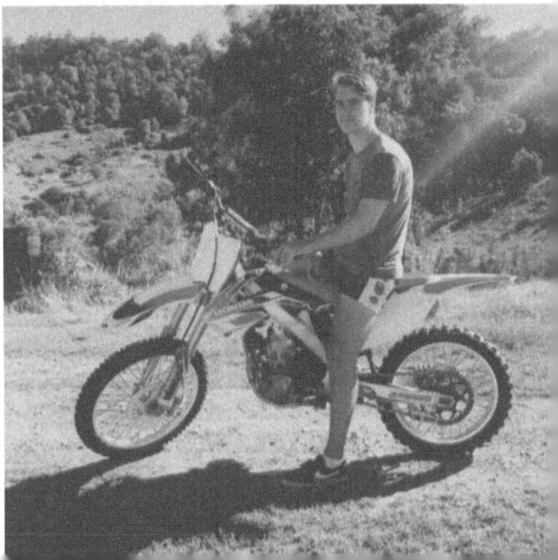

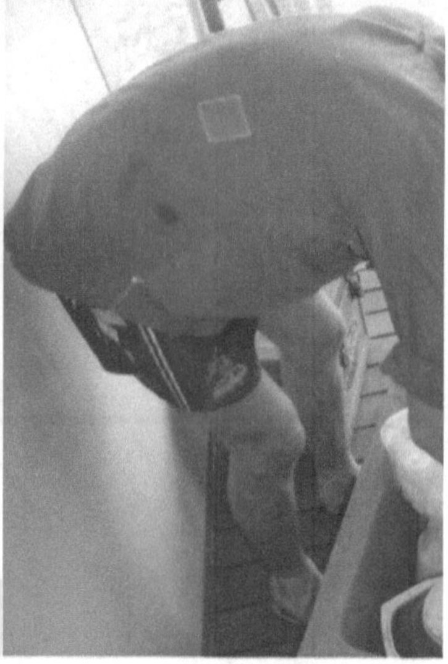

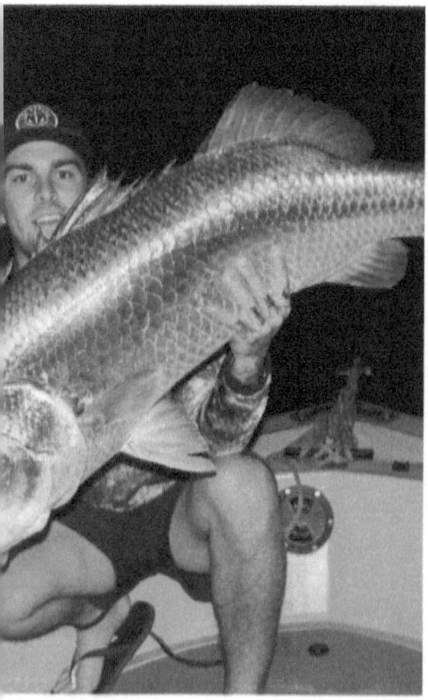

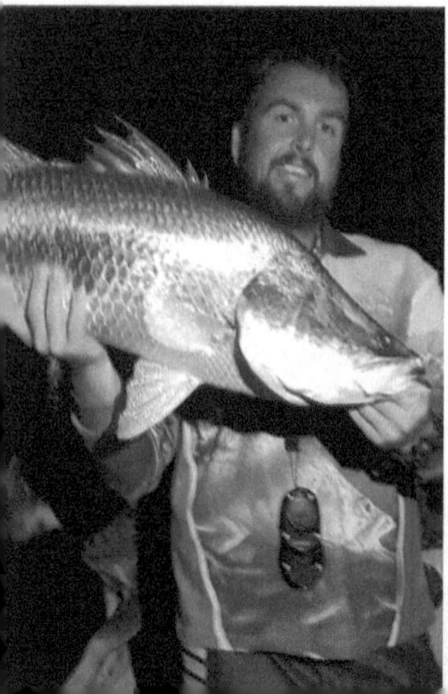

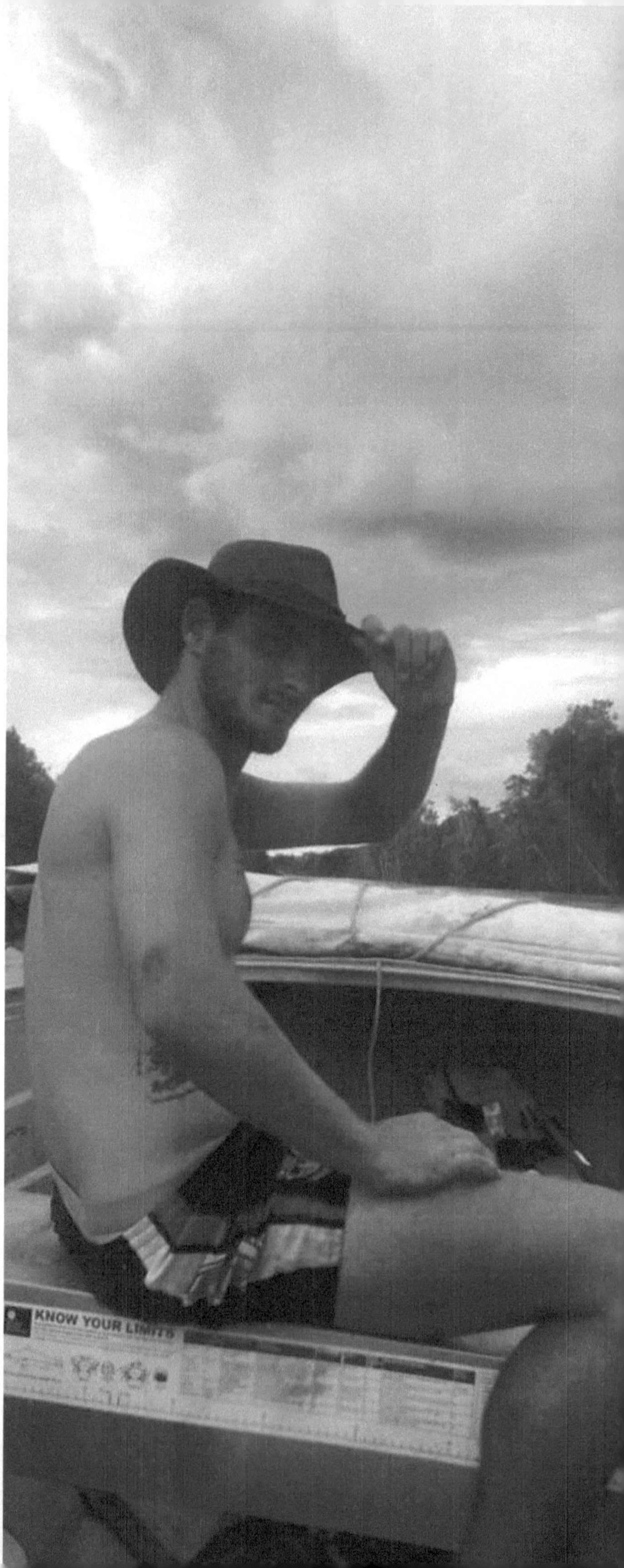
KNOW YOUR LIMITS

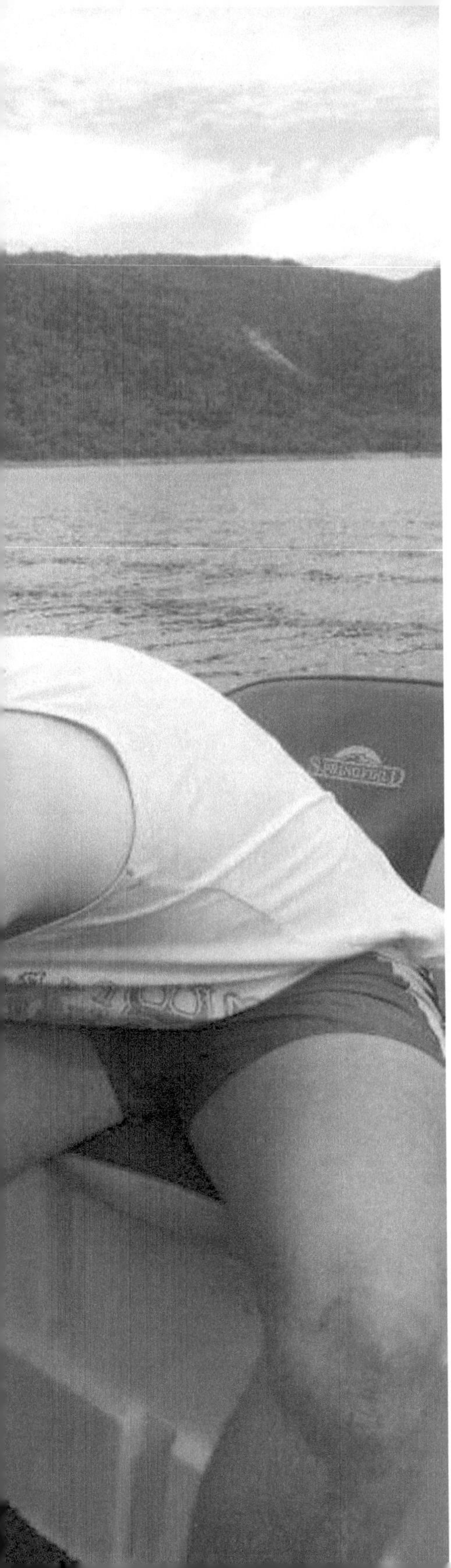

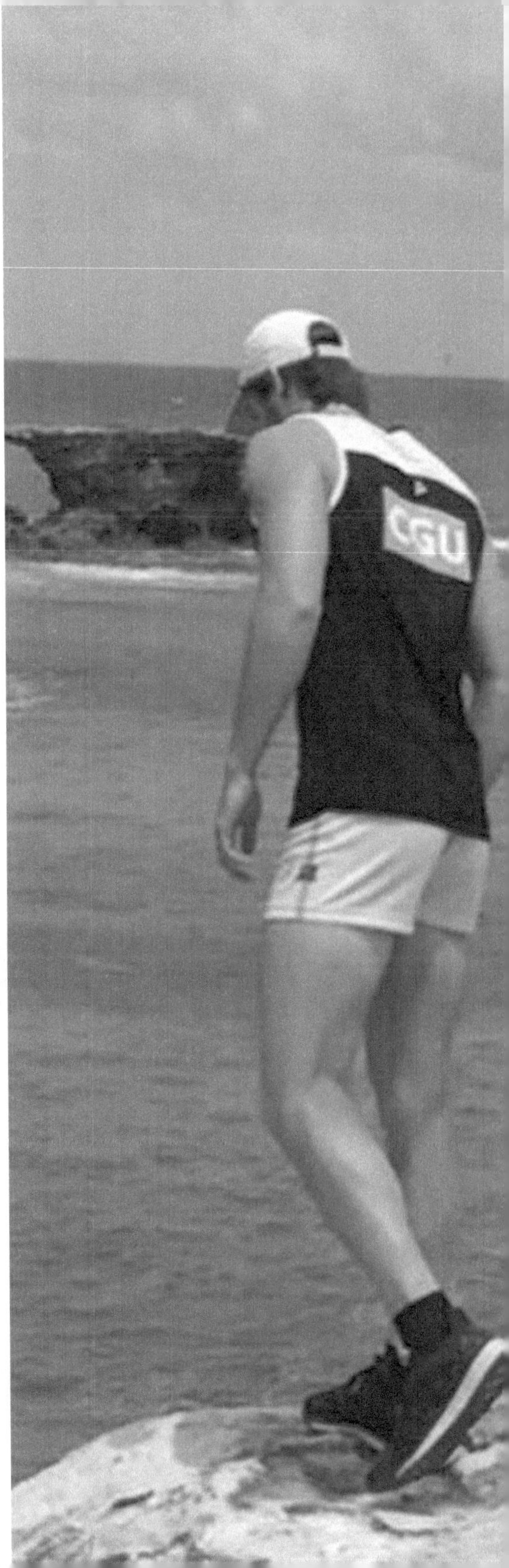
CGU

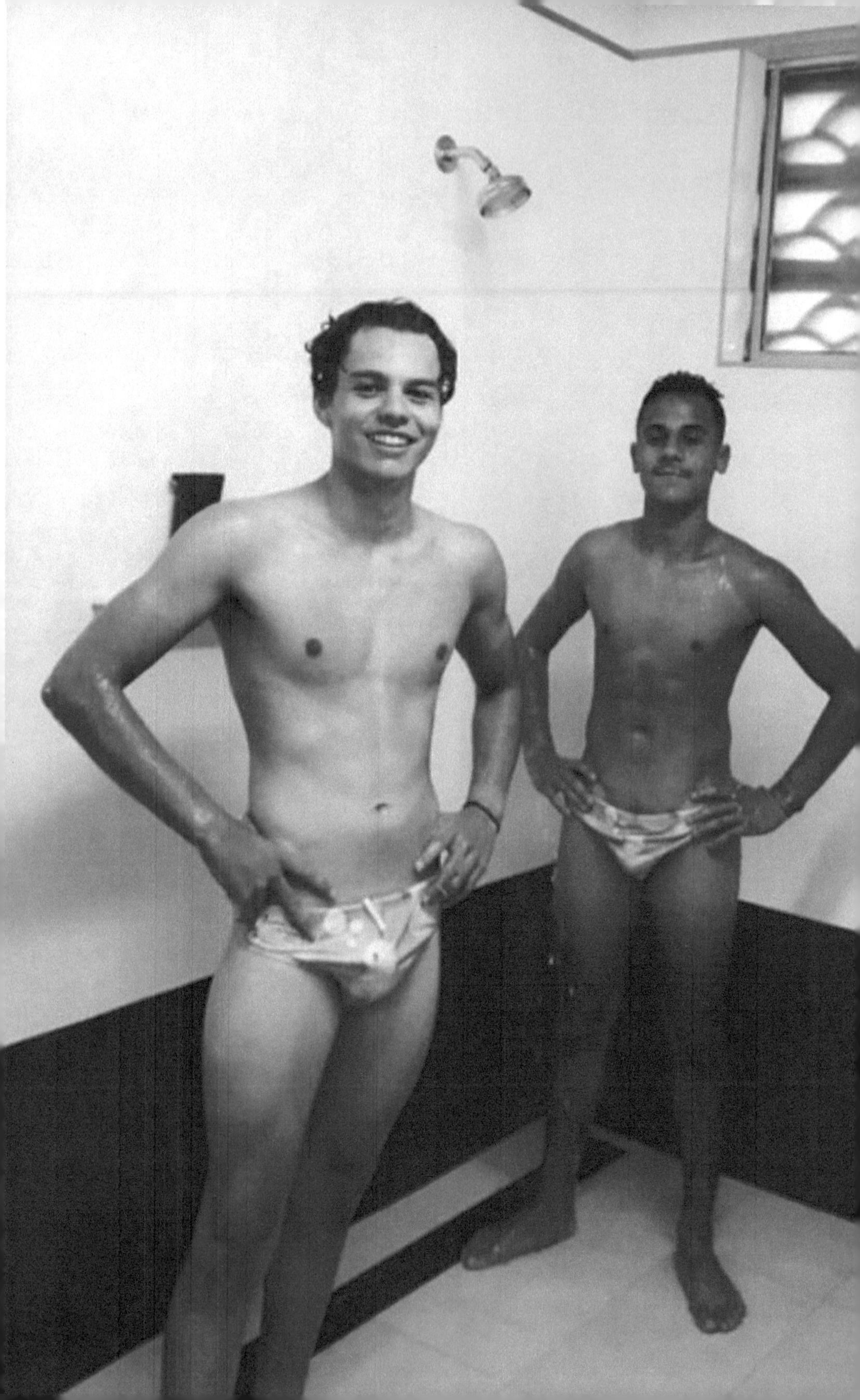

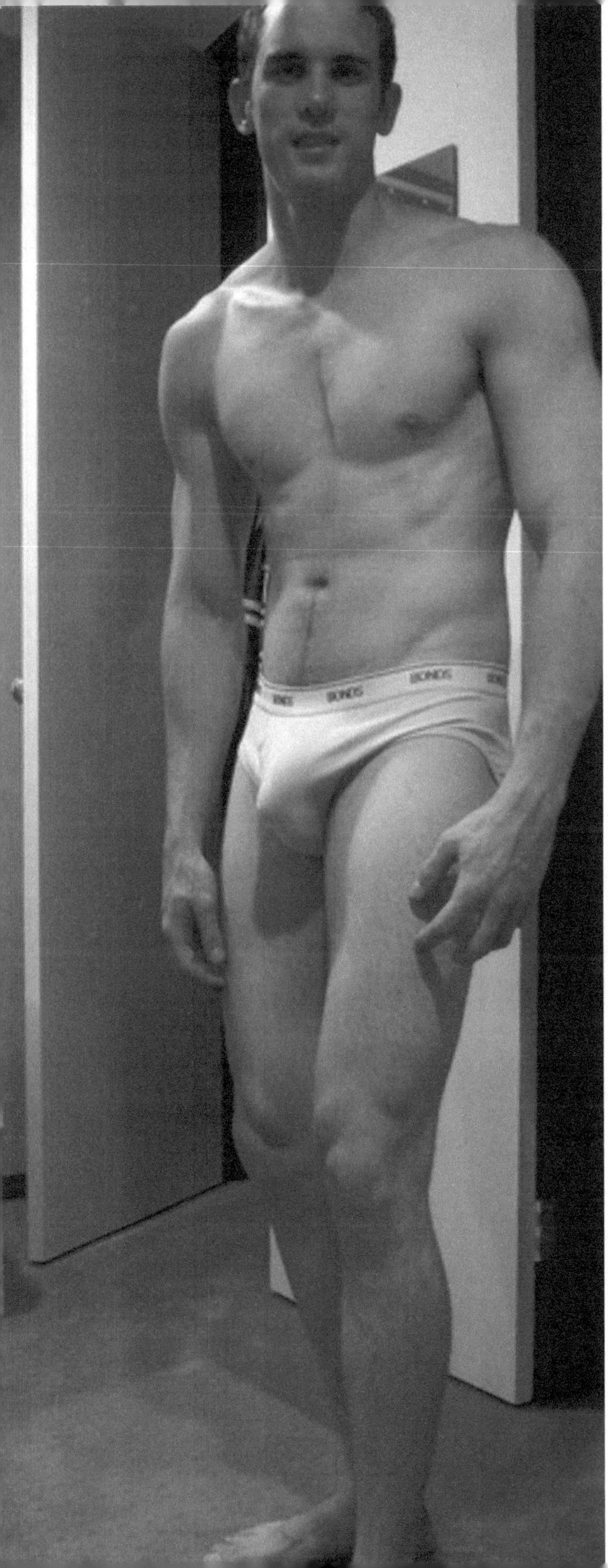
BONDS

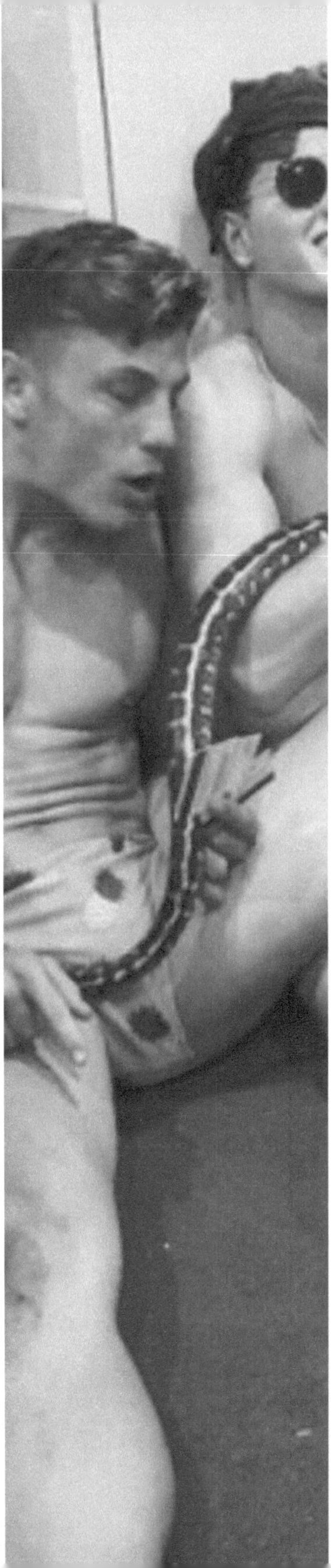

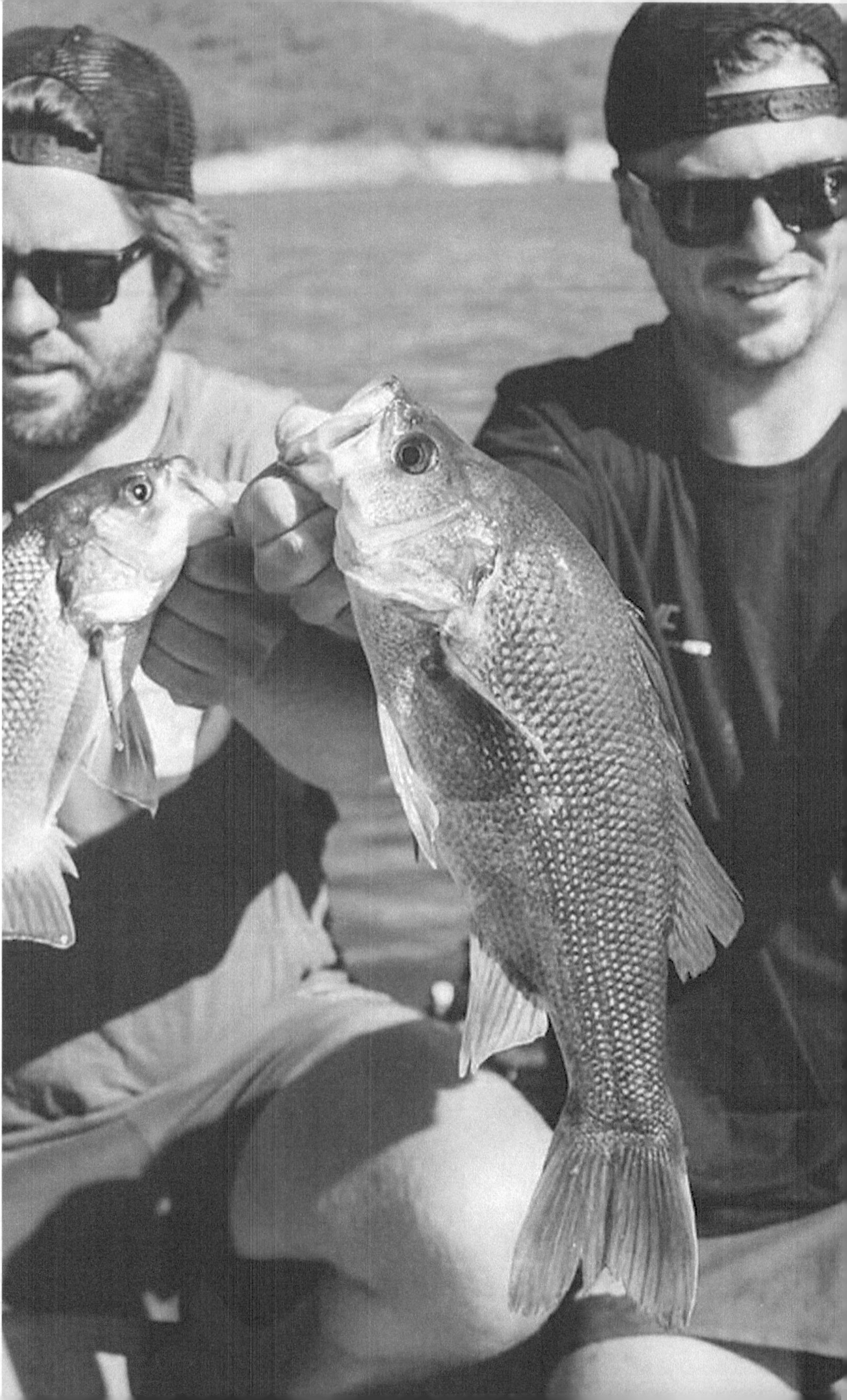

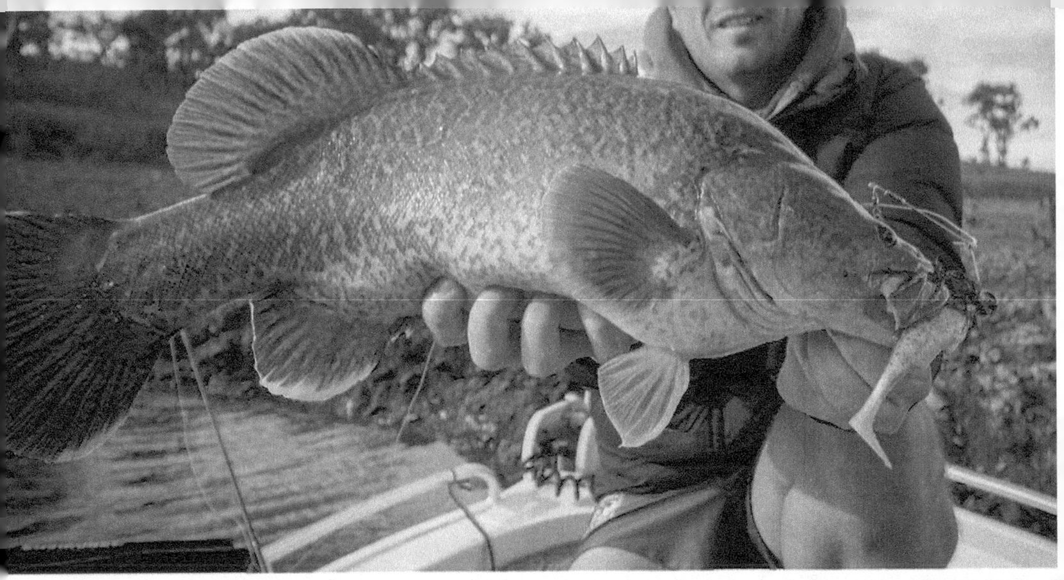

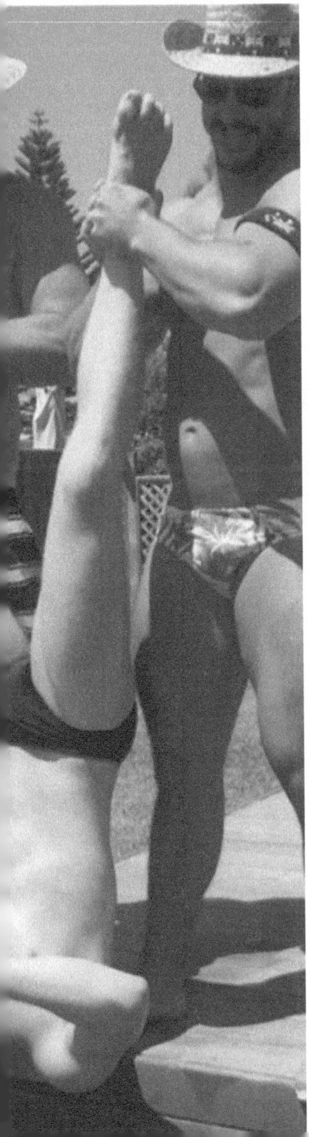

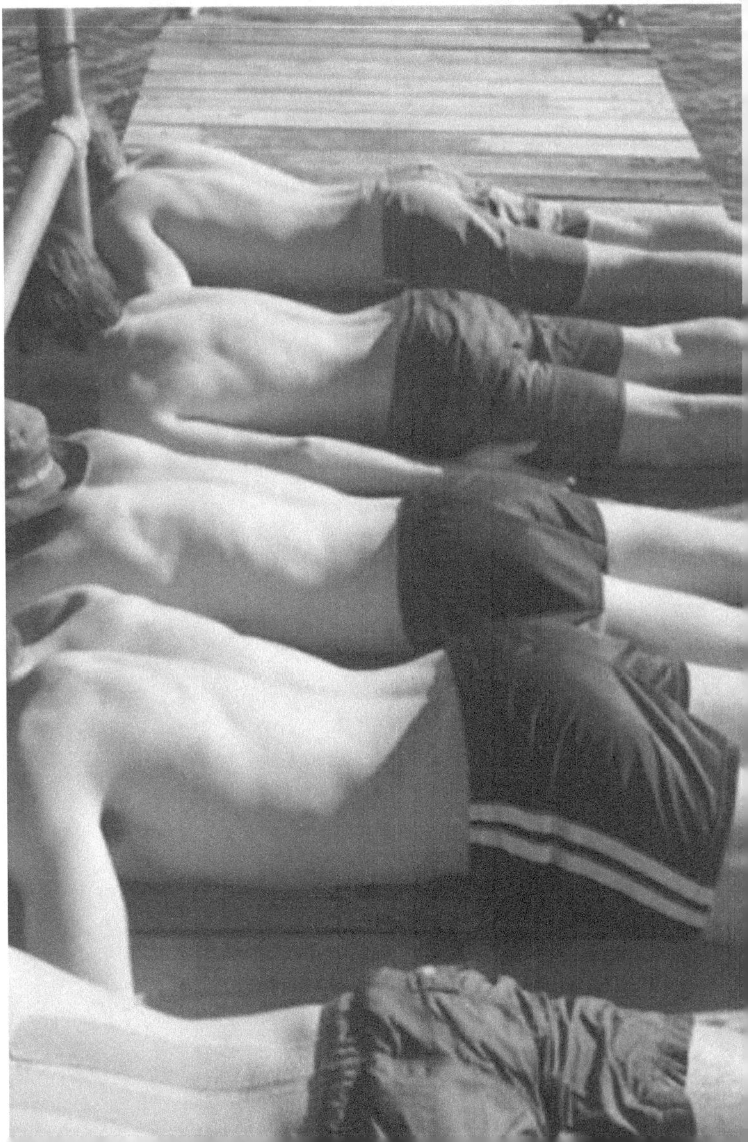

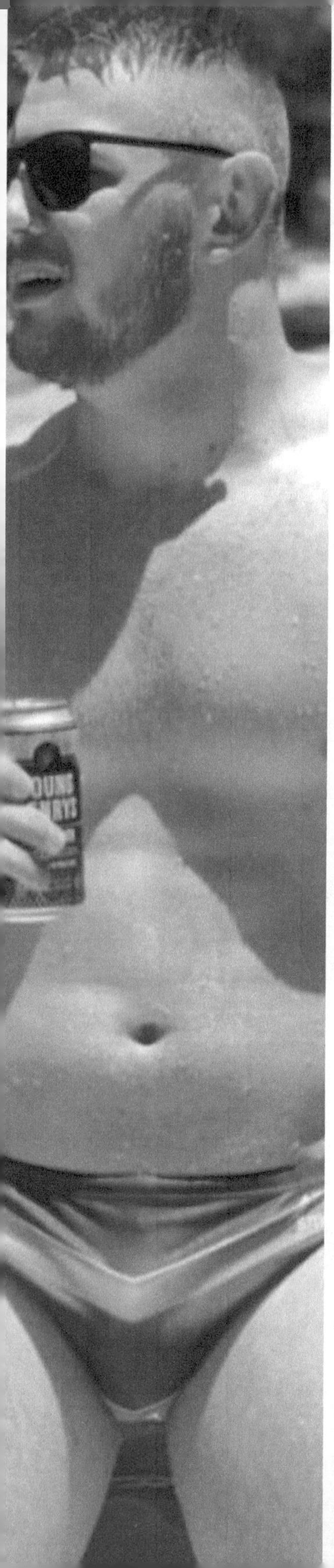

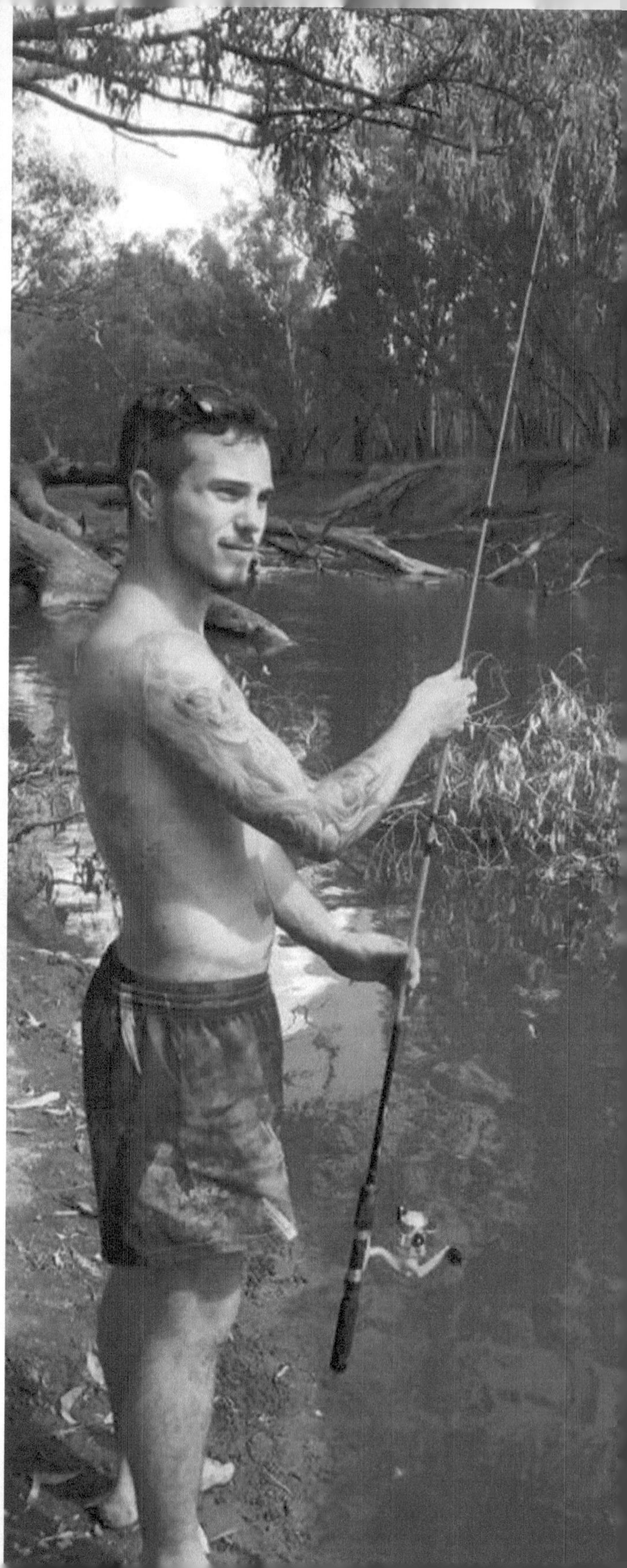

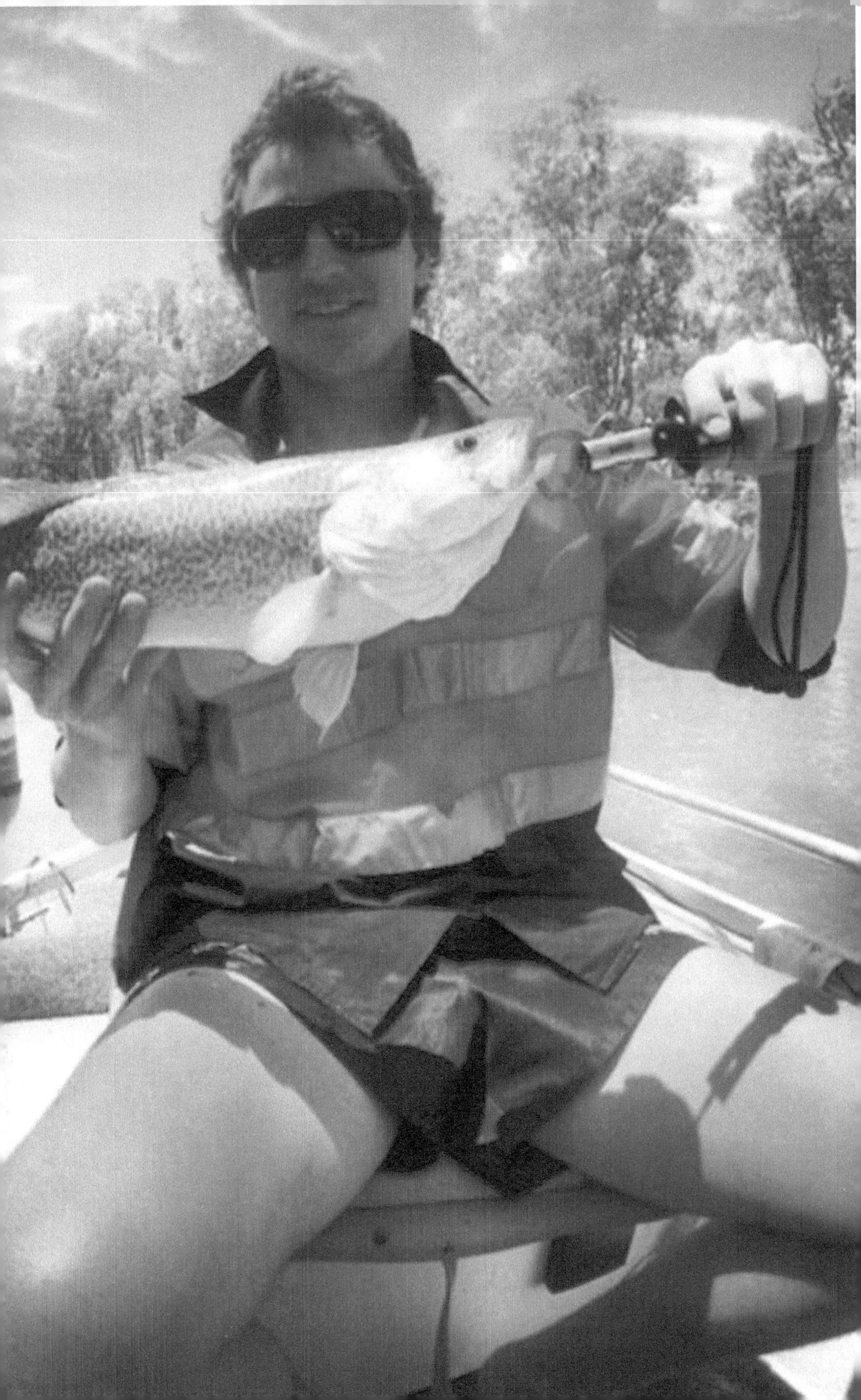

www.ingramcontent.com/pod-product-compliance
Lightning Source LLC
Chambersburg PA
CBHW021007180526
45163CB00005B/1920
* 9 7 8 0 3 5 9 9 6 5 3 1 1 *